IMAGES
of Aviation

GOWEN FIELD

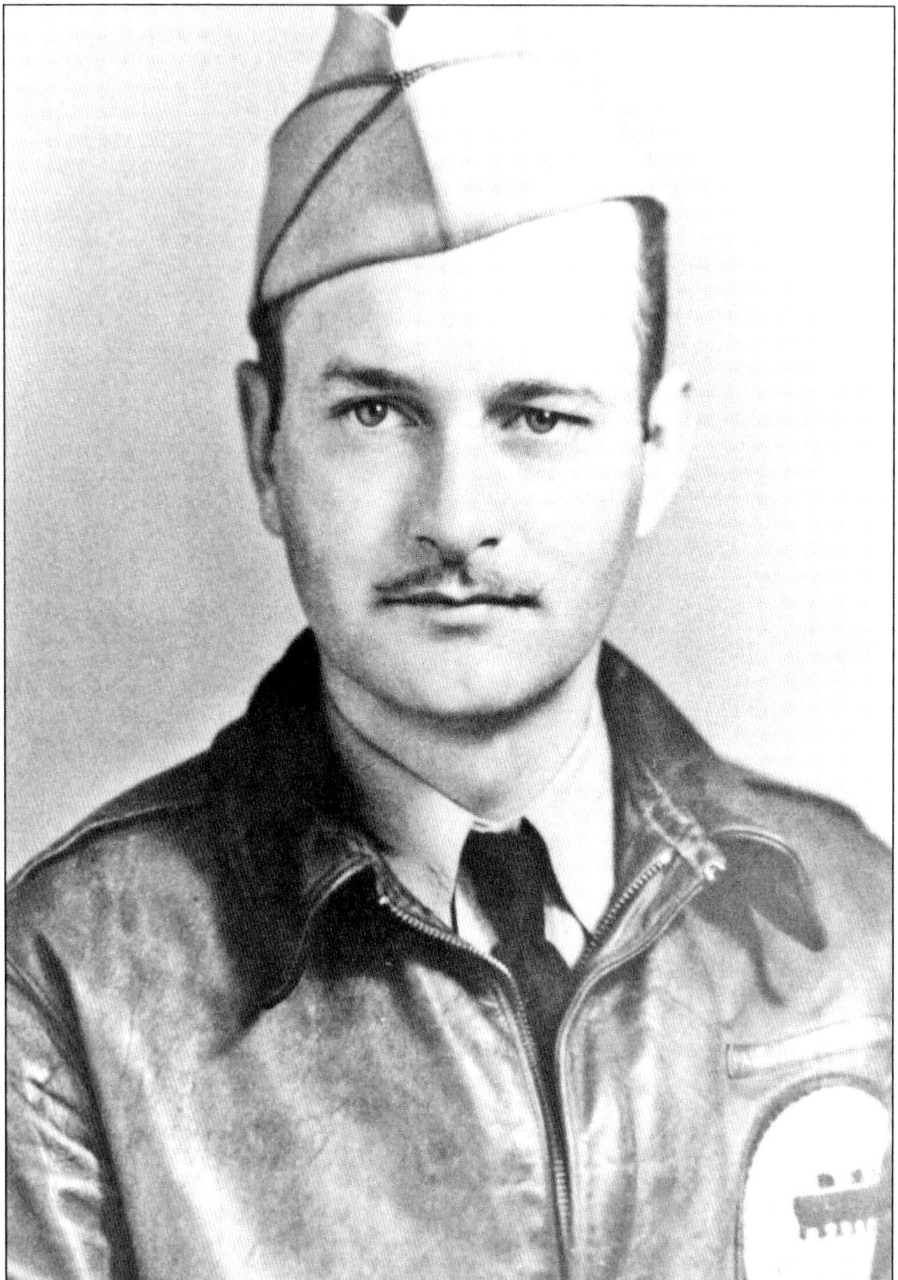

Lt. Paul Gowen of Caldwell, Idaho, was commissioned from the U.S. Military Academy at West Point. He earned his aviator's wings and flew bombers out of Howard Field, Panama. Lieutenant Gowen was killed in 1938 when his B-10 bomber developed an engine fire during takeoff and crashed. The Boise Airbase was renamed Gowen Field in honor of this Idaho aviator.

ON THE COVER: Taken from the vast Idaho Military Historical Society photograph collection, this snapshot shows pilots in front of an F-86L. The 124th Fighter Interceptor Group received 25 of these aircraft in 1959 and operated the planes for almost five years.

IMAGES
of Aviation

GOWEN FIELD

Yancy Mailes and Gary Keith

ARCADIA
PUBLISHING

ISBN 978-0-7385-4823-4

Published by Arcadia Publishing
Charleston, South Carolina

Printed in the United States of America

Library of Congress Catalog Card Number:

For all general information contact Arcadia Publishing at:
Telephone 843-853-2070
Fax 843-853-0044
E-mail sales@arcadiapublishing.com
For customer service and orders:
Toll-Free 1-888-313-2665

Visit us on the Internet at www.arcadiapublishing.com

*To those who gave their blood, sweat, and tears
to build and sustain such a valuable piece of Idaho's history*

Contents

ACKNOWLEDGMENTS

This project was a monumental task, one we could not have completed without the assistance of many giving people. We would like to thank the people and organizations whose contributions made the completion of this book possible. First and foremost, we must acknowledge the Idaho Military Historical Society (IMHS) and its board of directors for their unwavering cooperation. Second, we must recognize the individuals who entrusted their collections to the IMHS. Without these great collections, we could have never produced this publication. We only hope our effort does the photographs justice. Third, the following individuals answered questions and identified faces in photographs: Col. Michael Bates, retired; Stephen Bonde; Garald and Virginia Call; CMSgt. Pete Glick; Lt. Col. Dean Jackson, retired; Col. Larry Kauffman; Col. William Miller, retired; Brig. Gen. Gary Sayler; MSgt. William Stein, retired. As always, we must thank Joe Eastman for his fantastic scanning support. Joe scanned numerous negatives and cleaned up hundreds of images. Lastly, we would like to thank our wives, Lisa and Gaye, for the countless hours we spent on the phone or away from home. We appreciate your patience and your support.

INTRODUCTION

In the mid-1930s, Walter York, with the backing of a few other air-minded individuals, urged the Boise Chamber of Commerce to raise the necessary funds to purchase the initial 40 acres required to build a new airport. At the time, Boise operated its fledgling airstrip from the location of the present-day Boise State University football stadium, but the proposed site was, as the crow flew, some seven miles south of the Boise River. Convinced, the Boise administration began leasing and buying not only the first 40 acres, but a total of 400, between 1936 and 1938. With the land secured, the airport's founding fathers turned the first spade full of dirt on what would become at the time the nation's largest runway, at 8,800 feet.

Concurrent to the airport construction, at the urging of the Air Corps, Pres. Franklin D. Roosevelt began a program to beef up the air arm of the U.S. Army. Idaho's first answer to this call came when the state's adjutant general, Gen. Mervin G. McConnel, attempted to attract a National Guard observation squadron to the new airport. When rebuffed, he regrouped and penned a letter to the 9th Corps army headquarters, located in San Francisco, inquiring as to Boise's chances of housing an Air Corps training facility. Incidentally, Walter York had been called to active duty and charged with selecting sites to be developed as aviation training facilities. In his travels, he not only selected sites in the Midwest but also had a hand in choosing all of Idaho's airbases.

After reviewing the Army Air Corps site report, on December 3, 1940, the adjutant general of the U.S. Army wired Mayor James Straight of Boise, Idaho. In that communiqué, the general announced that, because of the Boise Airport's climatic and physical conditions, construction of the Boise Air Base had been approved. A short time later, an agreement was settled stating that the government would pay $1 per year for land and could renew the lease annually for 25 years.

On New Year's Day in 1940, the *Idaho Statesman* ran an extensive front-page article detailing the agreement and providing the public with some insight into the airport's new mission. The text announced that work would begin that very month and that the base would eventually house the 42nd Bombardment Group, the 16th Reconnaissance Squadron, and the 39th Air Base Group with a mission to support and operate the B-18 Bolo. The original project called for the construction of a temporary standard cantonment area totaling 120 buildings and providing facilities to house, mess, and administer a troop garrison of 2,500 officers and men. The cost was estimated at $2,115,130.

In order to facilitate the development of the base, the Army Corps of Engineers hired J. A. Terteling and Sons of Boise to grade the roads to both the cantonment and aircraft parking spaces and then resurface the runway to support the bomber operations. In addition, a four-mile railroad spur was designed to transport the construction materials. In March 1941, Gov. Chase Clark ceremoniously turned the first spade full of dirt, thus symbolizing the construction's commencement. That same month, construction reached its zenith, and the 900 men who had been hired to build the base began to find work elsewhere, as the soldiers had started arriving. Boise Air Base's first commander, Col. Robin A. Day, assumed his role on March 12, 1941, with

Col. Arthur J. Melanson as his executive officer. Colonel Melanson would eventually take command of the Boise base, then move on and build Mountain Home Air Base.

On Easter Sunday, April 15, 1941, the original cadre of 20 soldiers forming the 39th Air Base Group arrived, but were housed at the Boise barracks as no quarters were available until the 25th. In this early time period, the jackrabbits challenged the soldiers for space in the tents while the mud dried into an annoying dust. It was impossible to maintain an army image, but Colonel Melanson summed up the situation when he said, "It's all right to have dust on your shoes under the circumstances, but don't let me see yesterday's dust on your shoes today."

As construction continued at a hurried pace, the Army Air Forces induced yet another change to the Idaho air field. Under General Order No. 8, dated July 29, 1941, the army officially renamed the base Gowen Field in honor of Lt. Paul R. Gowen, a native of Caldwell, Idaho. Lieutenant Gowen had died at the controls of his B-10 while on duty in Panama in 1938. The choice of name proved popular with Idaho residents and further strengthened the bonds between the civilian and military personnel. This came at a good time, as bombers soon arrived, developing friction for the commercial air traffic operating in and around the base.

In August, Colonel Day asserted that the staff was adequate to begin operating the field as an army air base, and in turn the 42nd Bombardment Group received six twin-engine Douglas B-18 Bolo bombers. However, the B-18 aircraft were quickly replaced in October by the faster, twin-engine B-26 Marauder bomber.

With the bombing of Pearl Harbor, Gowen Field, like the rest of the nation, went on high alert; changes came quickly. First, in January 1942, the 42nd moved its headquarters to McChord Field near Tacoma, Washington, and in its place the 303rd Bombardment Group arrived. The unit landed at Gowen to prepare and train for war using its newly fielded B-17 Flying Fortresses. This arrangement was short lived, as the unit moved on in June 1942 to be replaced by the 29th Bombardment Group, which operated the B-24 Liberators. In September 1943, Gowen Field became a combat crew training school for the B-24, and Liberators became a familiar sight in the Idaho skies. This continued until the end of World War II.

At the close of the war, the fate of the airdrome was unknown, and by early 1946, the army had closed its lease and returned the land to Boise. This did not last long. Idaho's adjutant general, Gen. Harry Abendroth, requested that Lt. Col. Tom Lanphier build the Idaho Air National Guard that would lease the land from the city. On the same day that the National Guard activated the 190th Fighter Squadron, 37 charter members joined the Idaho Air National Guard. A few months later, the squad received its first F-51 Mustang. A short 10 years later, the unit operated the F-89 with over 600 men, calling themselves the "Raggedy Ass Militia."

Since that meager beginning in 1946, the Idaho Air Guard has centered its operations from Gowen Field, flying multiple aircraft including the F-86, F-102, F-4C, and most recently the A-10 and C-130. With its inception as a training base in World War II, Gowen Field played a key role in training air crews for the rigors of combat. With the Idaho Air Guard as the present steward of the base, Gowen Field now stands ready to meet the nation's call.

One

Gowen Field

Due to Boise's location, the Army Air Corps opted to build a training base near the city. The site for the base was remote yet close to potential bombing ranges, and weather was mild enough to allow year-round operations, unhindered by winter. Construction began in March 1941, and the base grew rapidly. At a time when the Great Depression had affected even remote Boise, Idaho, 900 civilians found employment constructing the buildings and runways at the new base.

During the summer and fall months of 1941, construction moved at such a rapid pace that flying units were able to move in and set up operations. The first flying unit, the 42nd Bomb Group, arrived to begin training with the Douglas B-18 bomber. The B-18s were soon replaced with the Army Air Forces' newest heavy bomber, the B-17 Flying Fortress.

By March 1943, Gowen Field was in full swing for training personnel, but the mission changed slightly. B-24 Liberators replaced the B-17s, and base personnel made the transition without missing a beat. The base also housed a maintenance sub-depot, which meant the intense training schedule could be met by keeping the bombers flying with more in-depth maintenance.

World War II formed a bond between Gowen Field and the city of Boise. This occurred due to the logical and natural interaction between the base's airmen and the citizens, as well as the economic ties that developed. The end of the war did not mean the end of this relationship.

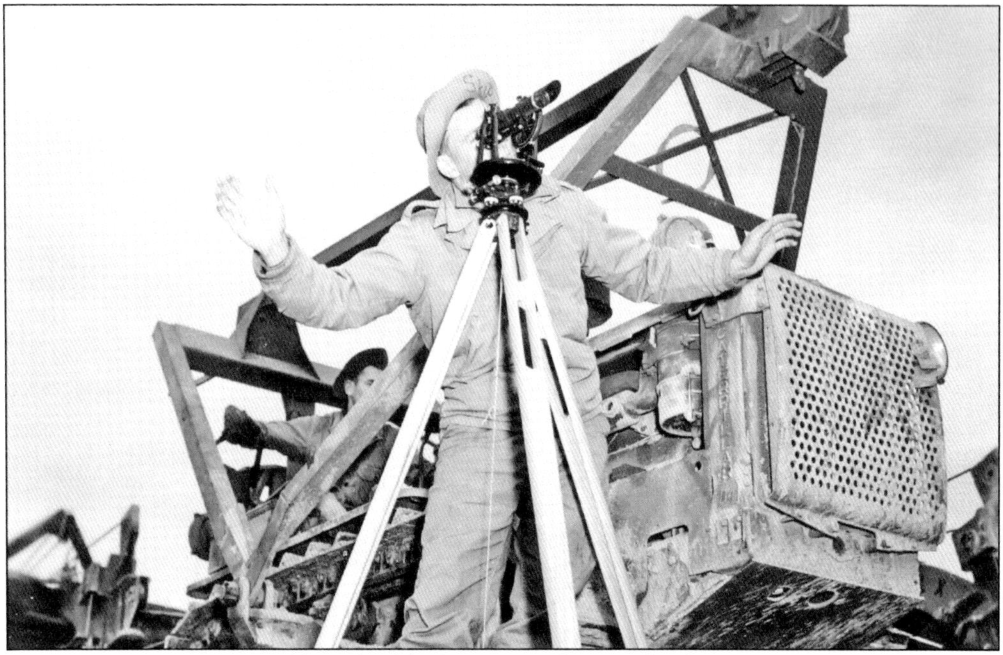

Construction on Gowen Field involved both Boise civilians and military personnel. These soldiers worked on one of many ongoing construction projects during World War II. President Roosevelt was urged in the late 1930s to expand the tiny Army Air Corps to prepare for a likely war with Germany and Japan. The new base was the result of Roosevelt's decision to do so.

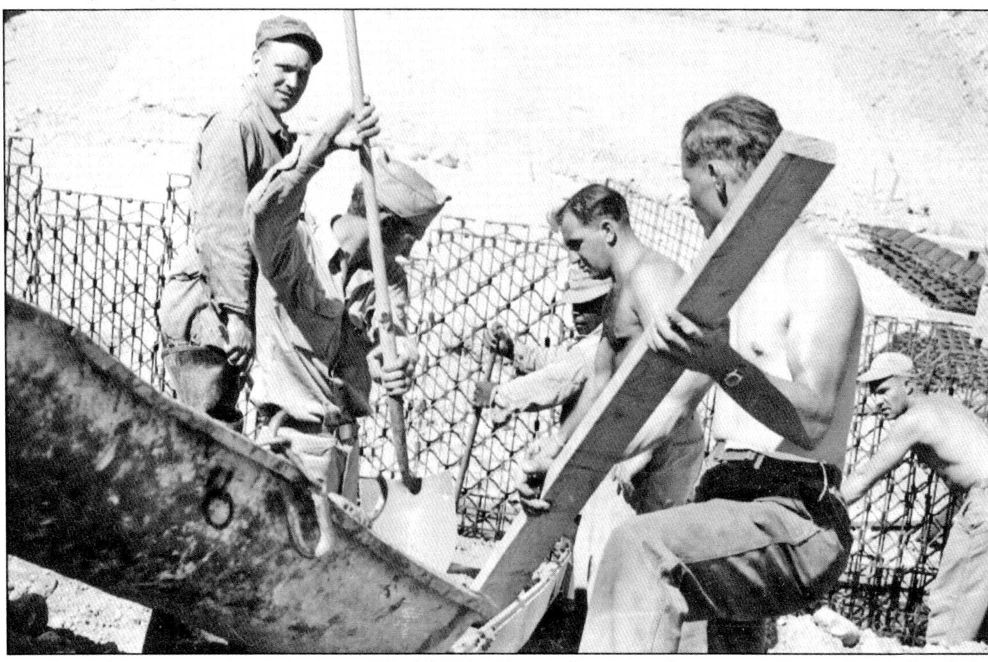

Prior to the country's entry into World War II, civilian employees performed much of the construction of Gowen Field. After the war started, military personnel assumed the majority of construction tasks, as seen here. For these soldiers, this was also a means of refining skills they would use in the combat theaters of operation.

Soldiers from one of the aviation engineer battalions that formed at Gowen Field are pictured here with a large grader. These soldiers later played an important role in the invasion of Europe during 1944 and into 1945. As Allied forces advanced, close air support was provided by the Army Air Forces' fighters and medium bombers that flew from small airfields built by the aviation engineers.

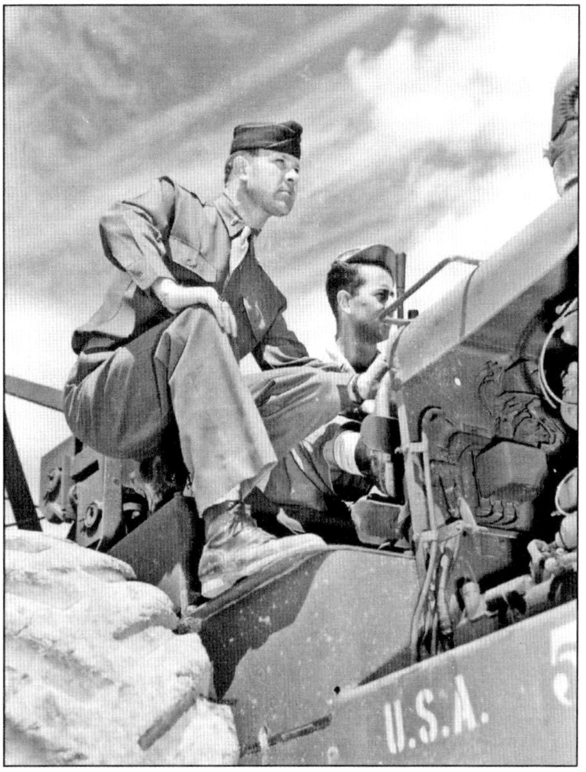

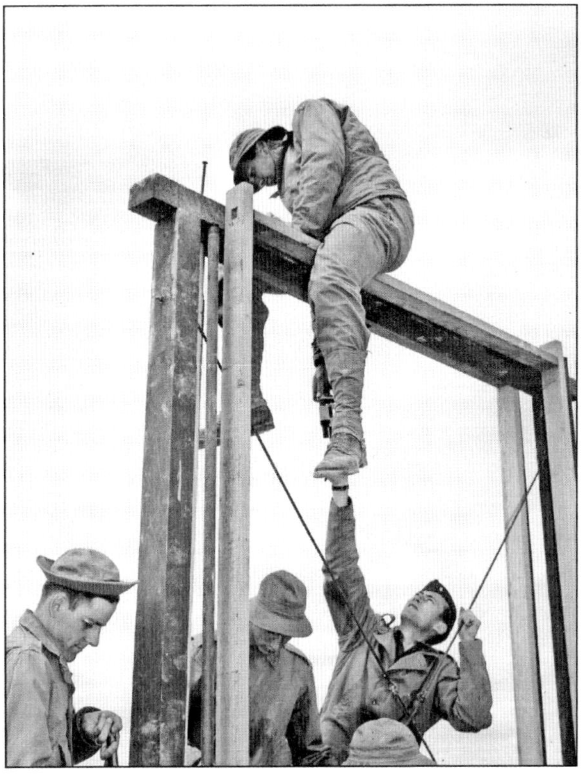

Construction was an ongoing task at Gowen Field, as the demand for training did not cease until the end of World War II. These soldiers built a vast number of structures on Gowen Field, many of which were used until the 1980s and 1990s. Bases like Gowen Field sprang up around the country with temporary buildings that eventually became permanent.

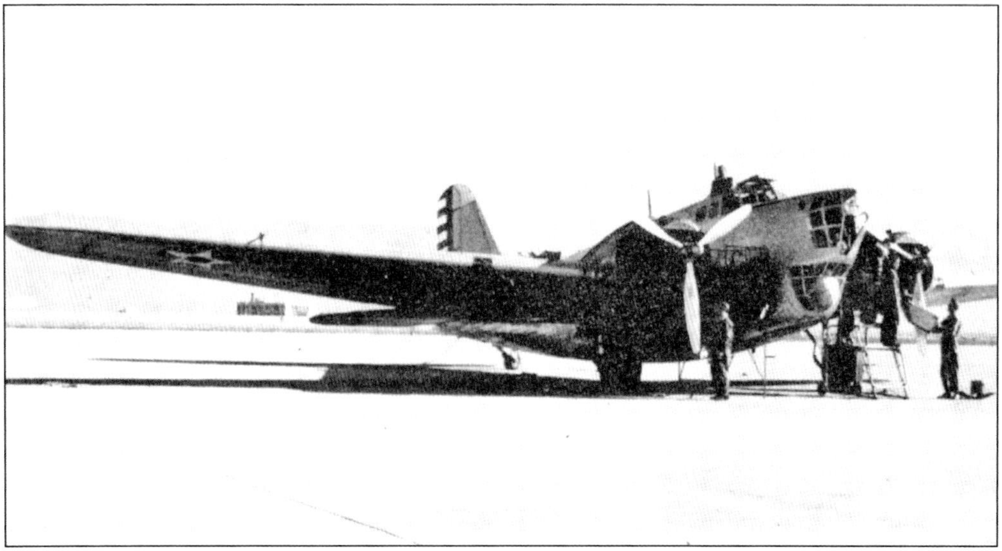

The B-18 Bolo bomber, pictured, was the first type of aircraft assigned to Gowen Field. During the late 1930s, the Army Air Corps tested different bombers and selected the B-18, but it quickly proved inadequate in range and payload. Thus, the B-17 soon became the standard bomber of the corps.

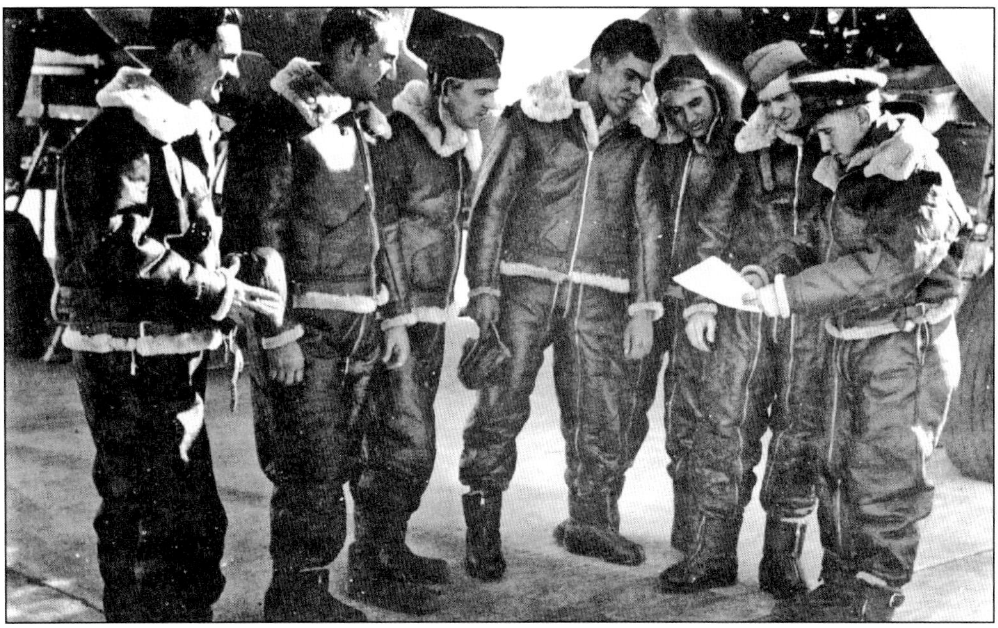

These B-18 crew members are wearing sheepskin-lined leather flight suits for high altitude. The suit seemed like a good idea, but in actual use it was found to be ineffective and did not provide adequate warmth. It was replaced by an electrically heated flying suit soon after the nation entered World War II. The surplus leather suits were issued to ground crew to wear in cold weather.

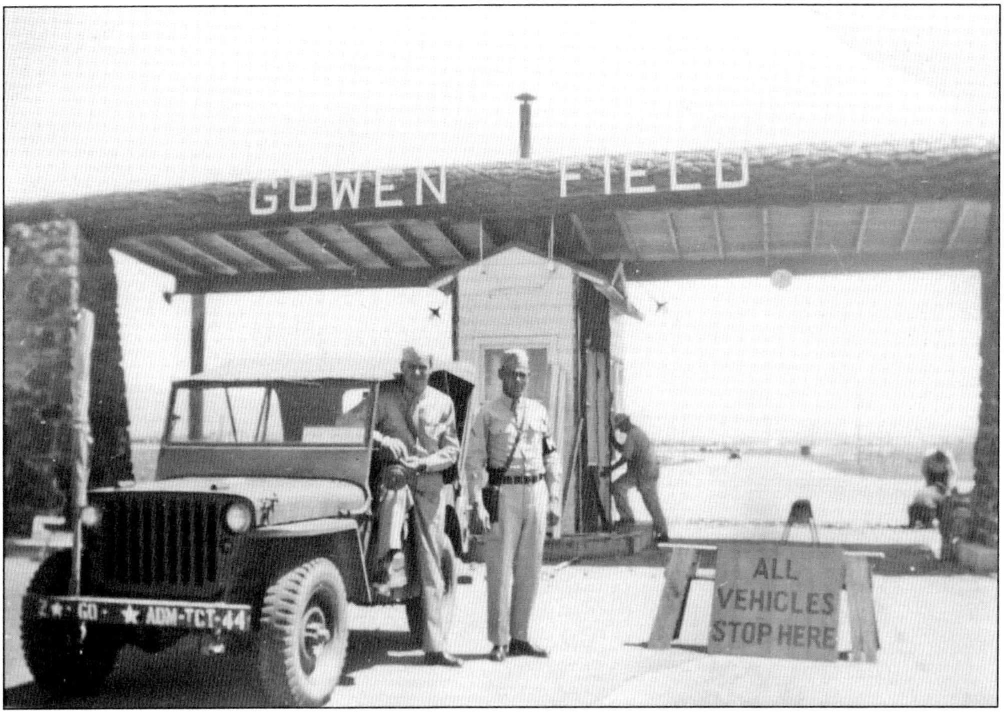

The main gate of Gowen Field was located on the southwest corner of the base's perimeter, as seen in this view to the east. All that remains of the gate are the two stone pillars, which were moved to the Idaho Military History Museum's facility.

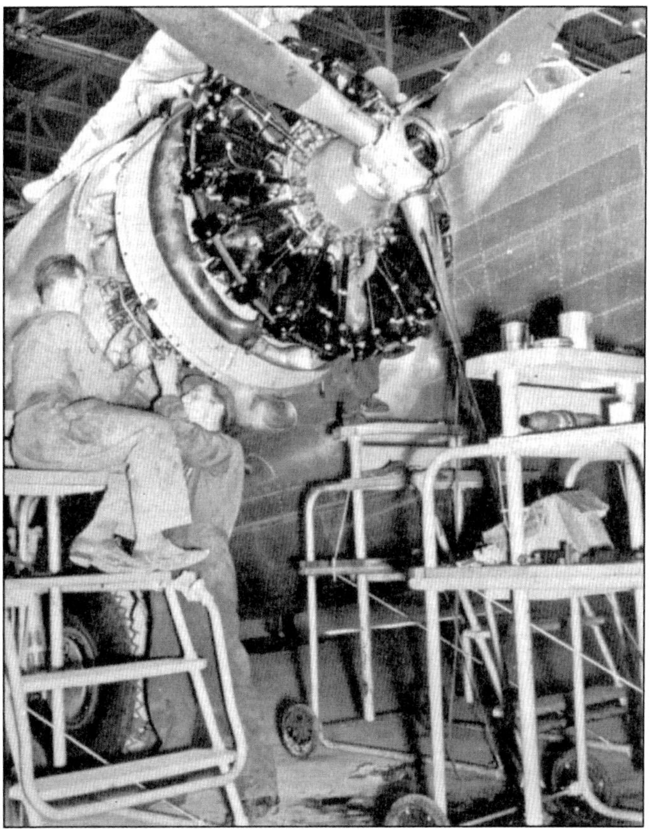

Flying crews were not the only ones who received training at Gowen Field. With the rapid growth of the Army Air Corps came the need for trained and competent ground crews. Here a ground crew works on a B-18 engine. The B-18s were powered by a pair of 930-horsepower Wright R-1820-45 radial engines with a maximum speed of 217 miles per hour, which was outclassed by the B-17 and B-24 bombers.

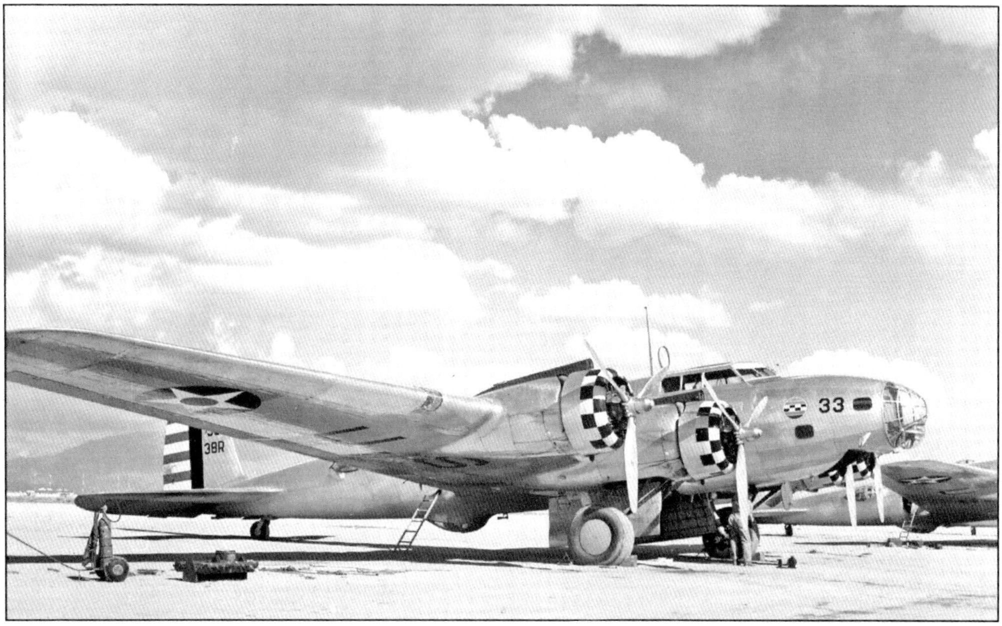

The first variant of the B-17 produced for the Army Air Corps, the Y1B-17, sits on the ramp at Gowen Field. Boeing only built 13 of these aircraft. These first B-17s were assigned to Langley Field in Virginia, but they visited Gowen Field at some point. The "blisters" on the side and bottom held defensive machine guns and were replaced with turrets or flat windows on later versions of B-17s.

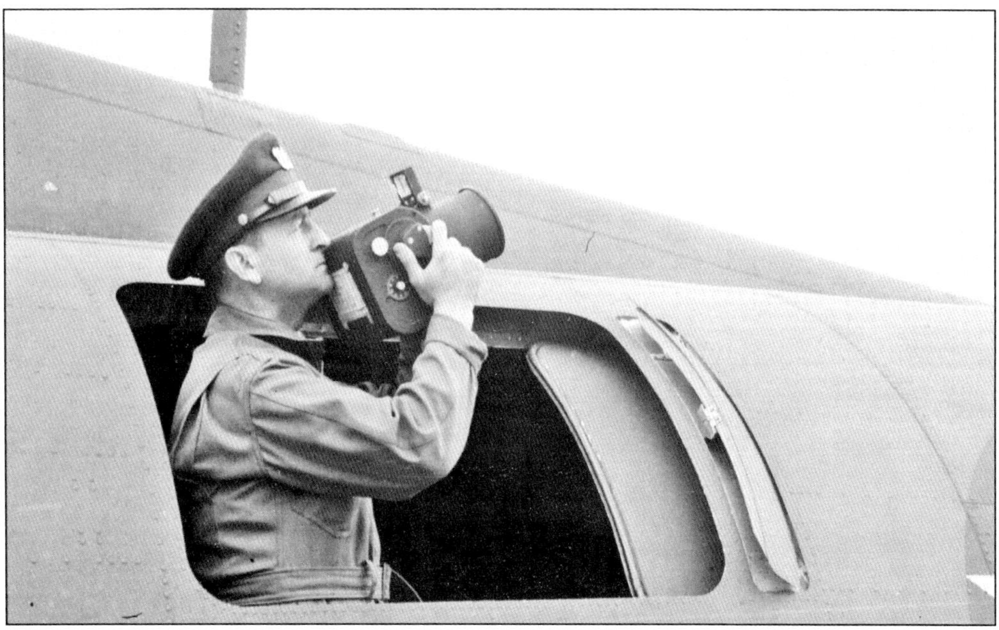

One of the first squadrons assigned to Gowen Field at the outbreak of World War II was the 16th Reconnaissance Squadron. This unit's mission was to train new crews on how to fly photoreconnaissance missions and operate the cameras. This warrant officer, identified by the cap device, demonstrates a method of using a camera from a waist position on a B-17, just forward of the tail.

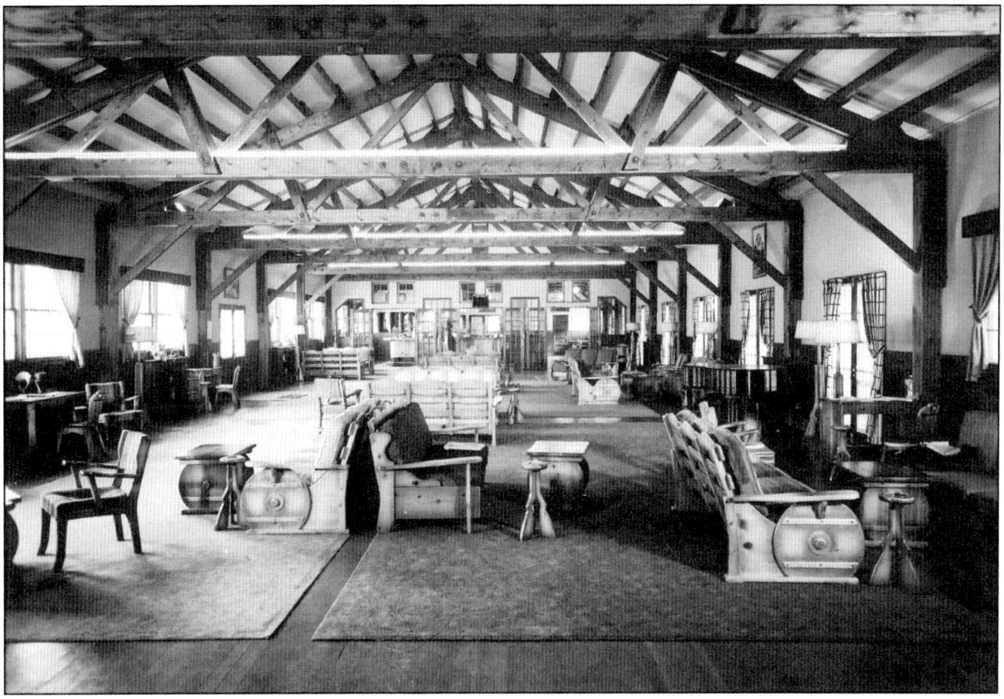

The Gowen Field Officer's Club, the center of social activity on the base, is still in use as an officer's club. The interior has been modified since World War II, but veterans of Gowen Field from the 1940s can still recognize the building from the outside.

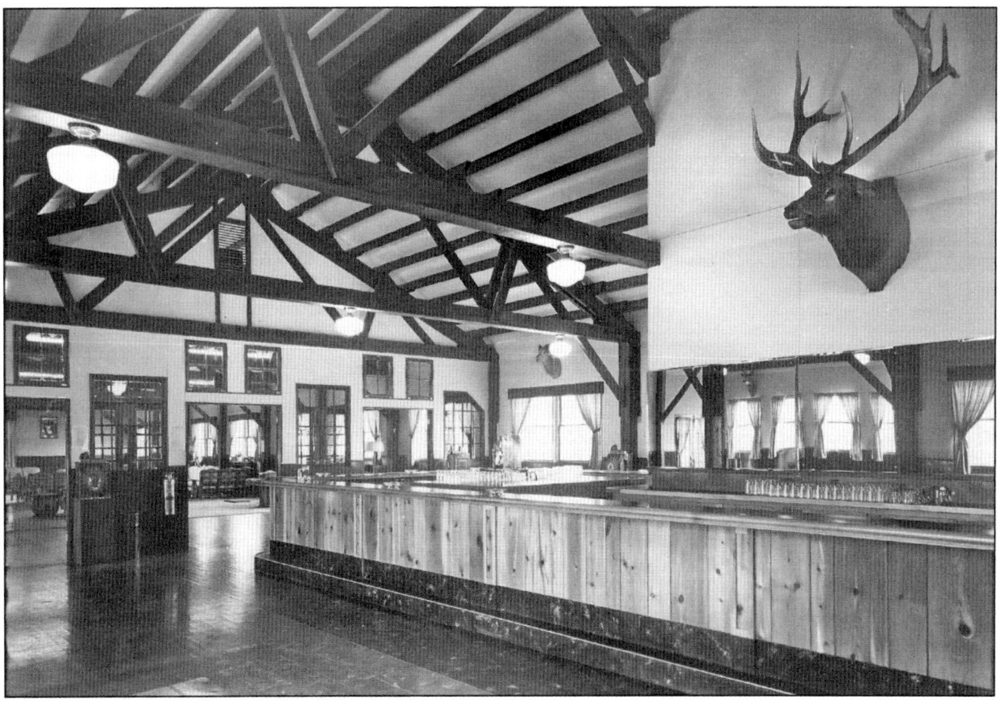

Shown in another view, the Gowen Field Officer's Club was regarded as one of the finest in the 2nd Air Force.

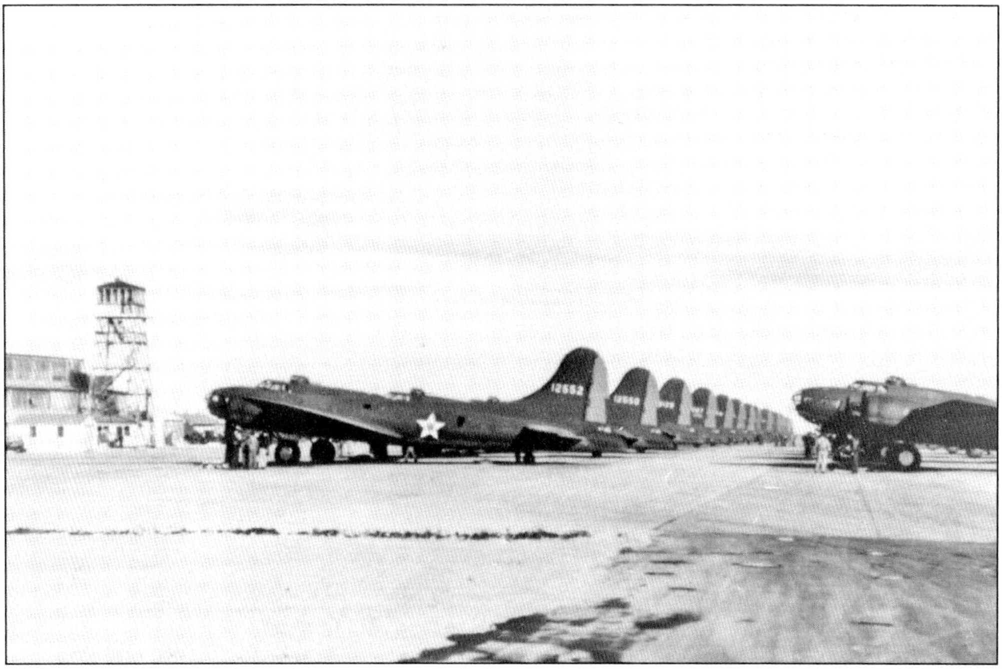

The first aircraft stationed at Gowen Field were originally B-18 Bolo bombers, but these were obsolete by the time the country entered World War II. The new Boeing B-17 Flying Fortress, seen here, was the first operational combat aircraft to see widespread use at Gowen Field. Some of the hangars used for B-17 operations are still standing today, more than 60 years after their construction.

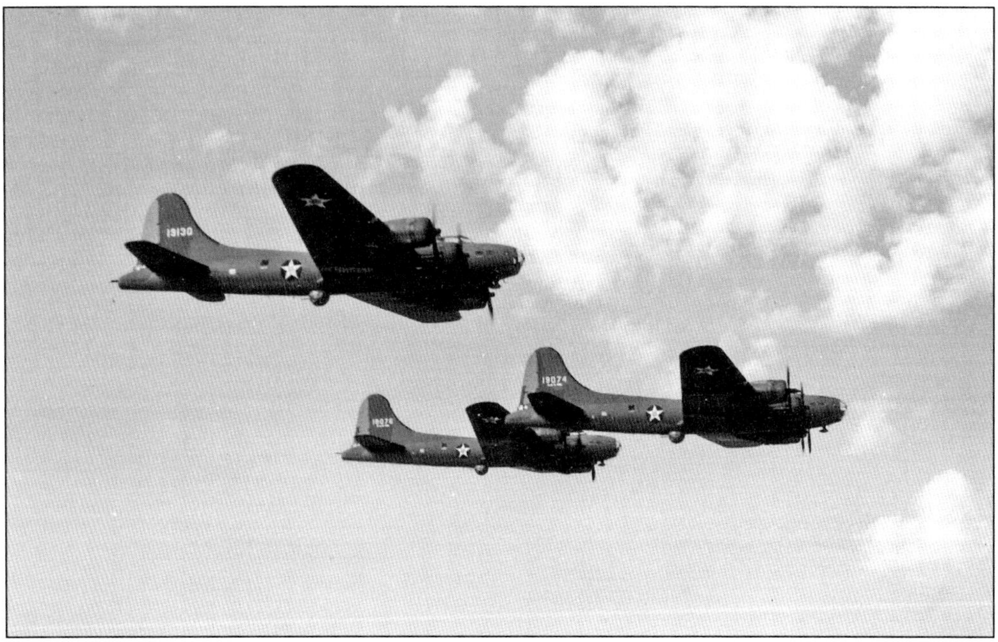

The three B-17s in this V formation are in the most basic pattern of combat configuration: the element. Two elements make up a squadron, with one forward and one back and offset, or echeloned. Basic flying skills such as these were routine instruction at Gowen Field, and as the war progressed, veterans of combat returned to serve as instructors.

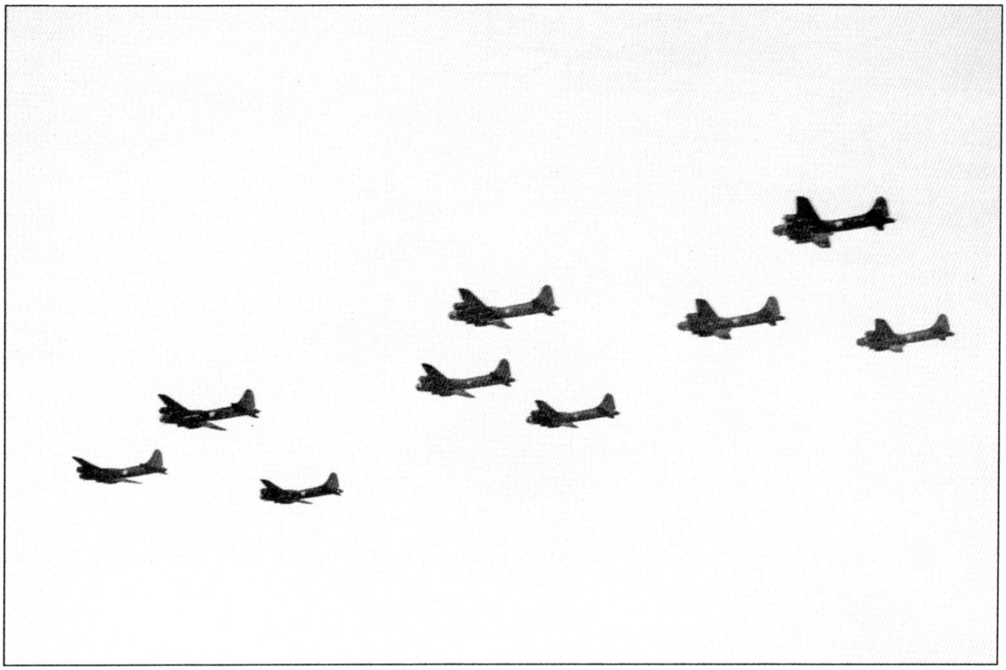

Formation training was an important part of instruction at Gowen Field and other airfields across the country during World War II. Crews were taught how to safely fly close and maximize the defensive features of the B-17 Flying Fortress: its multiple .50-caliber machine guns. Flying a tight formation allowed dozens of guns to fire at attacking enemy aircraft.

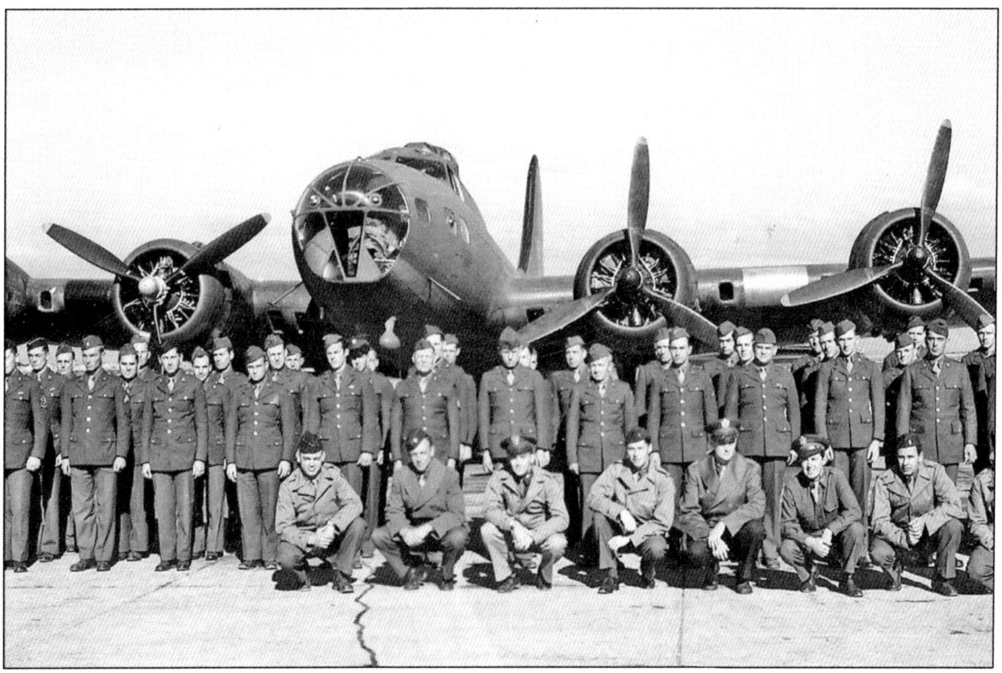

The reason for Gowen Field's existence is front and center—bomber crews for the U.S. Army Air Forces to take the fight to Germany and Japan. Graduates of Gowen Field's aircrew training are seen here with the mighty B-17 Flying Fortress.

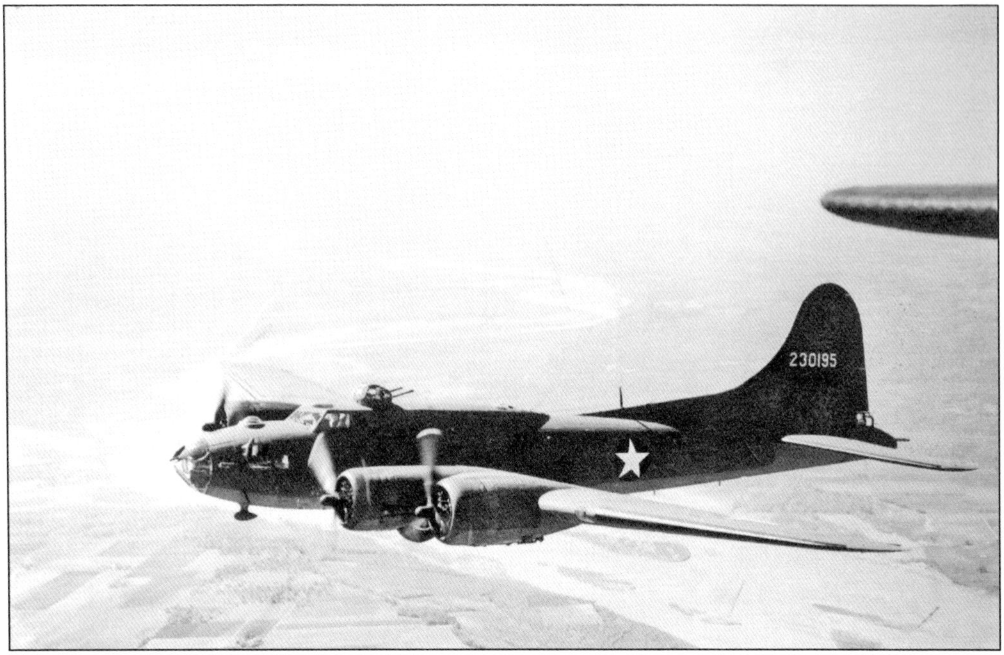

The Snake River runs through southern Idaho and also forms part of the state's border with Oregon. This B-17E of the 388th Bomb Group, No. 42-30195, is pictured on a training mission as it crosses over the Snake River. This aircraft, later named "Blind Date," was lost in a crash in England in 1944.

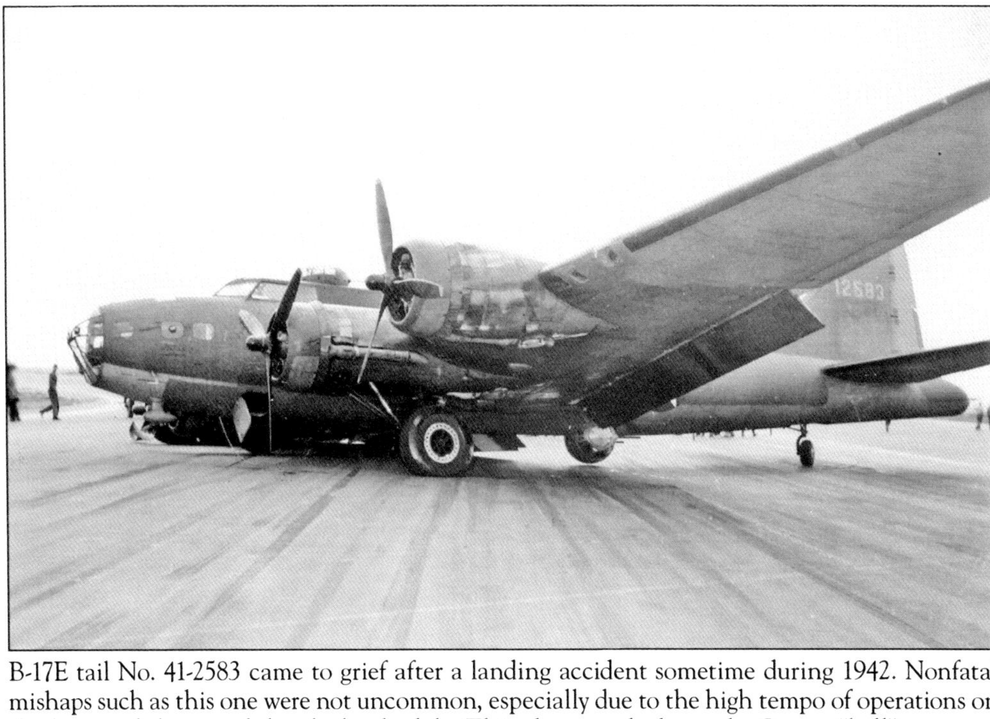

B-17E tail No. 41-2583 came to grief after a landing accident sometime during 1942. Nonfatal mishaps such as this one were not uncommon, especially due to the high tempo of operations on the base and the round-the-clock schedule. This photograph shows the Sperry "ball" turret on the bottom of the fuselage quite clearly.

Col. Robin A. Day, the first commanding officer of Gowen Field, is depicted in a drawing done by the Collias brothers for the base newspaper. Day's tenure in the role was brief, but during his time the base saw rapid growth. He departed Gowen Field on July 25, 1941.

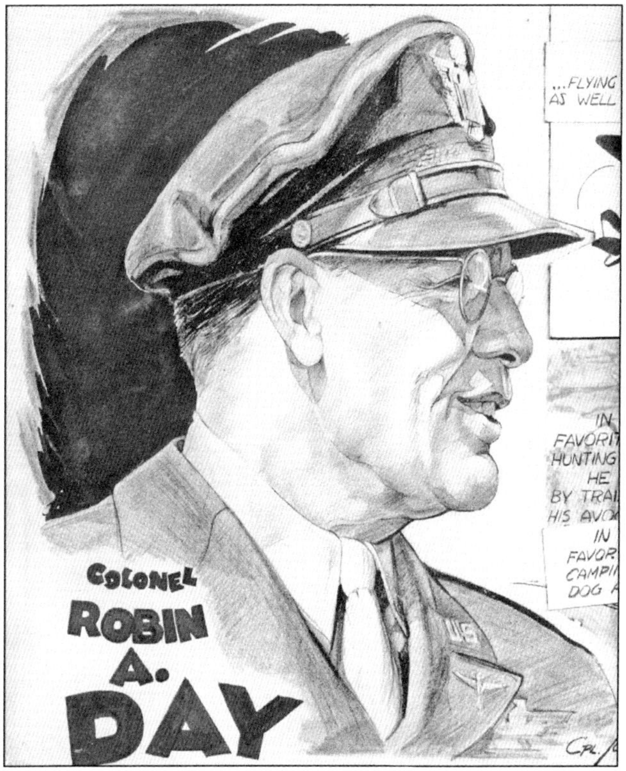

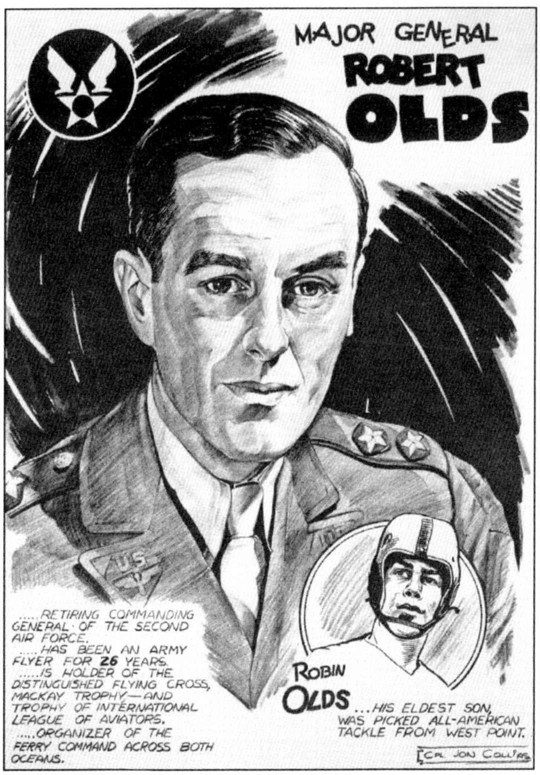

This is a sketch of Maj. Gen. Robert Olds, a former commander of the 2nd Air Force, done by brothers Nick and John Collias. The two Collias brothers served at Gowen Field working at the base newspaper, the *Gowen Beacon*. Of interesting note, Major General Olds's son Robin flew fighters in World War II and went on to earn fame in the Vietnam War as a commander of the 8th Tactical Fighter Wing.

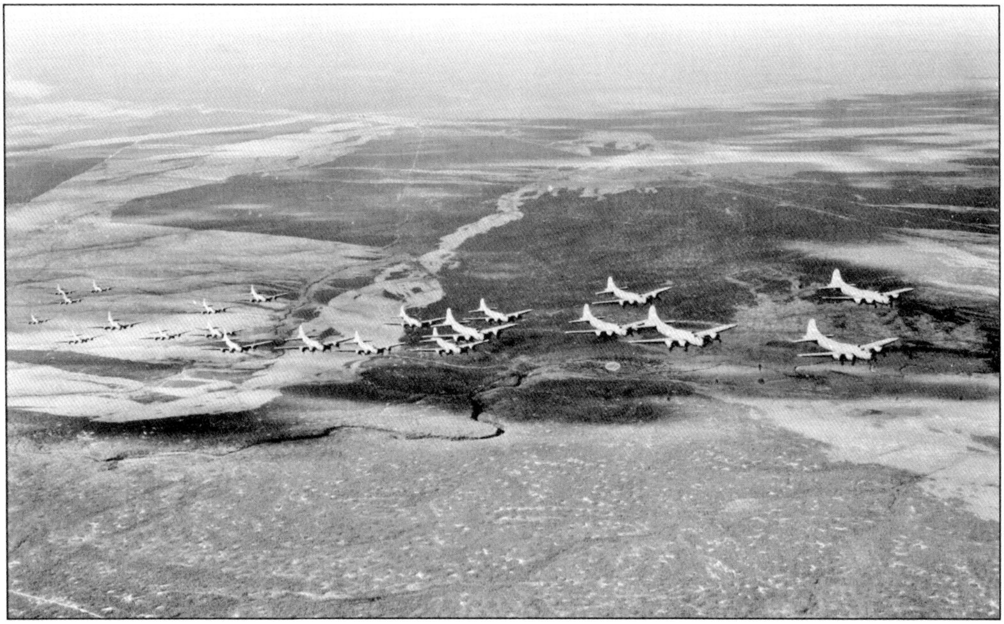

Seen over the southwest Idaho desert, this group formation represents an important part of the training that crews undertook while stationed at Gowen Field. The need to quickly and safely form up after takeoff was essential in England due to the vast numbers of planes in the air at the same time. Furthermore, English weather compounded the problem with heavy fogs that led to midair collisions.

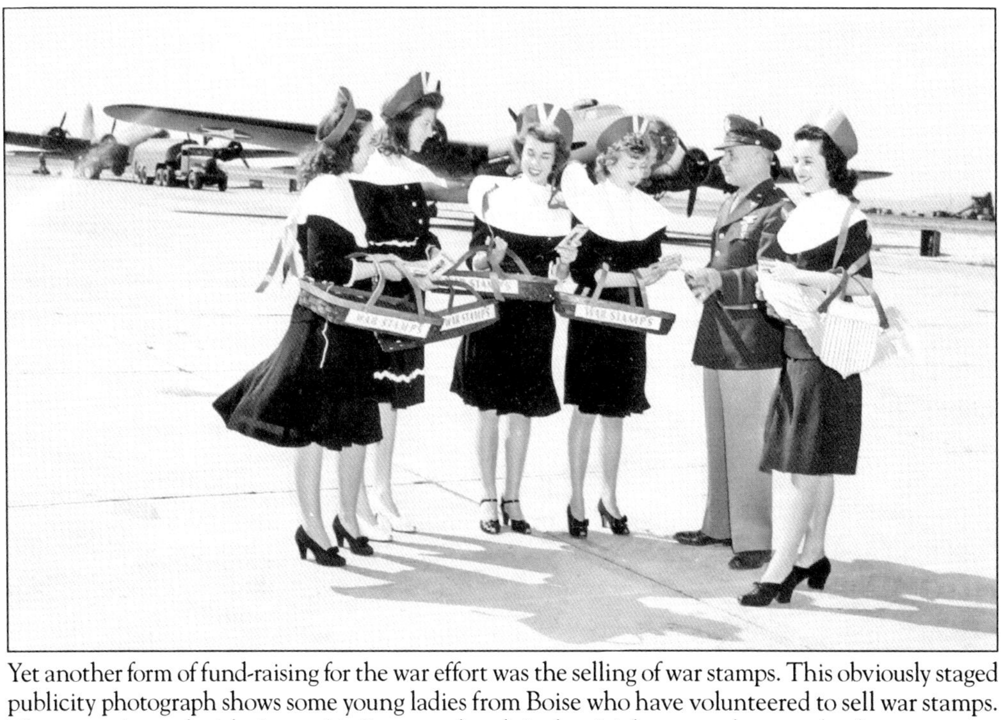

Yet another form of fund-raising for the war effort was the selling of war stamps. This obviously staged publicity photograph shows some young ladies from Boise who have volunteered to sell war stamps. They are pictured with Army Air Forces colonel Arthur Melanson, who was the first executive officer of Gowen Field and the first base commander of Mountain Home Army Air Field.

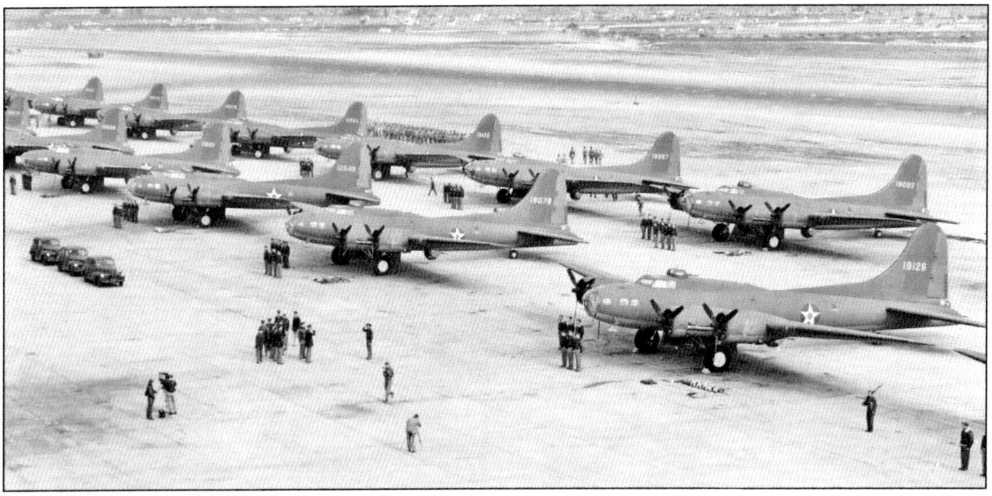

During an inspection of Gowen Field, B-17s sit on the ramp with their crews as 2nd Air Force officers review the aircraft. These are B-17Es, many of which were lost in combat during the early part of the Army Air Forces' bombing campaign against Germany. Fighter escort was not available on these missions, but later P-51s could travel the length of the assignments.

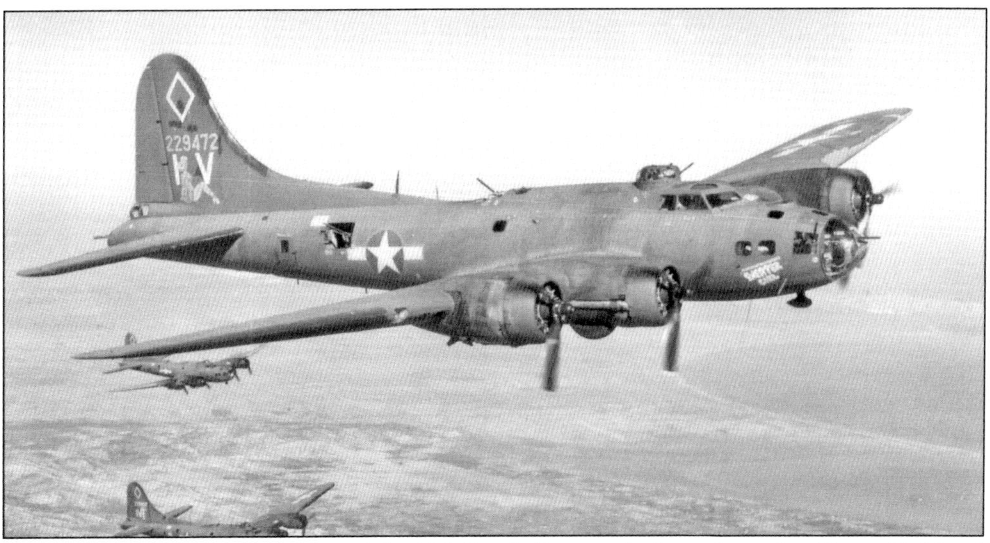

The B-17E "Sweater Girl" was part of the 99th Bomb Group, which was formed at Gowen Field and trained at the base for a brief period. The aircraft is seen here on a flight near the Mediterranean Ocean. The crew trained at Gowen Field in 1942.

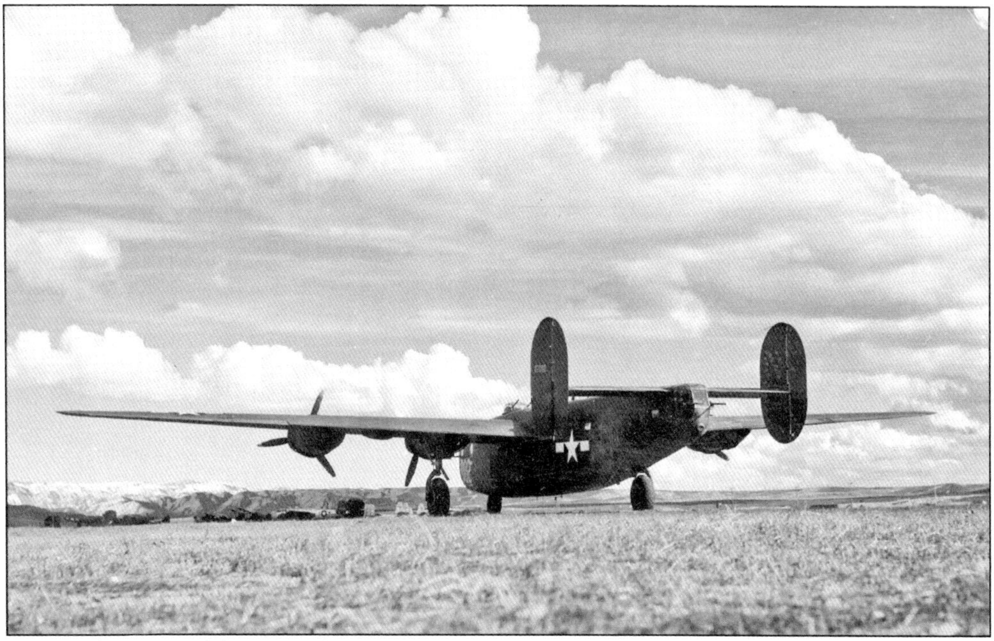

Despite their peaceful setting, these B-24s were an important part of the intense training schedule at Gowen Field. The base's first B-24 Liberators arrived in 1943 to be married up with awaiting aircrews. Once assigned an aircraft, crews began training and, once graduated, moved on to combat in either the European or Pacific theaters of war.

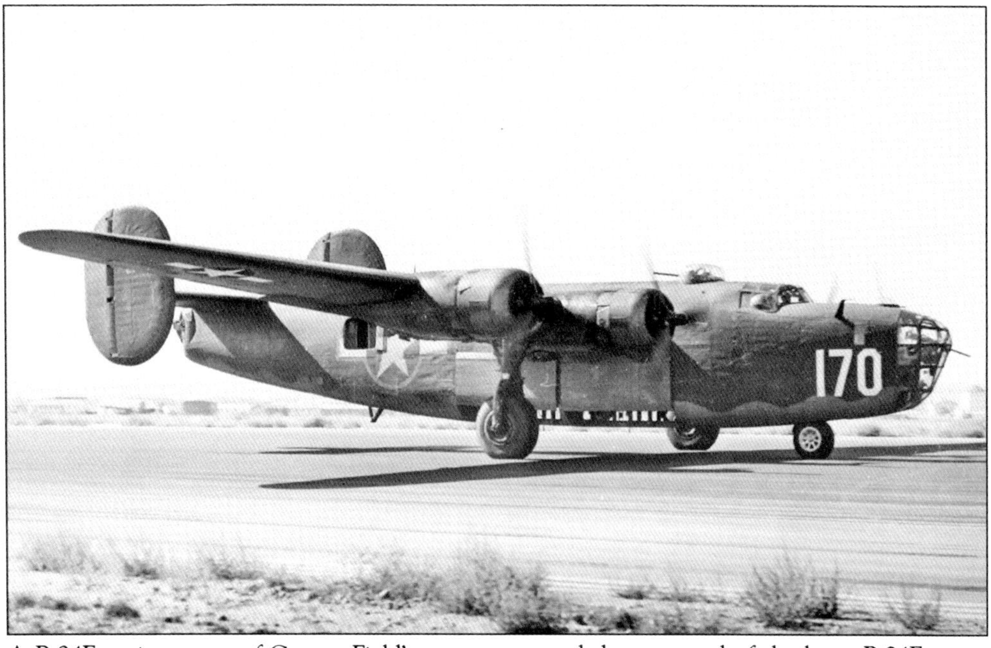

A B-24E taxis on one of Gowen Field's runways toward the west end of the base. B-24Es were powered by four Pratt and Whitney radial engines that each produced 1,200 horsepower with cruise speeds of 160 miles per hour. Later versions of the B-24 were even faster. Just beyond the nose, one of Gowen Field's Celestial Navigation Towers is visible. These strange-looking towers housed the equipment where navigators could practice their night navigational skills anytime of day.

While flying crews received much recognition, ground crews were often overlooked. Long combat missions and damage took their toll on the big bombers. Many times, the ground crews worked all night to get parts replaced and repair damage in order to ready the aircraft for the next day's mission. Here mechanics work on the gun turret of a B-24 Liberator.

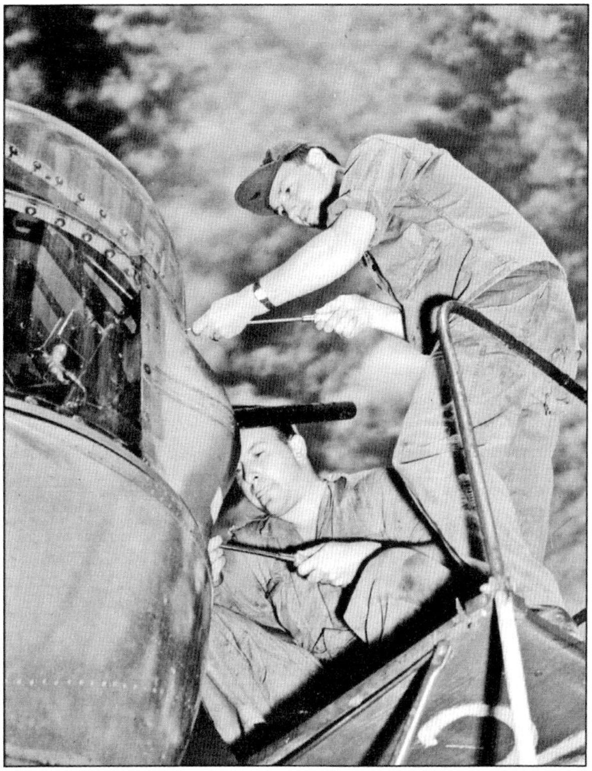

Actor Jimmy Stewart volunteered for the U.S. Army when the country entered World War II, becoming a qualified bomber pilot and training at Gowen Field. He kept out of the spotlight and focused on learning to fly the B-24 Liberator. His unit, the 445th Bomb Group, deployed to Europe and became part of the famous 8th Air Force. Eventually promoted to major, Stewart flew 20 combat missions over Europe.

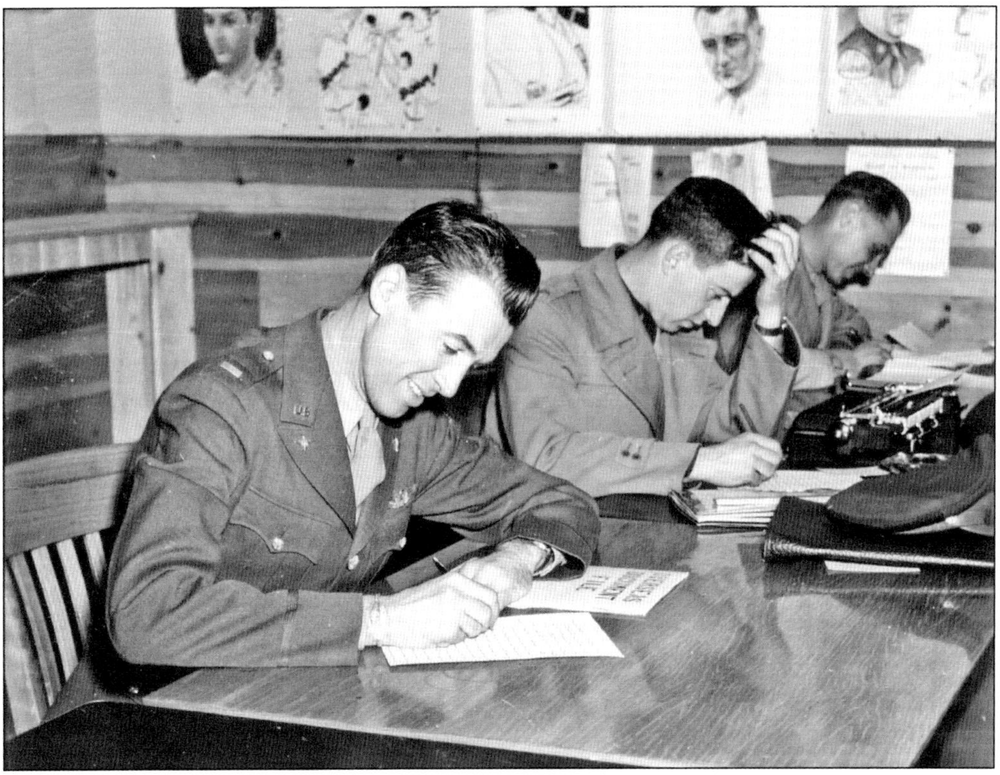

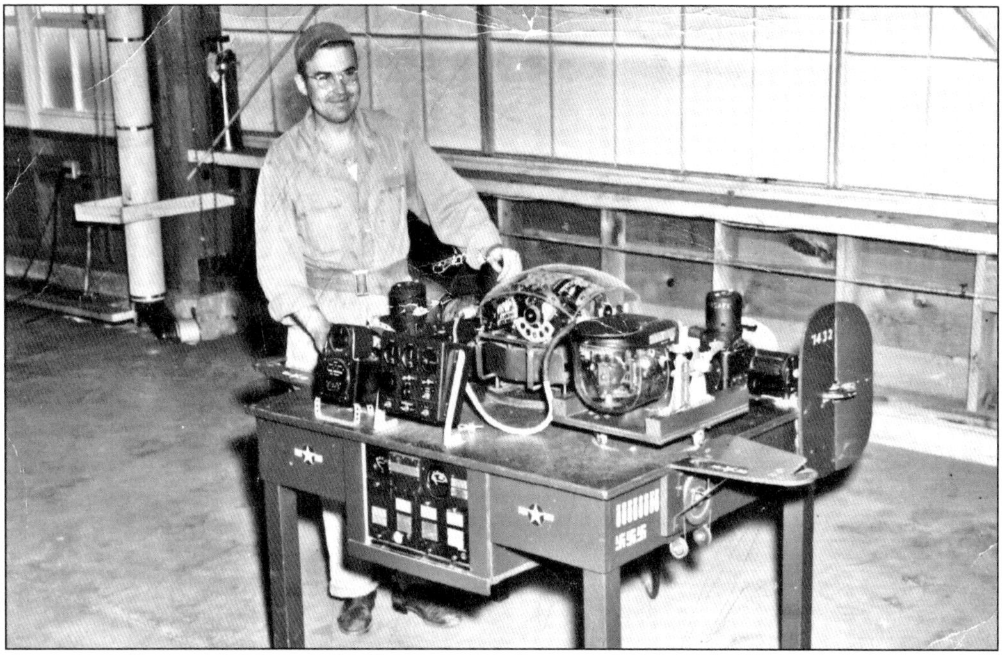

One of many noncommissioned officers assigned to Gowen Field, TSgt. Robert Nagel taught photo-navigation, bombing, and air strategy. He devised modifications to the A-7 Bomb Trainer and A-2 Auto-Pilot Trainer that allowed accurate simulated flight conditions. With a few valves added and adjustments to the autopilot, he was able to accurately simulate a bombsight in actual flight. These modifications were adopted at all army airfields nationwide.

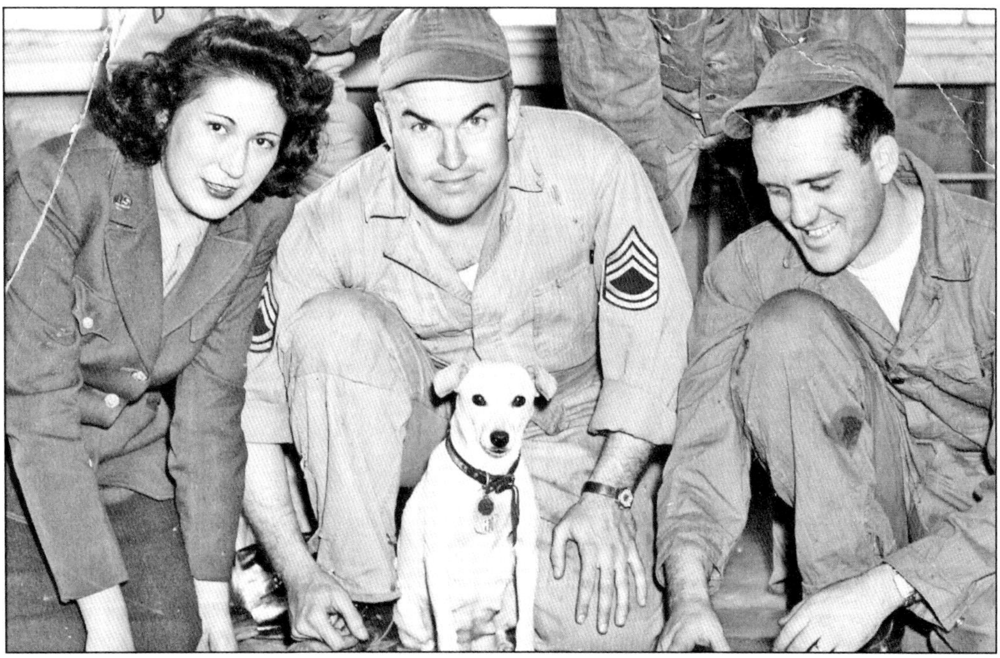

Technical Sergeant Nagel (center) and two unidentified Gowen Field soldiers admire Nagel's dog Lady, who has just had a litter of puppies. Lady must have been Nagel's constant companion, because on one occasion he even took her to a violin concert in Boise.

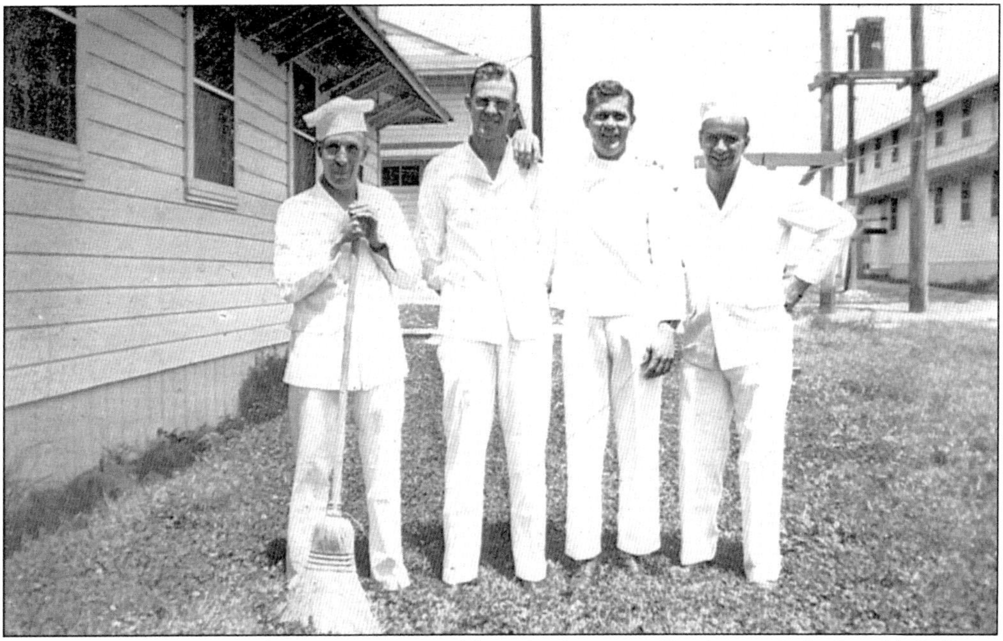

Pictured from left to right are Gowen Field cooks Sergeant Erickson, Cpl. Garald Call, an unidentified sergeant, and Sergeant Noff. Corporal Call, a butcher before the war and a grandfather to Gary Keith, was injured in basic training and rendered unfit for combat. In a rare act of common sense, a personnel officer changed his military occupational specialty to meat cutter. (Courtesy Garald Call.)

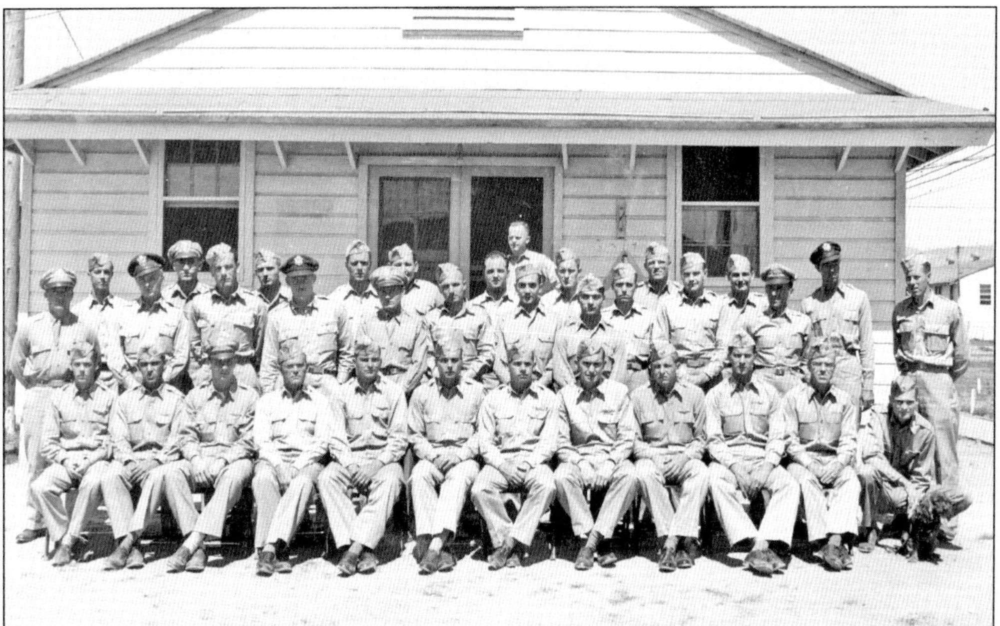

These officers and men are members of the 411th Bomb Squadron, one of the training units of the 29th Bomb Group based at Gowen Field. In 1944, the 29th was re-designated a very heavy bomb group and departed the base to train in the B-29. The group later joined the 20th Air Force in the Pacific and participated in the aerial campaign against the Japanese mainland.

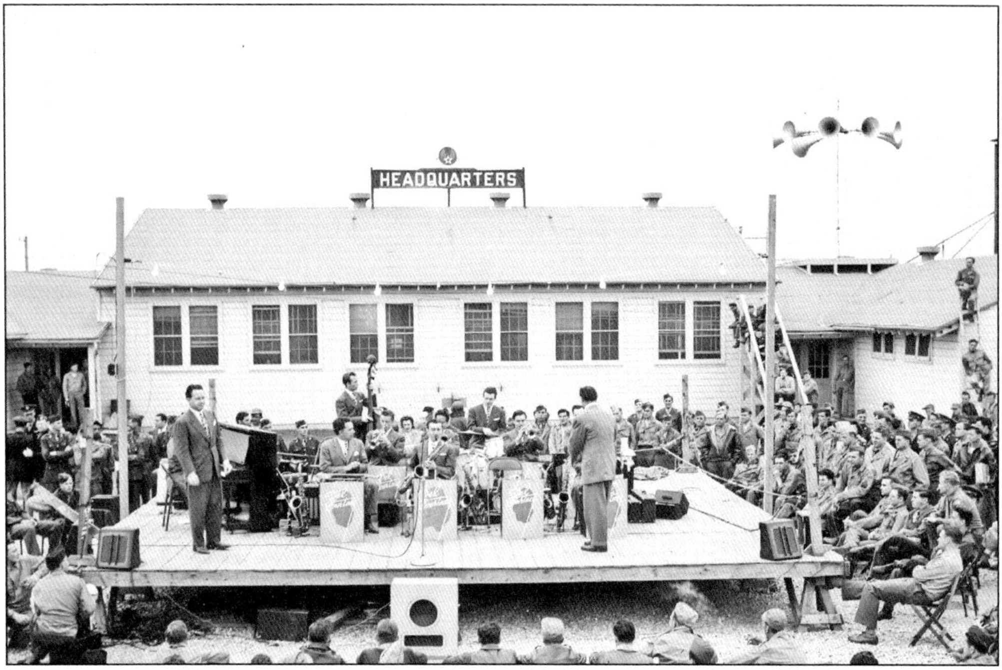

Del Courtney and his band entertain some of Gowen Field's airmen in front of the base headquarters building. Bands played an important part in boosting morale during the war and frequently made stops at bases both within the country and overseas. Del Courtney loved to keep big band music alive as much as he could, performing well into his 80s.

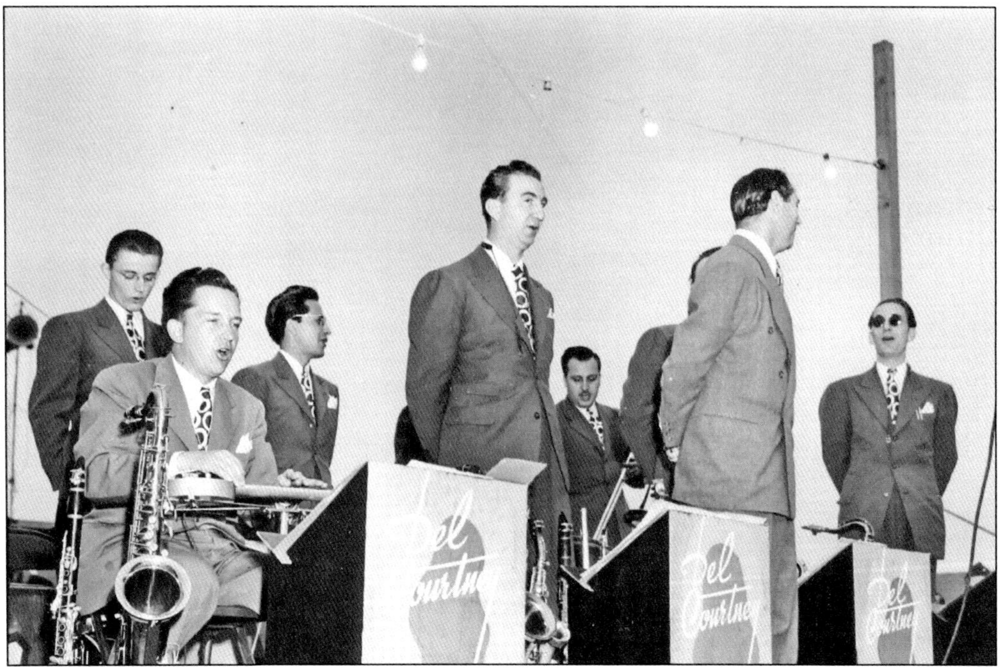

This provides another angle of the Del Courtney Band during its performance at Gowen Field. A variety of concerts, shows, and plays were arranged so that airmen did not have to take the bus into nearby Boise.

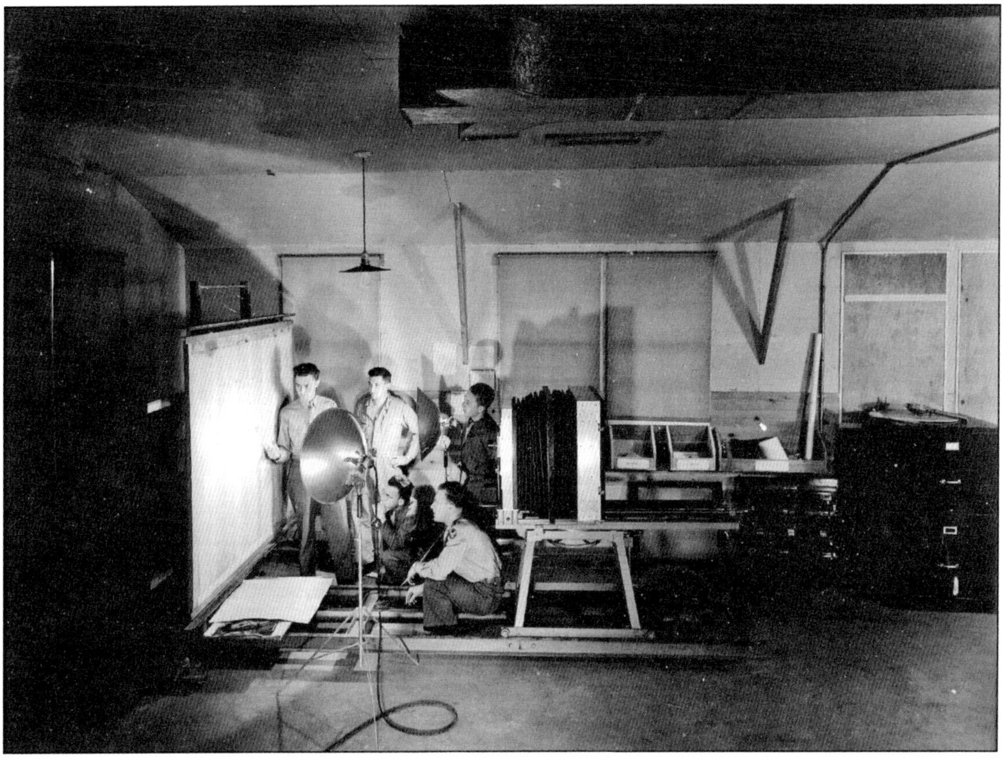

The base's photography shop personnel are busy at work. In the days before computers and editing software, graphics work was accomplished by hand. One method was to superimpose one photograph over another to achieve a desired result. The authors believe that process is what is occurring here.

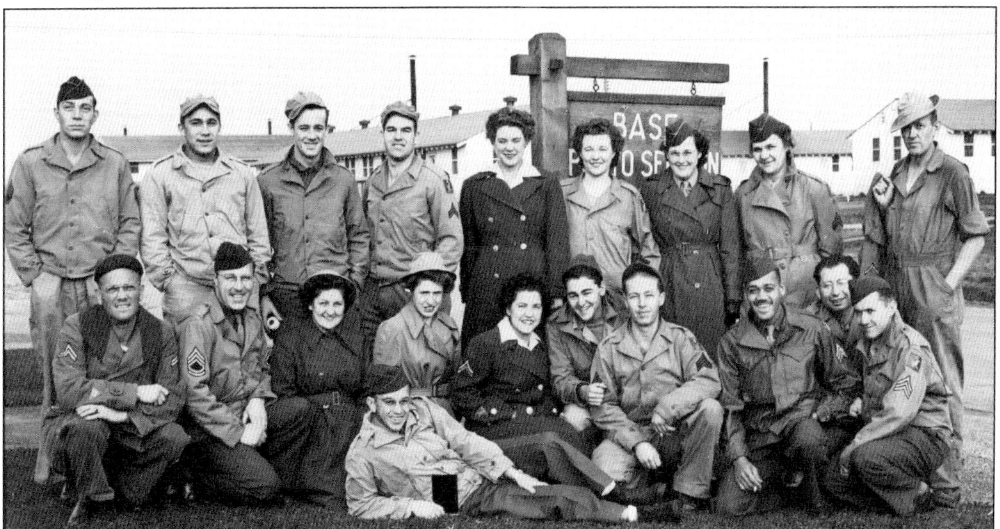

Civilians and Army Air Forces personnel are shown at the base photography division, which not only took photographs but created posters and educational materials used on base. Sgt. David Regensberg, the photographer who took many of the views in this chapter, leans on his right side in the center foreground.

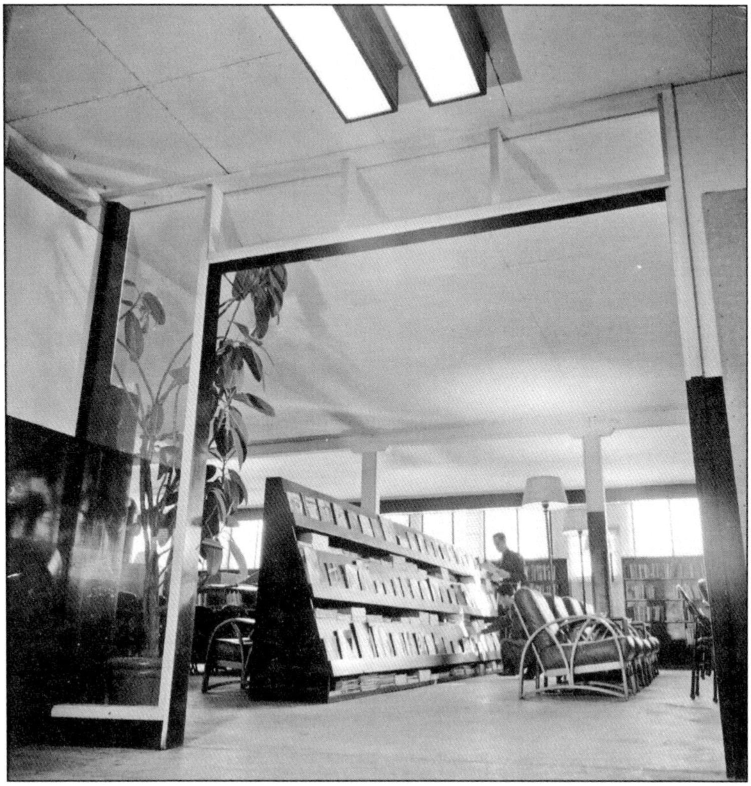

Gowen Field was close to the city of Boise and its recreational opportunities, but there were also facilities on post for personnel to enjoy. In 1942, the Post Exchange was remodeled into a library. This library held more than 3,000 volumes, along with easy chairs and floor lamps. To keep pace with the busy training schedule, the facility was open 24 hours a day.

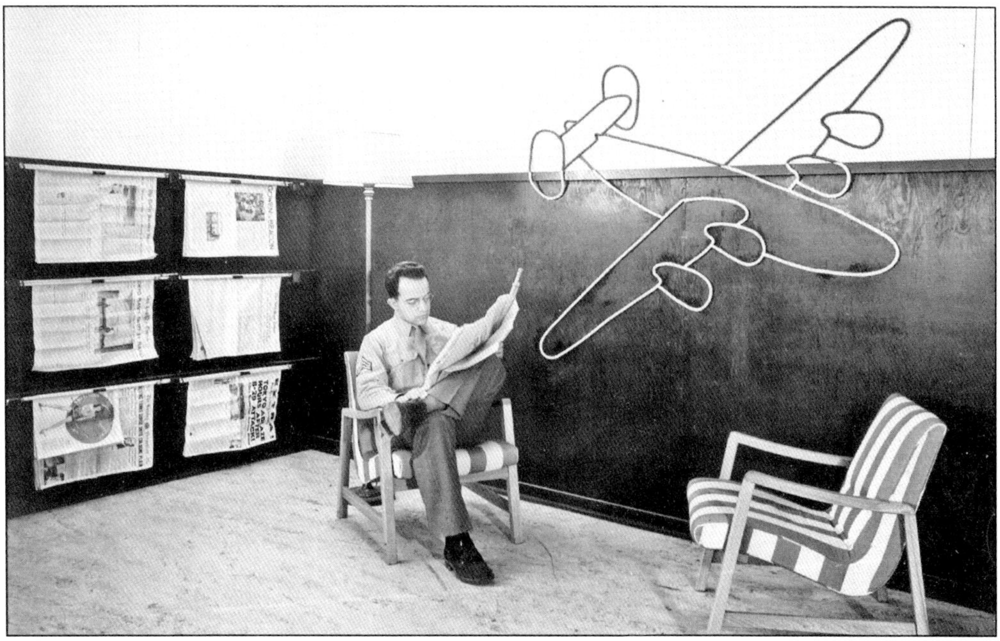

A sergeant relaxes in one of Gowen Field's day rooms; it is stocked with papers such as the *Idaho Daily Statesman*, the *New York Times*, and the *Gowen Beacon* (the base newspaper). The aircraft painted on the wall next to him is a B-24 Liberator, an indication that this photograph was taken after the B-17 Flying Fortresses had left Gowen Field.

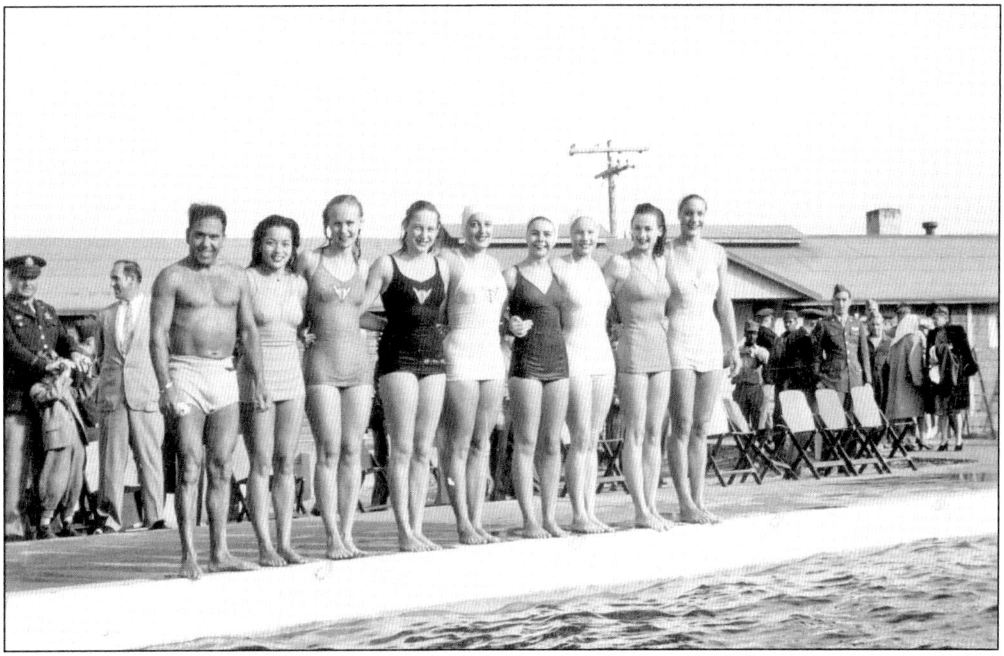

Gowen Field boasted excellent recreational facilities, which included a swimming pool that became the center of many social activities and swim meets. It was used for many years after the war but eventually fell into disuse. The pool was demolished in 2006.

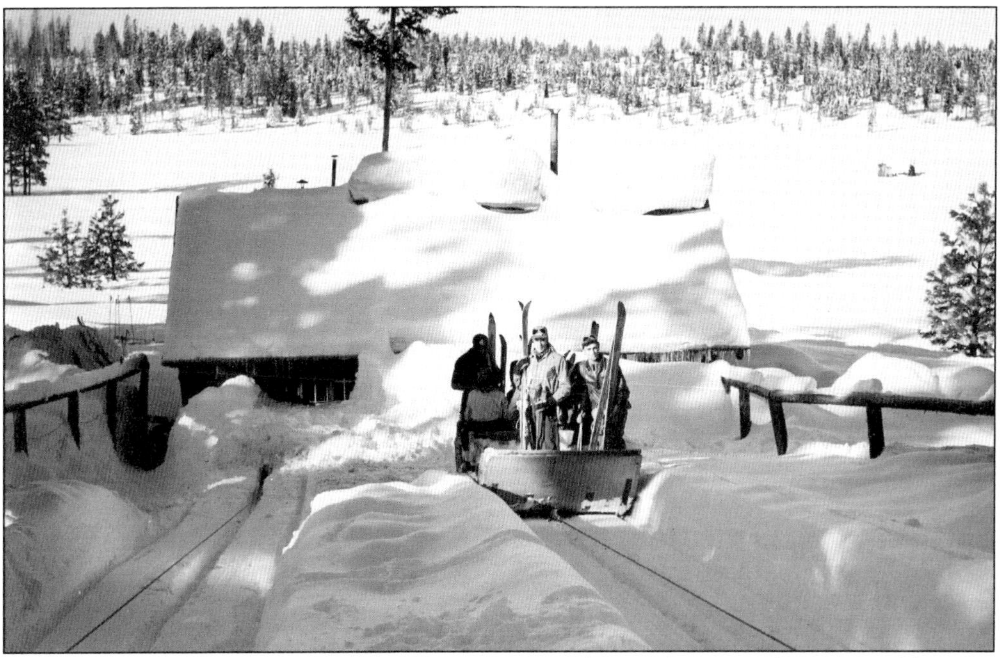

There were—and still are—several ski resorts within driving distance of Gowen Field. Bogus Basin is the closest, situated in the mountains just north of Boise. Often when airmen received a three-day pass to leave base, they chose the popular pastime of skiing. As a side note, according to the February 10, 1944, *Gowen Beacon*, the U.S. Army transformed Bogus Basin into a physical training center.

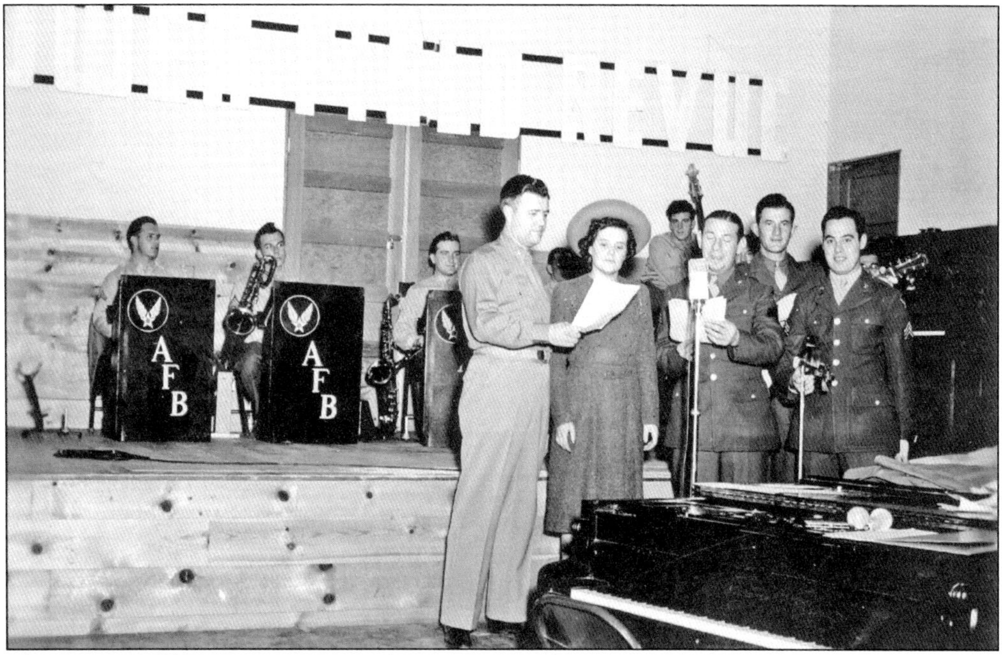

The Gowen Field Revue was an annual program started in 1942. In January 1943, the *Gowen Beacon* described the Revue as an "elaborate musical stage show composed of a variety of acts." The Gowen Field Dance Band played an active role in the event, with live radio broadcasts transmitted for the soldiers' entertainment.

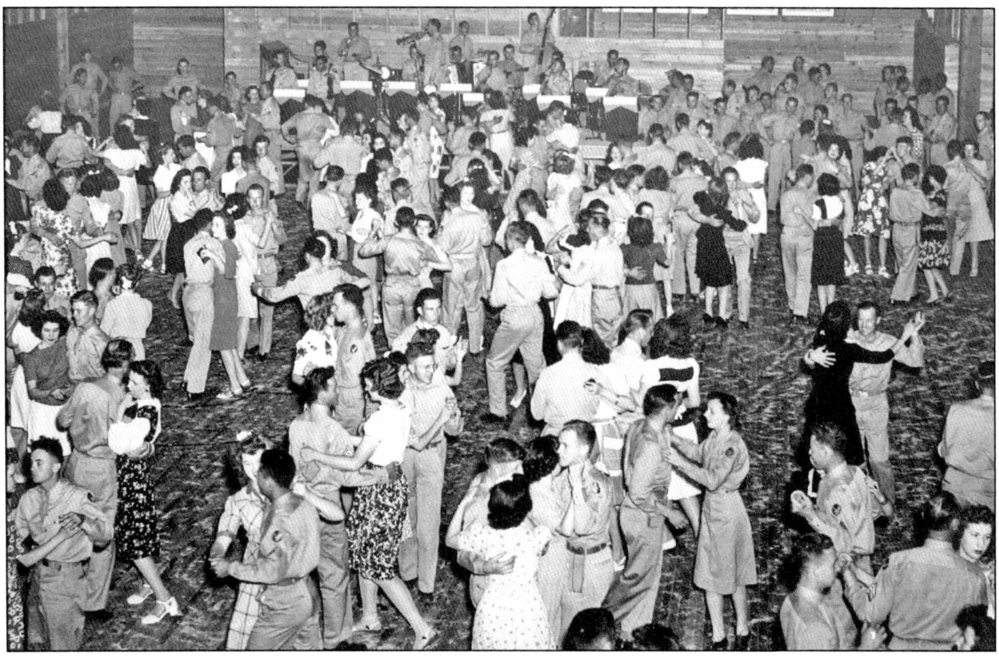

Taken at one of the many social functions between Gowen Field airmen and some of Boise's single young ladies, this photograph embodies the relationship between the airbase and the city. Dances were usually held downtown in Boise at USO halls and churches, unlike the one seen here in the base gymnasium.

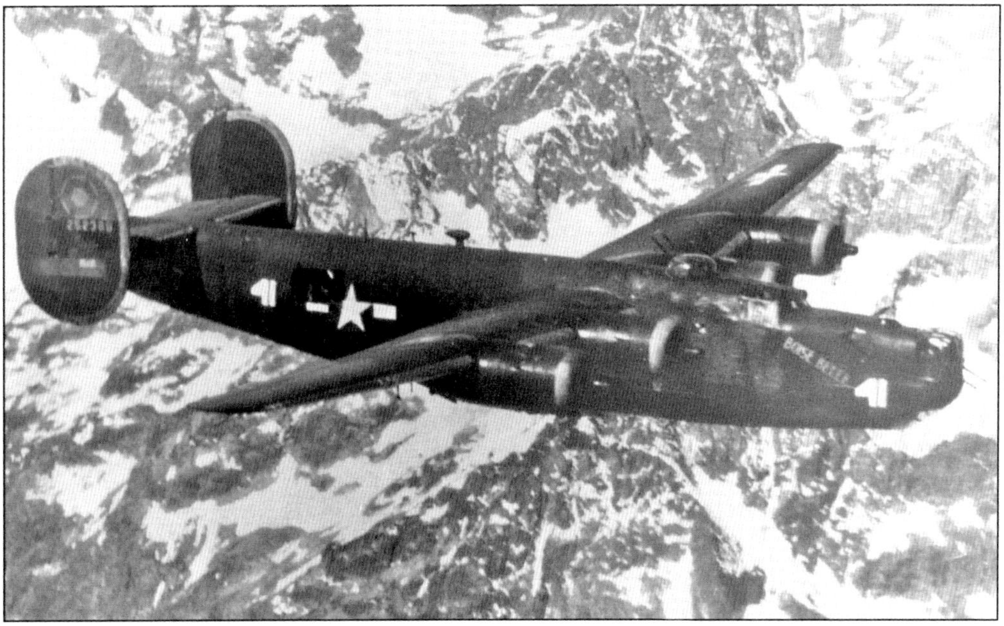

The "Boise Belle" was a B-24 Liberator assigned to the 766th Bombardment Squadron of the 461st Bombardment Group. The 461st formed and trained at Gowen Field from July until September 1943 and later served in the Mediterranean theater. The crew of the "Belle" flew with the airplane on one of the raids against the German oil refineries at Ploesti, Romania; despite heavy clouds, flak, and smoke over the target, the group hit its objective.

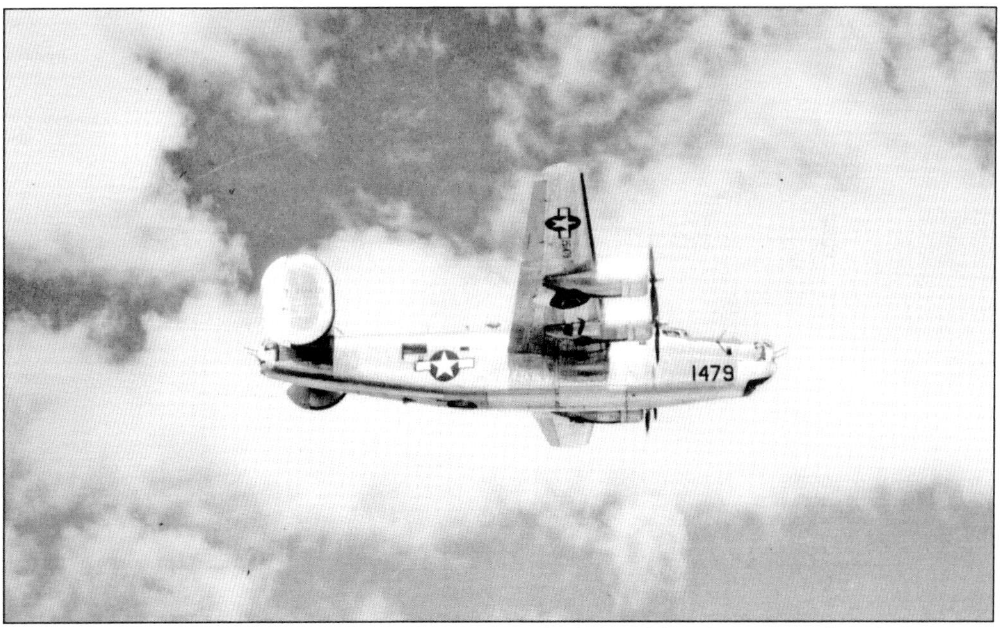

Climbing out of Gowen Field, this B-24J shows its multiple bomb bay doors, as well as the Emerson nose turret seen on the later models of Liberators. The electrically powered Emerson turret, with two .50-caliber machine guns, was used to protect the B-24 against frontal attacks. German Luftwaffe fighter pilots preferred fast, head-on attacks to minimize the defensive firepower of B-17 and B-24 machine guns.

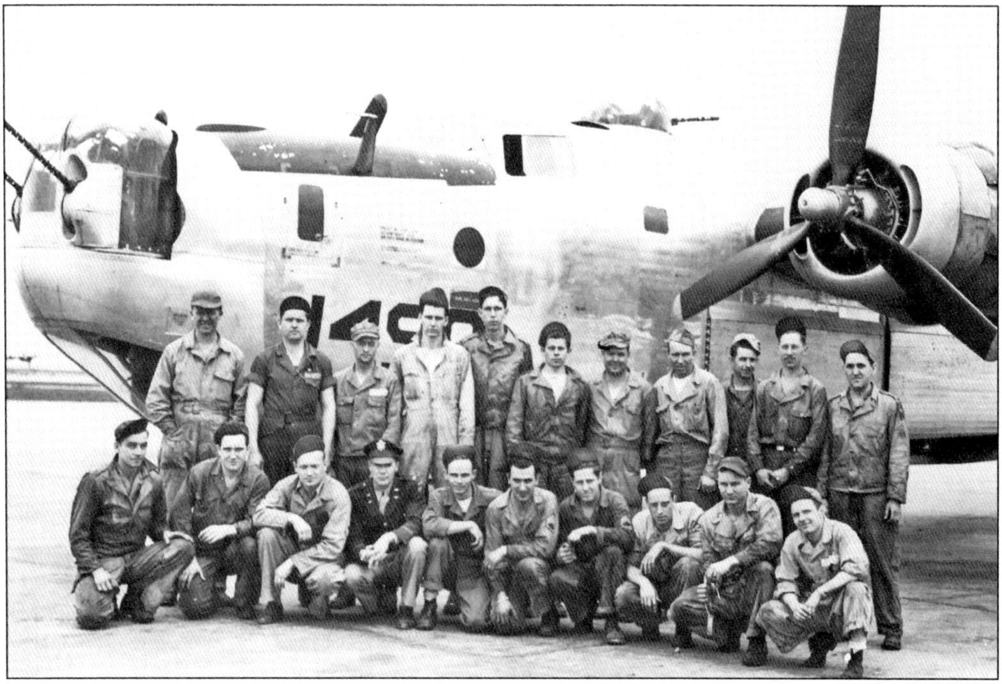

These fliers and ground crew were members of the 29th Bomb Group at Gowen Field from 1943 to 1944. When the Army Air Forces changed the policy of operational training units remaining at a base, the 29th left Gowen Field and traded its B-24 Liberators for the newer B-29 Superfortresses.

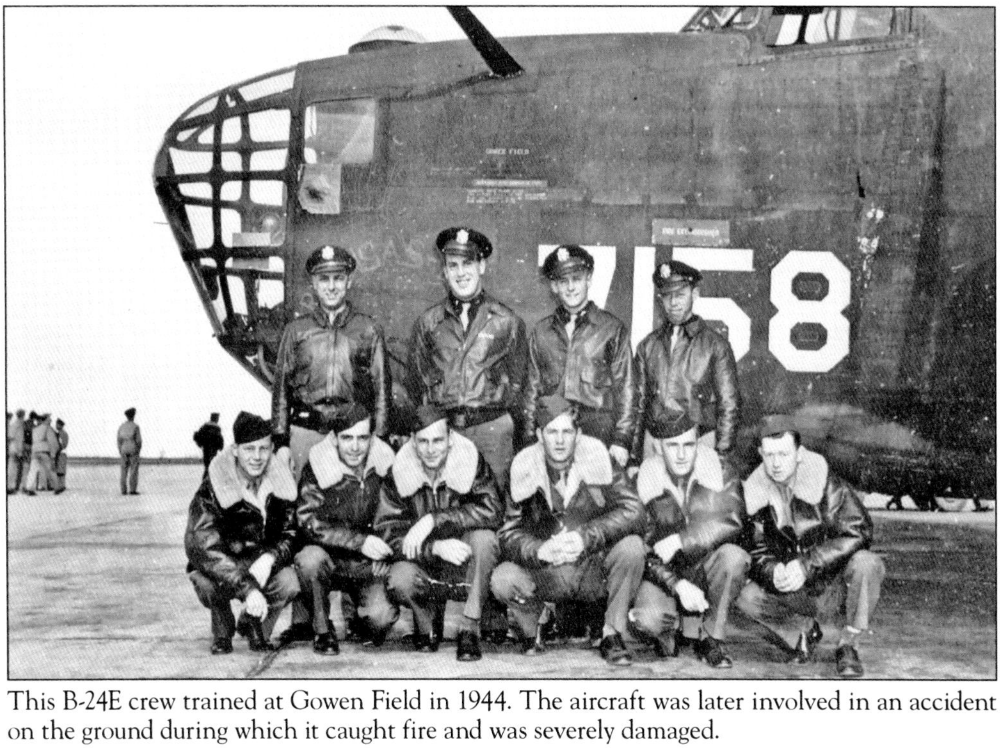

This B-24E crew trained at Gowen Field in 1944. The aircraft was later involved in an accident on the ground during which it caught fire and was severely damaged.

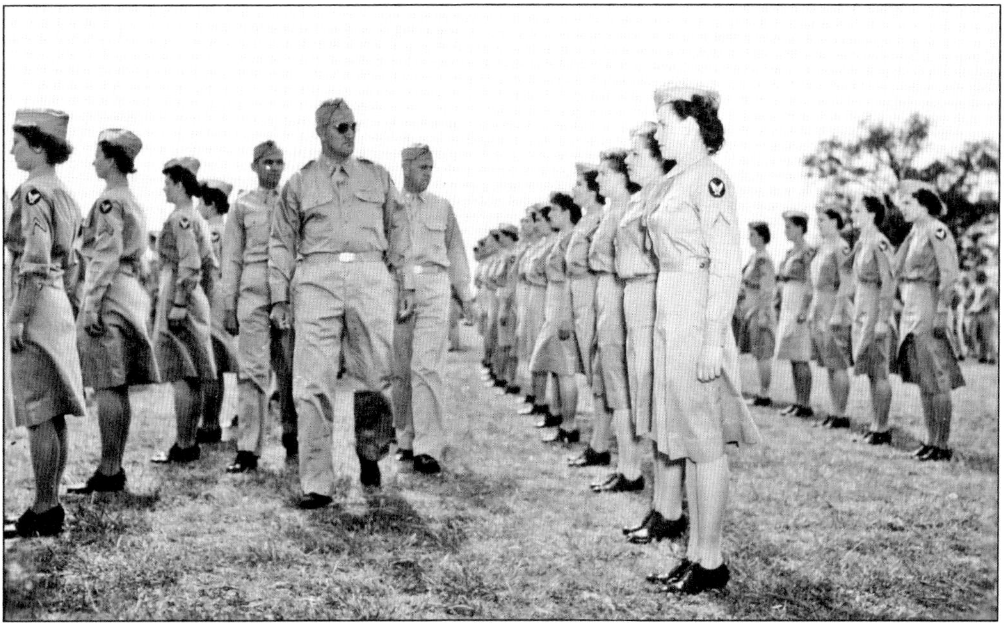

These Women's Army Auxiliary Corps soldiers represent some of the hundreds who served at Gowen Field during World War II. On their left sleeve, they wear the patch of the Army Air Forces. WAACs, as they were known, served in a variety of roles in the Army Air Forces and at Gowen Field such as administrative assistants and even aircraft mechanics.

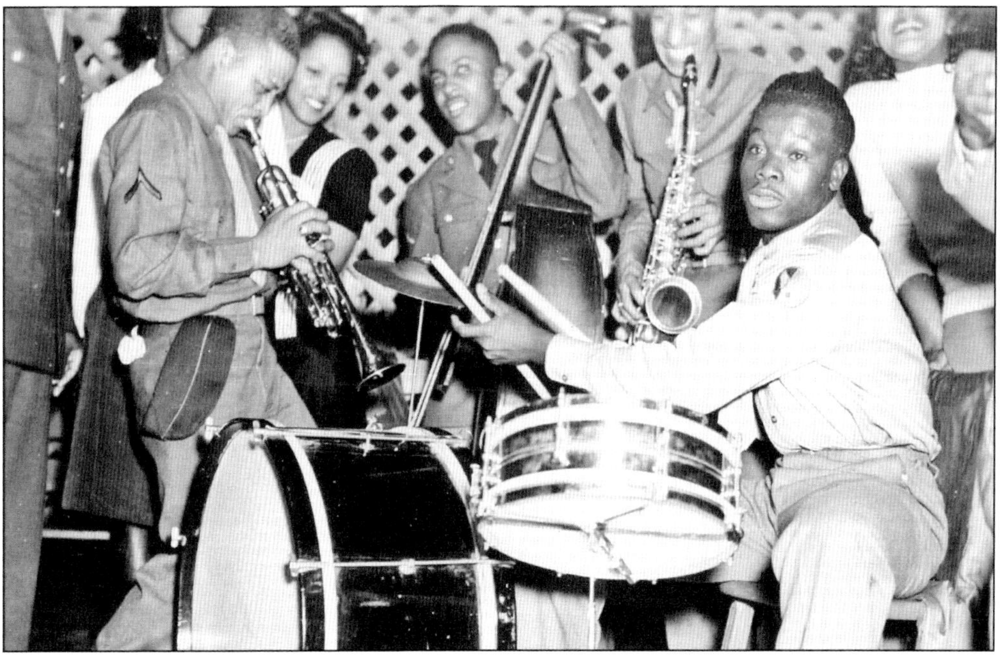

African American soldiers were not allowed in combat during World War II. Many served at Gowen Field in administrative roles and in mess halls to free up white soldiers to fill combat positions. The army was segregated at that time, and therefore Gowen Field had separate barracks, churches, and mess facilities for both races. During free time, music was just as important to African American soldiers as it was to other GIs.

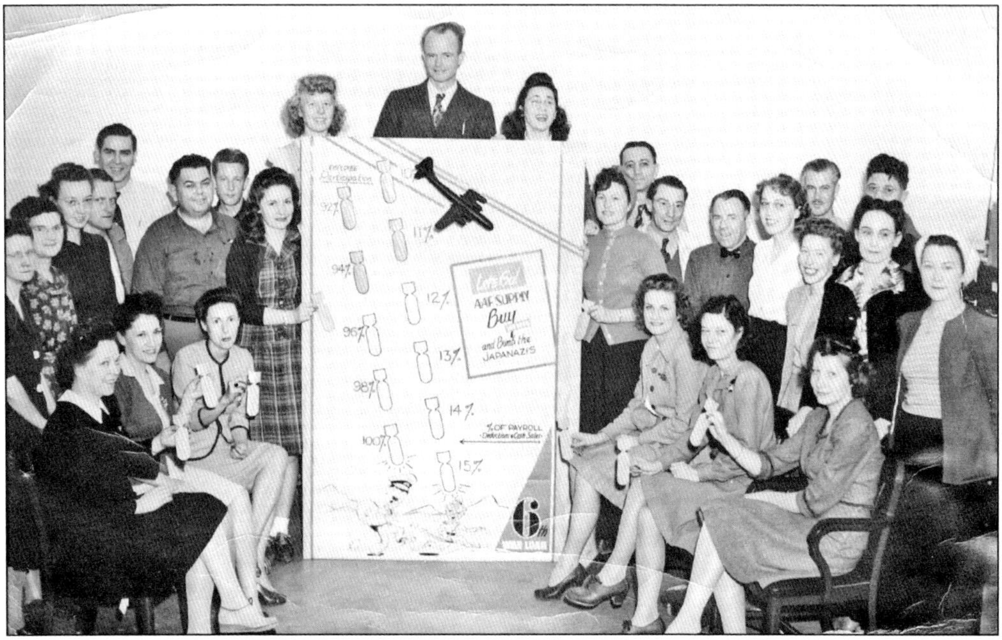

World War II impacted both those in uniform and the civilians on the home front. Employees in the government and private sectors were encouraged to buy war bonds as well as donate a portion of their wages to the war effort. Pictured are some of Gowen Field's civilian workers who contributed to the sixth war bond drive.

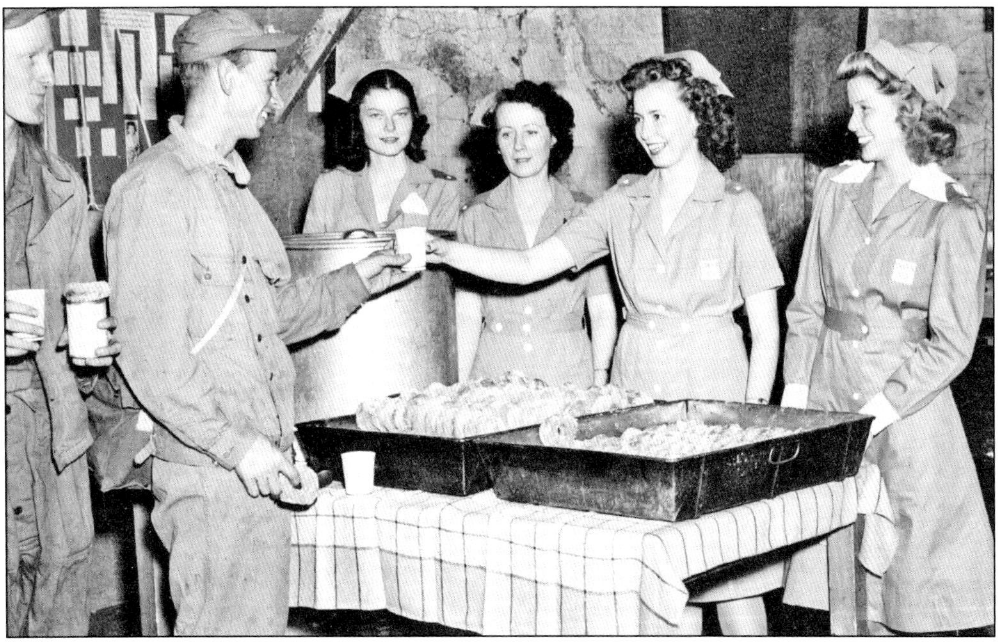

"Doughnut Dollies" was the affectionate nickname given by troops to female volunteers who handed out coffee and doughnuts. Different service organizations like the USO and Red Cross took baked goods, coffee, and reading materials to servicemen at train depots, posts, and halls in local towns. These canteen aides distributed snacks to the hardworking ground crewmen of Gowen Field.

Actress Ann Sothern visited Gowen Field as part of a Hollywood program to support the troops and build morale. Base airmen had a chance to meet famous movie stars up close with obvious positive results. During the 1940s, Ann Sothern starred in a series of 10 Maisie movies and later did television in the 1950s. In 2001, she died in Ketchum, Idaho, at the age of 90.

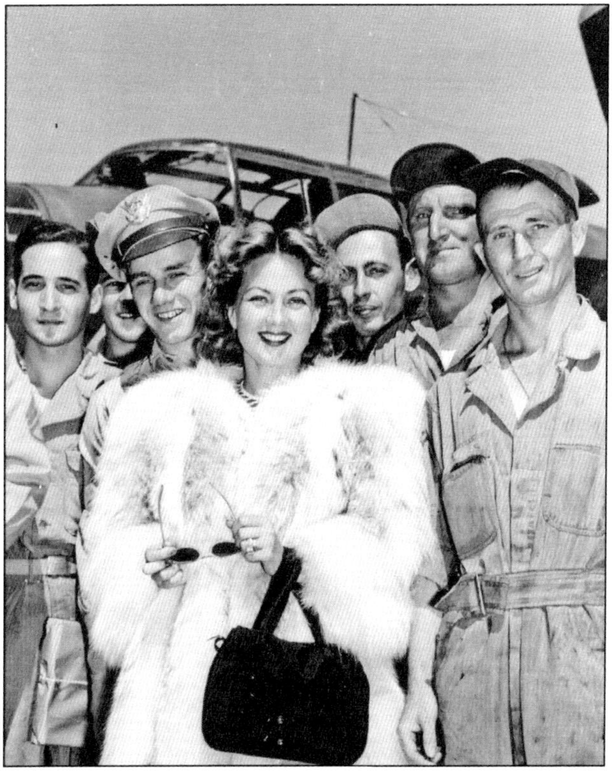

Gowen Field officers enjoy a sports event in Boise—and the company of one of the city's residents. Many airmen formed romantic relationships with Boise women that often resulted in marriages.

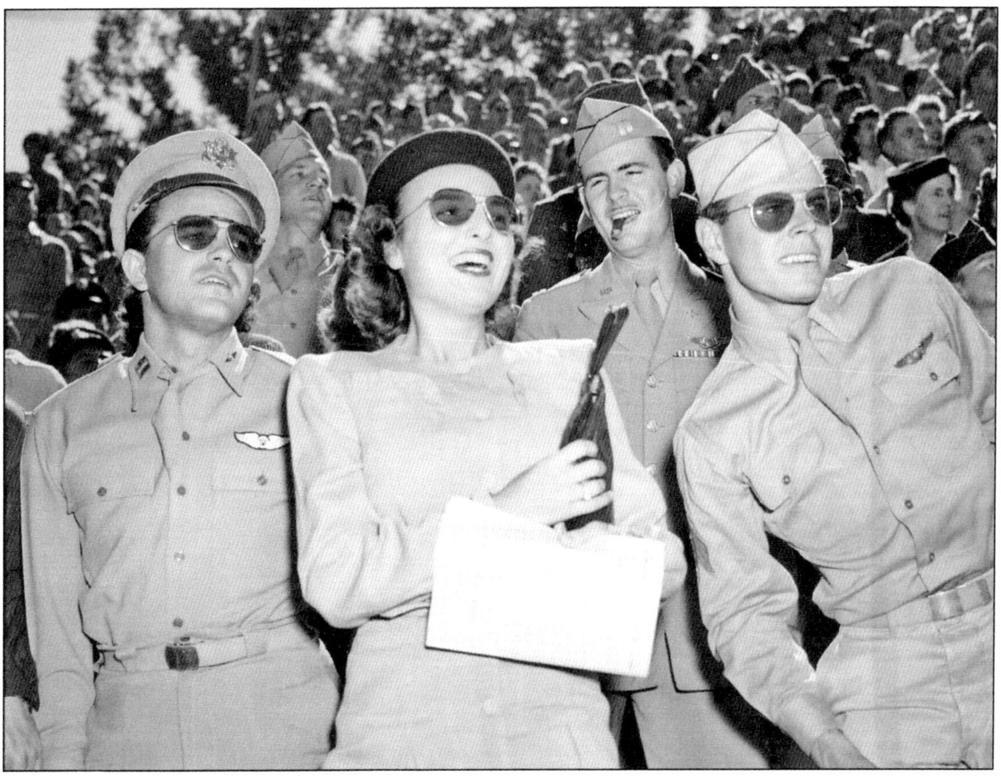

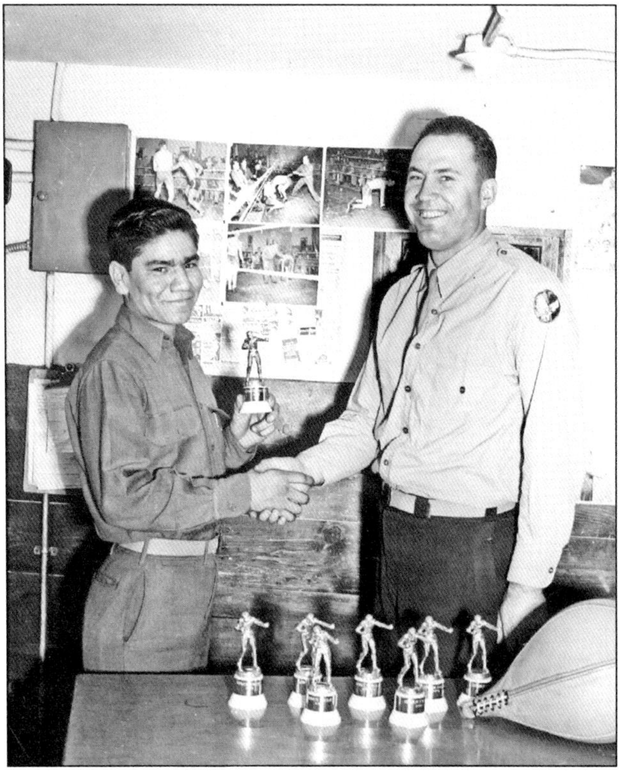

As a means of promoting morale and physical fitness, the army in general made sports facilities and activities a part of every military post. Special Services officers and men maintained the sports equipment and helped organize sports including these awards being given for boxing.

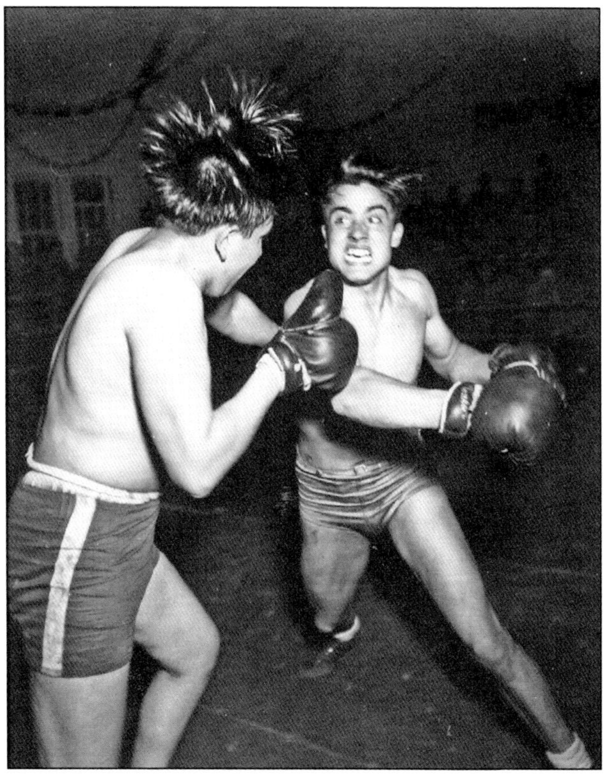

Boxing was one of many sporting activities available to personnel at Gowen Field, and matches were a form of entertainment to the spectator as well.

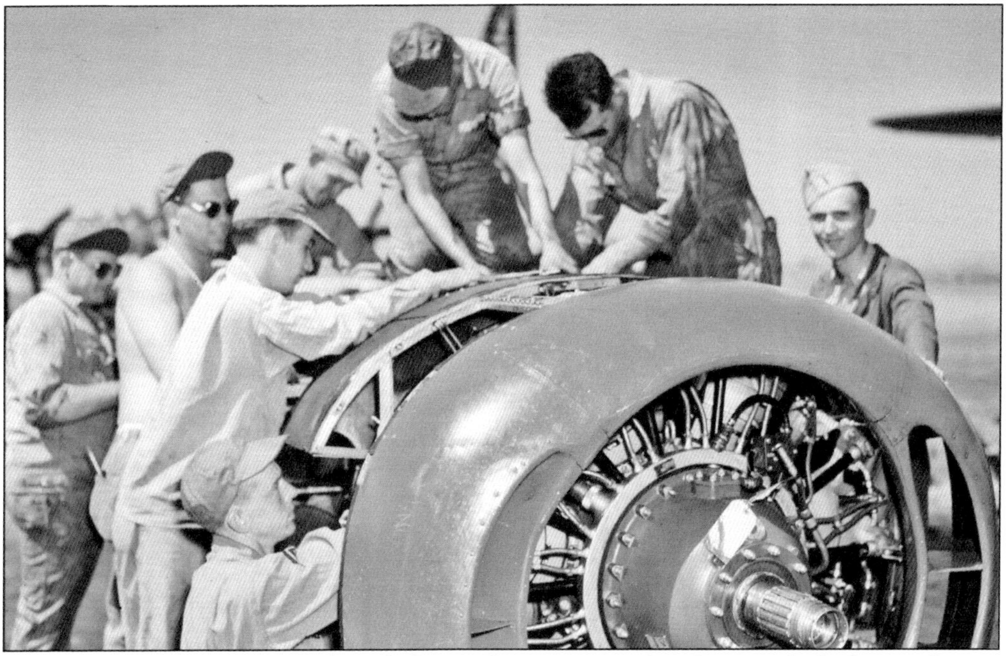

While the flying crews received much-deserved recognition, the often-overlooked ground crews kept the aircraft flying. Training the crews was critical. In 1942, 2nd Air Force headquarters recognized Gowen Field's 29th Bombardment Group as "outstanding among all groups in the Second Air Force." The ground crews were given due recognition when the 2nd Air Force stated, "In the maintenance of your aircraft, records show that you occupied the top position."

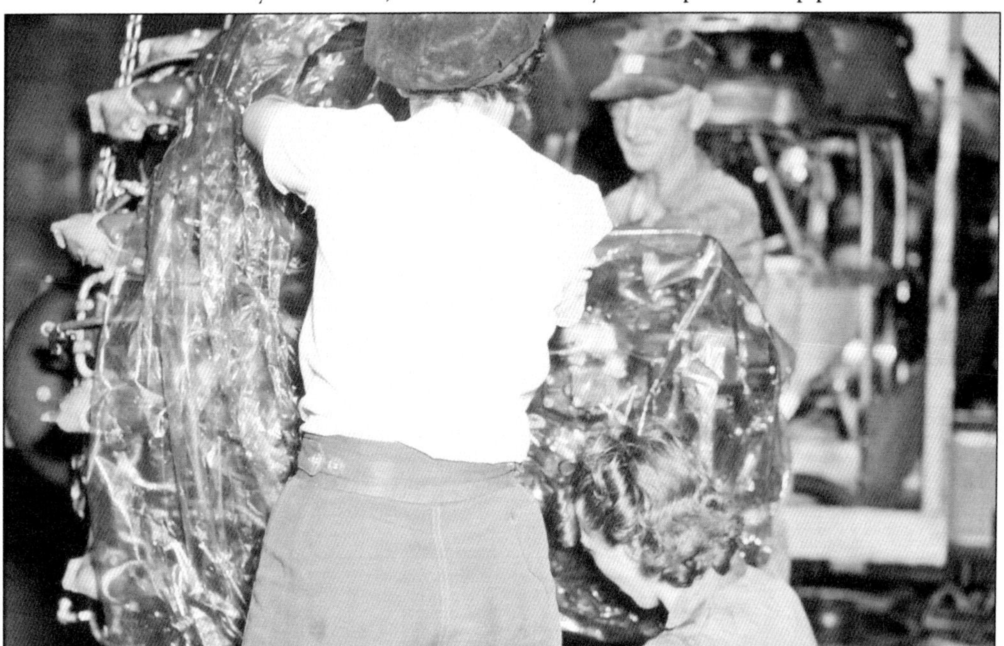

Not all members of the ground crew were men, as this photograph clearly shows. When the WAACs arrived at Gowen Field, they originally provided solely administrative staffing, but many ended up as aircraft mechanics. Here two unidentified WAACs work on a B-24 engine.

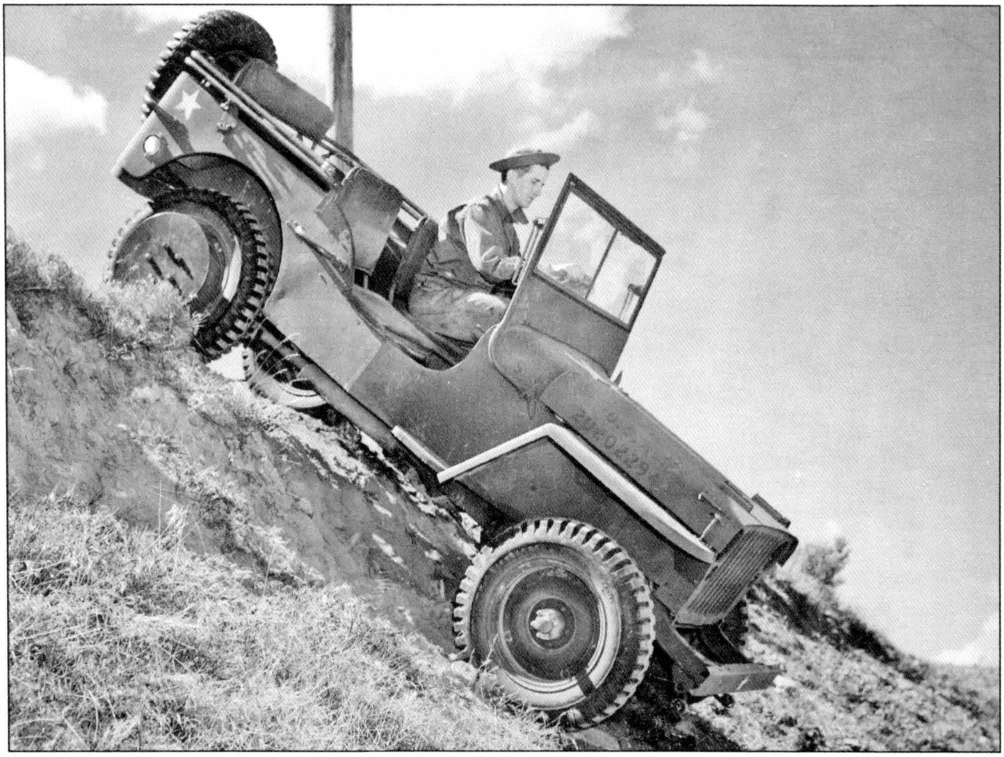

The famous Jeep was able to traverse the desert terrain surrounding Gowen Field. The driver is wearing a work (or fatigue) hat, nicknamed "the Daisy Mae." Soldiers coined the term after a popular comic character of the day who wore a similar hat. Its wide brim made it especially practical in the Idaho desert for soldiers who had to work in the sun.

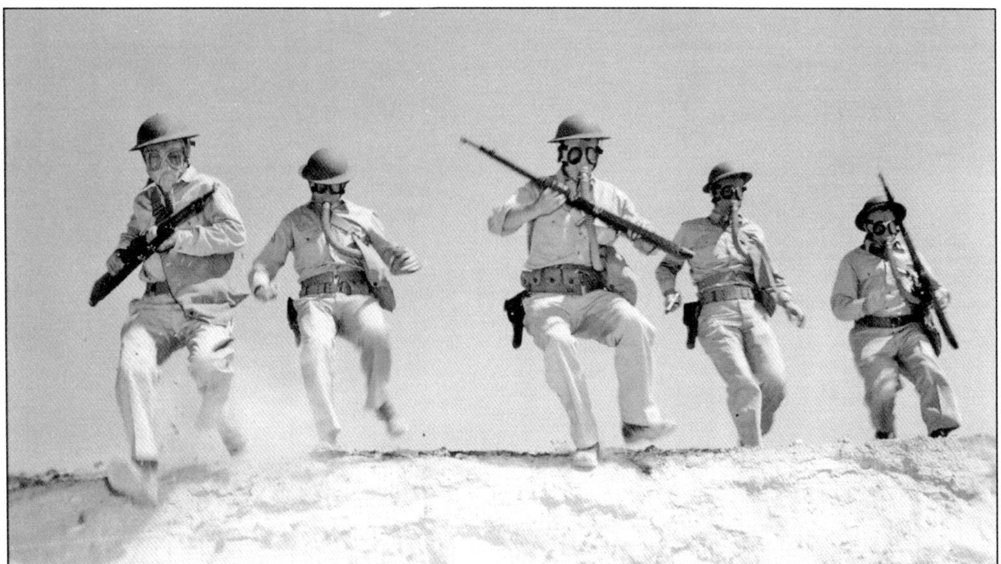

Members of Gowen Field's base defense unit trained in chemical warfare gear, since tear gas could have been used for defense or riot control. Their weapons are older, World War II–era M1917 rifles. By World War II, these were obsolete for frontline combat use but ideal for base security.

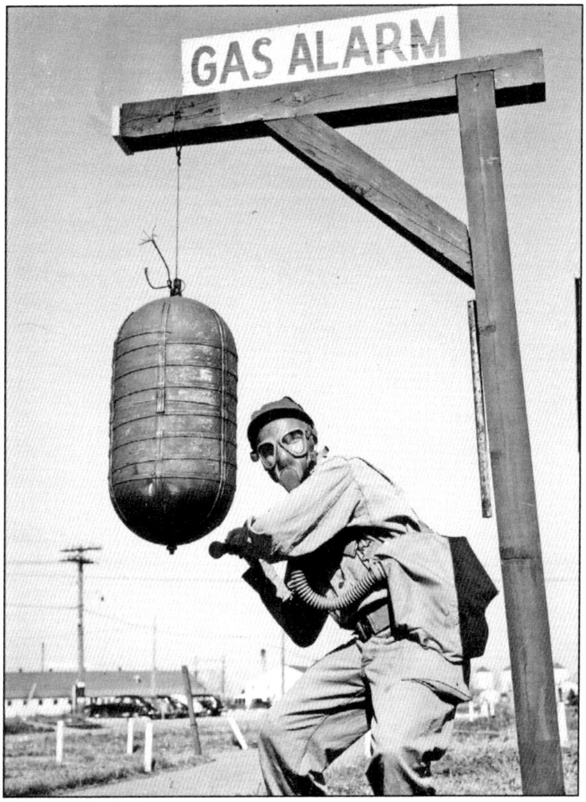

After the attack on Pearl Harbor, people feared that Japan's military forces might invade the western part of the country. Training in chemical warfare was common at Gowen Field in the early part of World War II. This airman is ready to strike the base gas alarm, which at one time was an aircraft oxygen tank.

Along with chemical warfare training, the base defense unit trained on marksmanship and simulated field conditions to prepare airmen for living at remote fields. This view, taken south of the base, shows Gowen Field soldiers aiming bolt-action M1903 rifles. The rifles were considered somewhat obsolete by the army for frontline service and were often issued to units within the United States.

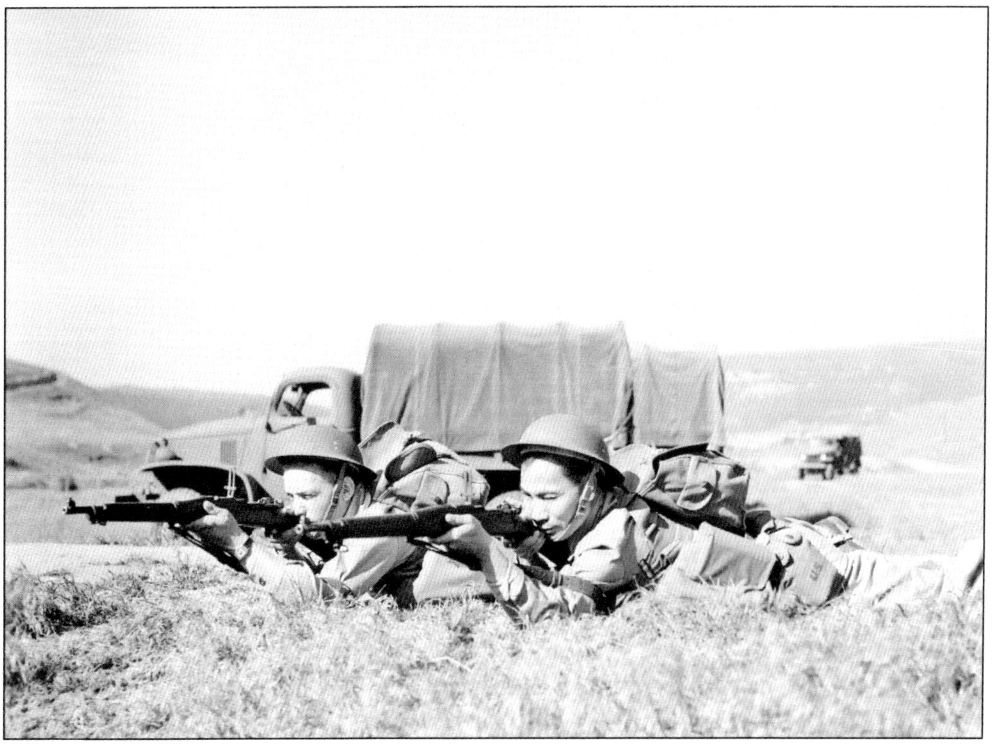

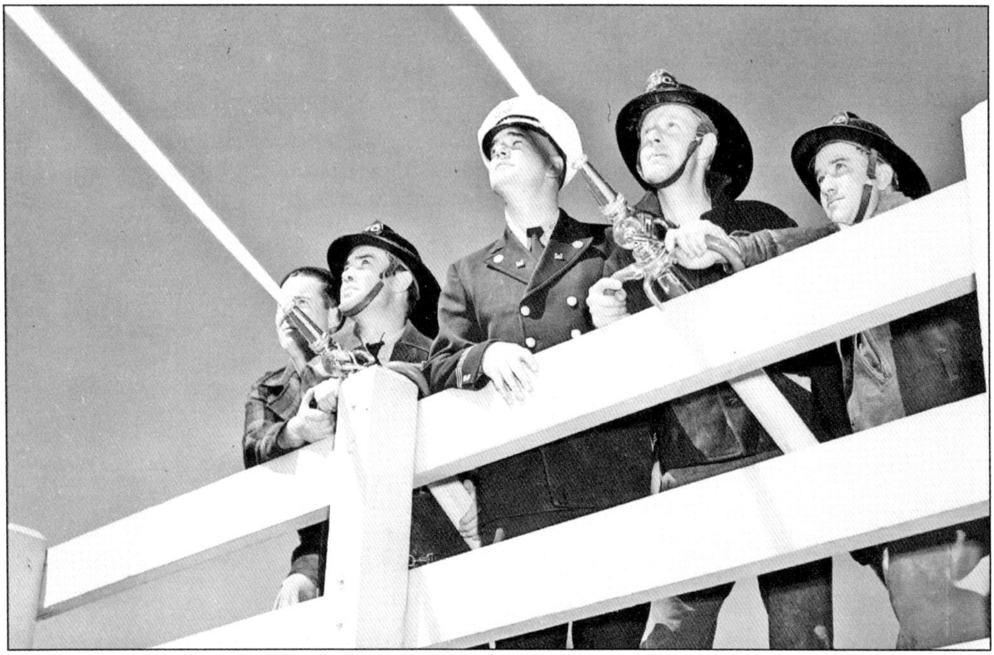

Members of Gowen Field firefighting department demonstrate the capability of their fire hoses, possibly for one of the many visits by local government officials. Despite the entire country being on a war footing with higher security, demonstrations like this one were not uncommon at Gowen Field. The department had an excellent reputation for fire safety and awareness on base.

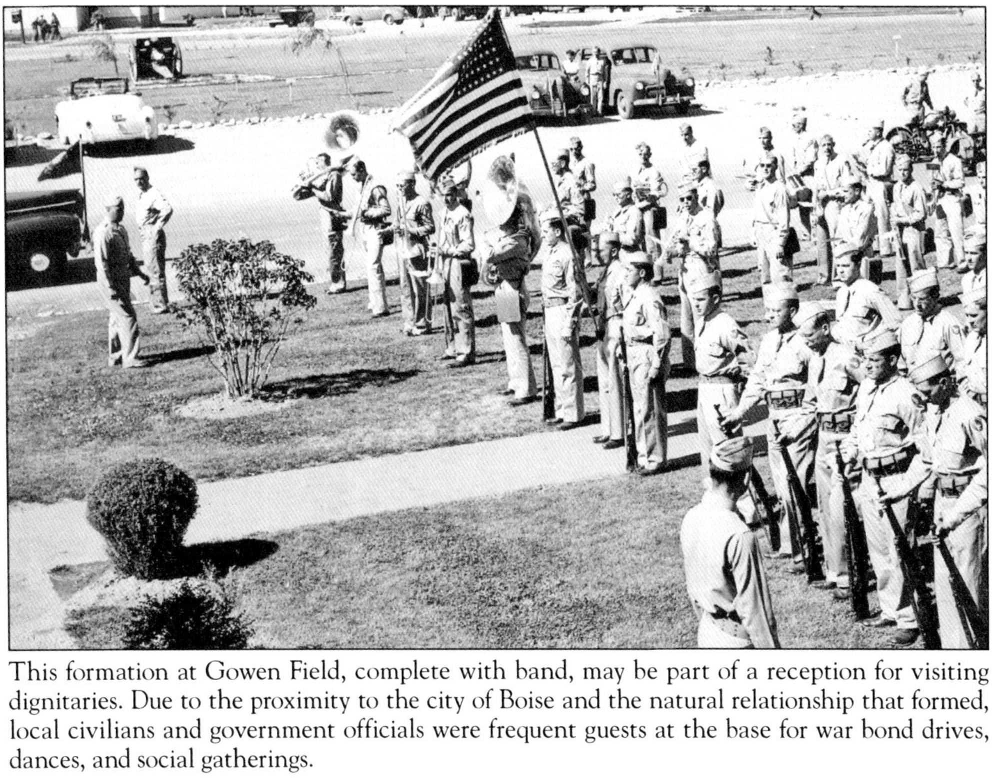

This formation at Gowen Field, complete with band, may be part of a reception for visiting dignitaries. Due to the proximity to the city of Boise and the natural relationship that formed, local civilians and government officials were frequent guests at the base for war bond drives, dances, and social gatherings.

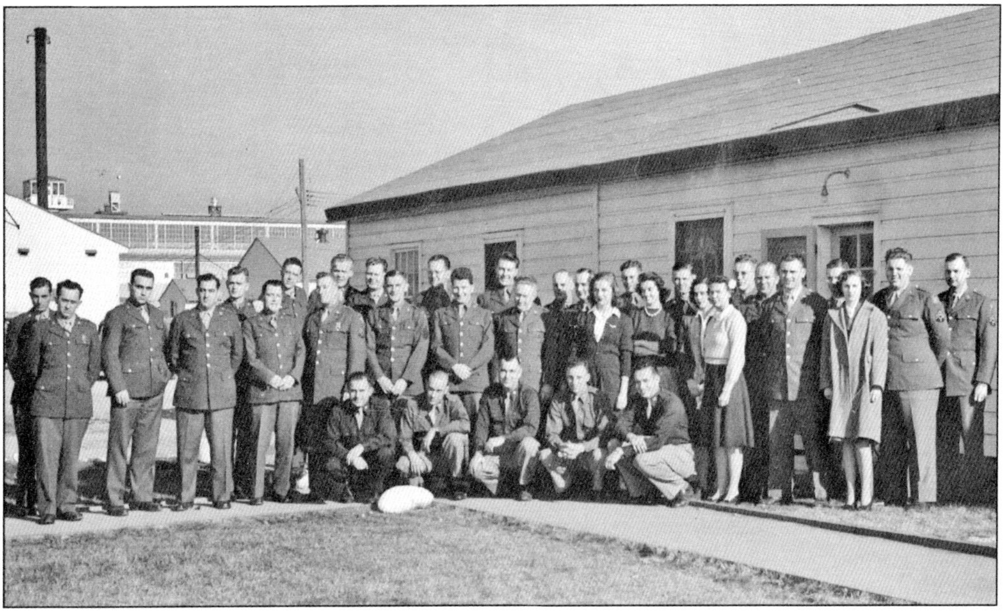

Gowen Field Finance Office personnel pose on January 22, 1944. Civilian workers were present in nearly every office at Gowen Field, performing many administrative duties to free up airmen for combat-related jobs.

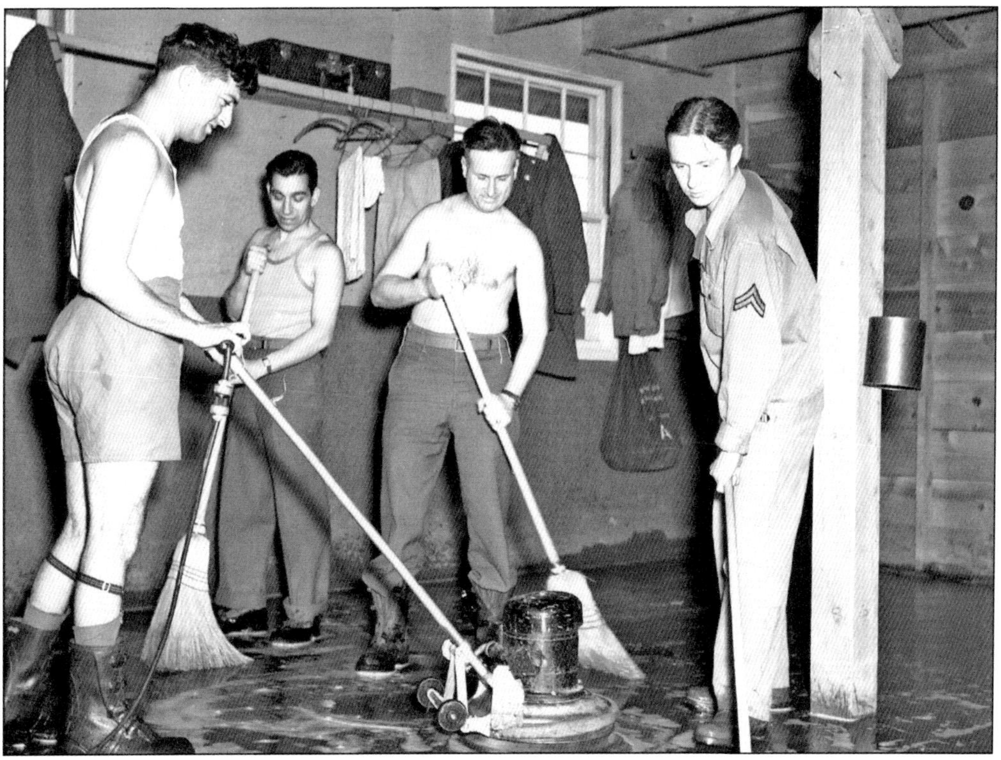

Fatigue duty was unpopular but important, as it taught soldiers discipline and cleanliness. These GIs clean one of the many Gowen Field barracks, some of which stood for years after World War II and were later used by the Idaho Air National Guard.

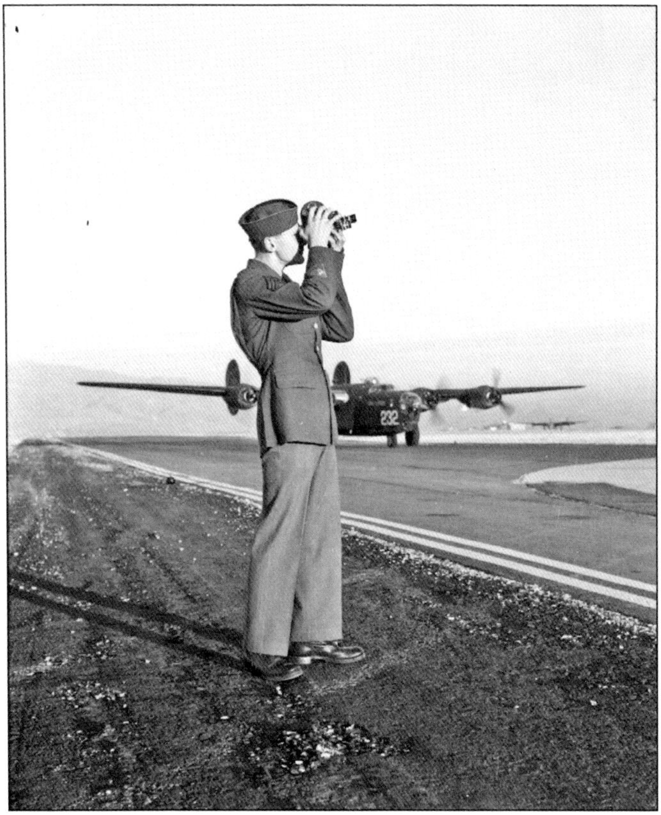

Filming takeoffs and landings had value as a training aid because it allowed instructors to debrief their student pilots on how well (or poorly) the flight went. This lone photographer represents the base photograph section, which had a quiet but significant role in documenting the daily life at Gowen Field during the war.

This may look like just another formation on Gowen Field, but the photograph reveals important details about the time and event. The church in the background was built late in World War II, and the flag is at half-mast, indicating a state of mourning in the nation. This formation may be a memorial service for Pres. Franklin Delano Roosevelt, who died in office on April 12, 1945.

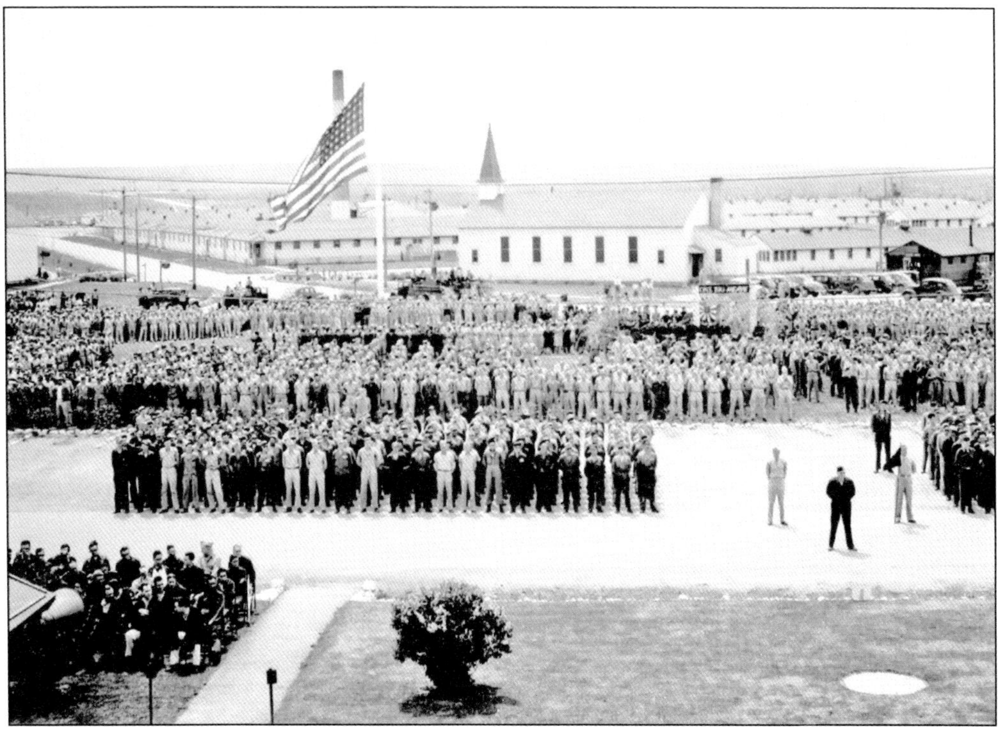

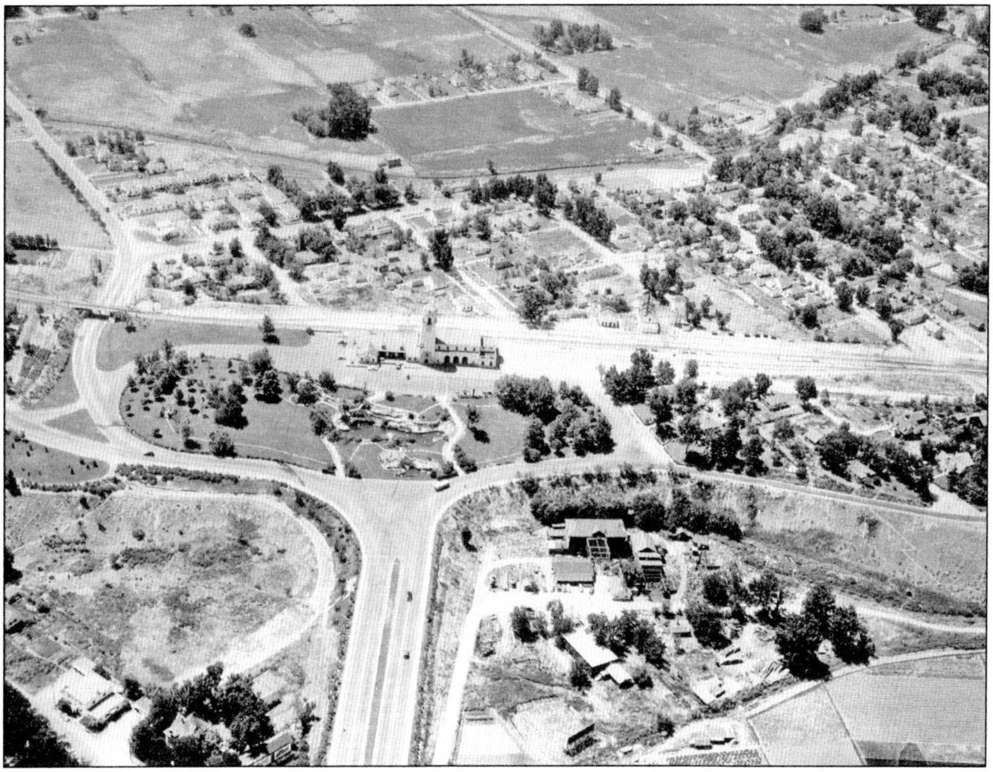

This aerial view of Boise was taken looking south, with the Boise train depot in the center. The train depot was a popular spot for Gowen Field airmen to have their portraits taken, usually posed on a rock with the hills to the north of town as a scenic backdrop. The depot still stands but is no longer used by passengers disembarking from trains. While well preserved, it mainly hosts events and social functions.

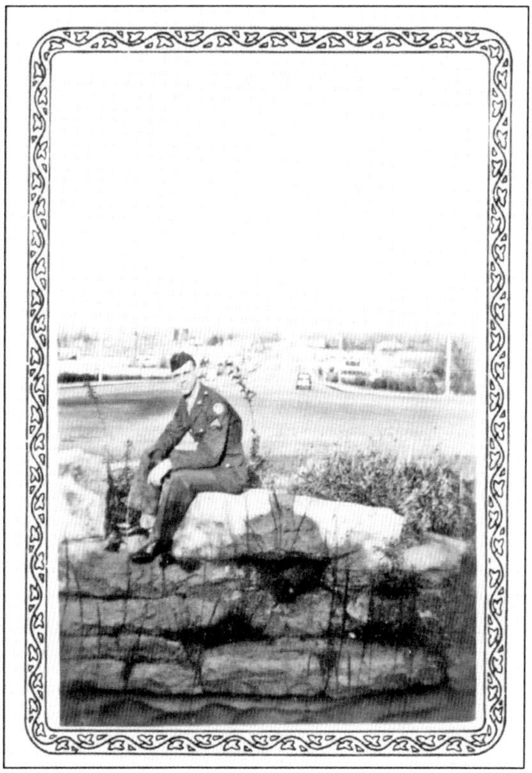

Cpl. Garald Call was one of the thousands of airmen who served at Gowen Field during World War II. While on leave in Boise, he poses in his dress (or Class A) wool uniform. On his left sleeve is the 2nd Air Force patch. Corporal Call married Boise resident Virginia Matthews and remained in the city after the war.

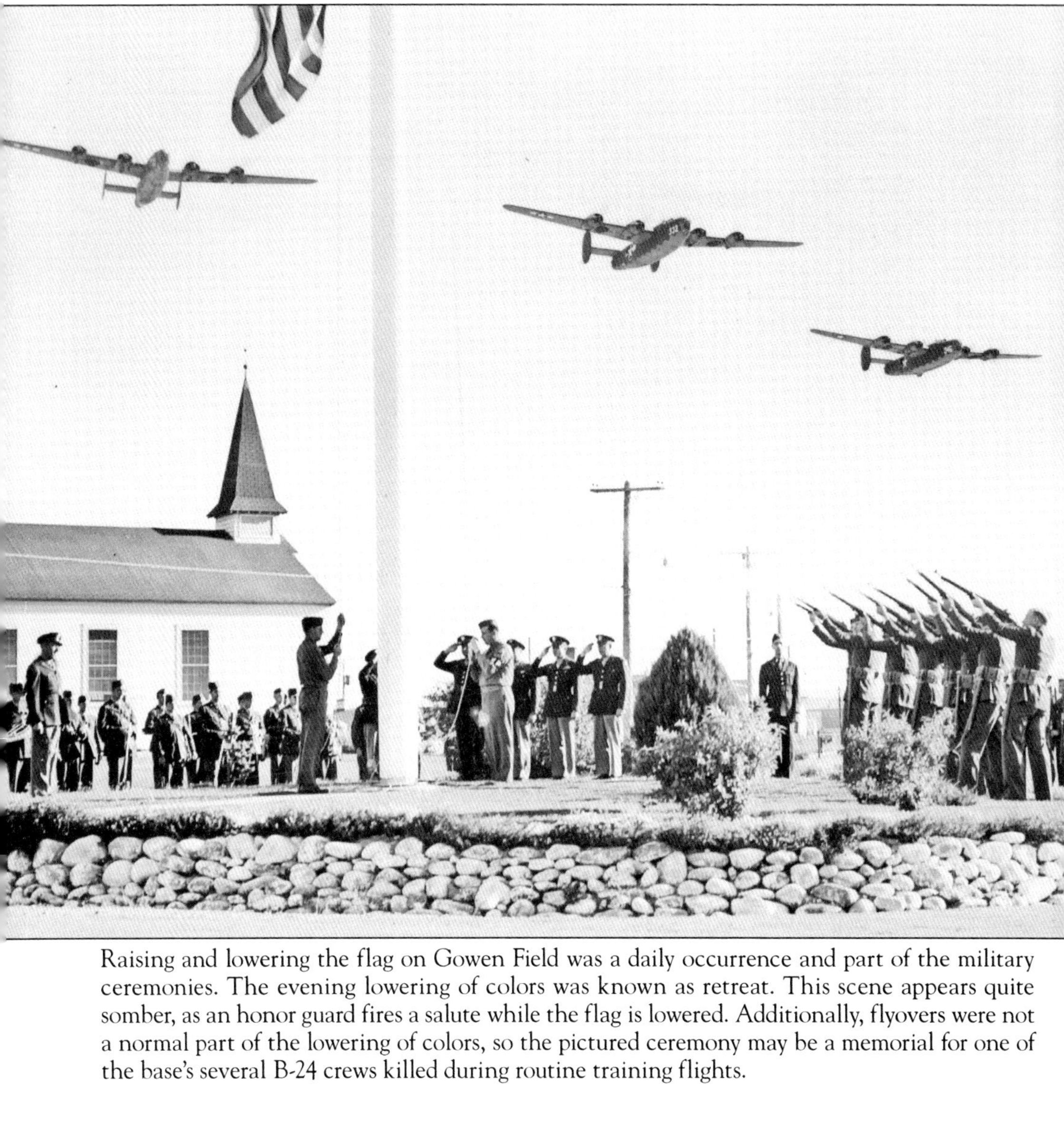

Raising and lowering the flag on Gowen Field was a daily occurrence and part of the military ceremonies. The evening lowering of colors was known as retreat. This scene appears quite somber, as an honor guard fires a salute while the flag is lowered. Additionally, flyovers were not a normal part of the lowering of colors, so the pictured ceremony may be a memorial for one of the base's several B-24 crews killed during routine training flights.

Two

The Idaho Air National Guard

In 1946, Idaho's adjutant general, Gen. Harry Abdenroth, requested that Tom Lanphier, editor of the *Idaho Daily Statesman* and famed World War II pilot, organize the Idaho Air National Guard. Due to his connections with the local paper, Lanphier ran an advertisement requesting volunteers. The local community answered his call, and on October 13, 1946, the same day that the Army Air Forces activated the 190th Fighter Squadron, 37 charter members joined the Idaho Air National Guard. Eventually the group grew to a cadre of 44 airmen and 23 officers, all of whom were World War II veterans.

After filling the ranks, Lieutenant Colonel Lanphier sought land for his operation. Gowen Field had been returned to the city after the war, with many of its buildings in caretaker status. After securing the real estate needed for air operations, the Idaho Air Guard began to receive its first 25 F-51 Mustangs.

The new members of the 190th knew that they would only be called upon in the event of a national emergency and relished the idea that they would deploy as a unit. Nonetheless, in this early time period, they recognized that their first mission was to ready the pilots and airplanes for combat. To do this, they needed more people; recruiting became the linchpin for their survival. The 190th needed to recruit at least 250 personnel to meet the criteria for a squadron.

In an interview conducted by retired colonel Bill Miller, Lanphier stated, "Our initial mission after we got P-51s was to acquaint the people of Idaho that there was such a thing as the Air National Guard. We flew to every little airport in the valley and put on our shows and displays to gain enlistments and build our strength." Lanphier went on to recruit Bernie Fisher, who would later be awarded the Medal of Honor for his actions in Vietnam. Others serving in the 190th recalled the days of going door to door asking to speak with the sons of Idaho. This was the genesis of the Idaho Air Guard and laid the foundation for contemporary operations.

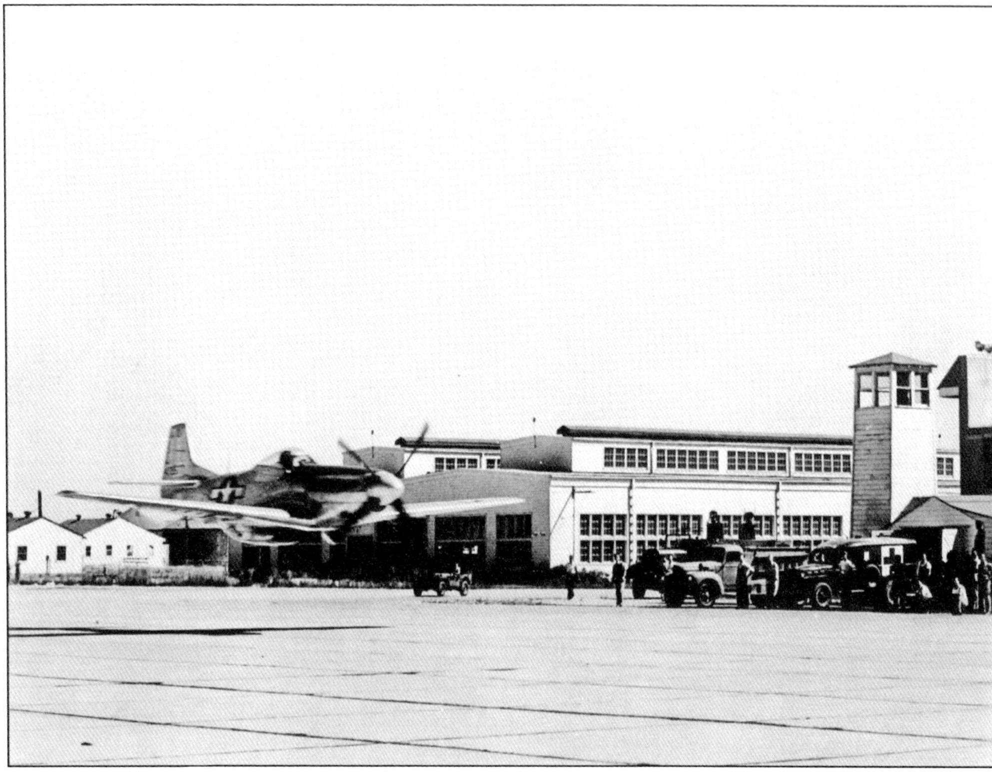

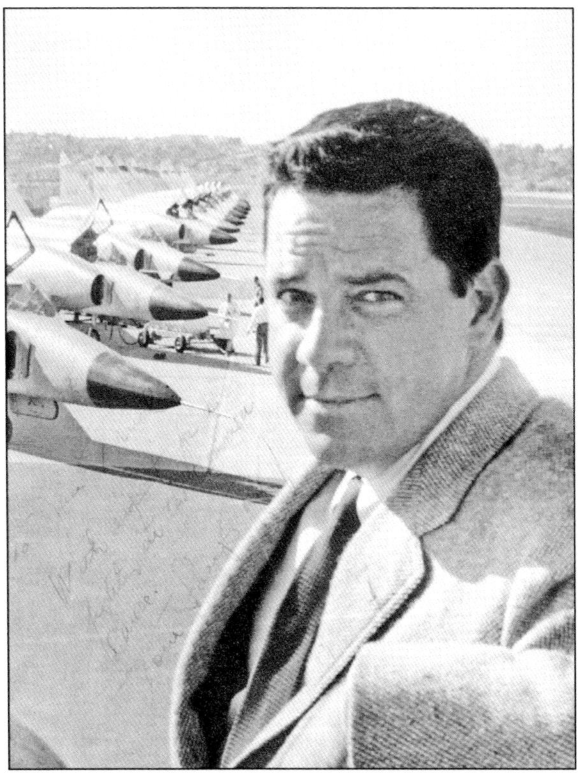

The 190th Fighter Squadron's first commander, Lt. Col. Thomas G. Lanphier, begins a double Immelmann off the deck of Gowen Field. This display of true airmanship attracted the recruits needed to fill the ranks of the fledgling Idaho Air National Guard. Many refer to Tom Lanphier as the founding father of the modern-day Idaho Air National Guard.

Tom Lanphier, years after leaving the Idaho Air Guard, is pictured on the flight line in front of multiple F-102s. He garnered fame during World War II when he received credit for five and a half aerial victories, including the downing of Admiral Yamamoto's aircraft. For his actions concerning the destruction of the bomber carrying Yamamoto, the navy awarded Lanphier the Navy Cross.

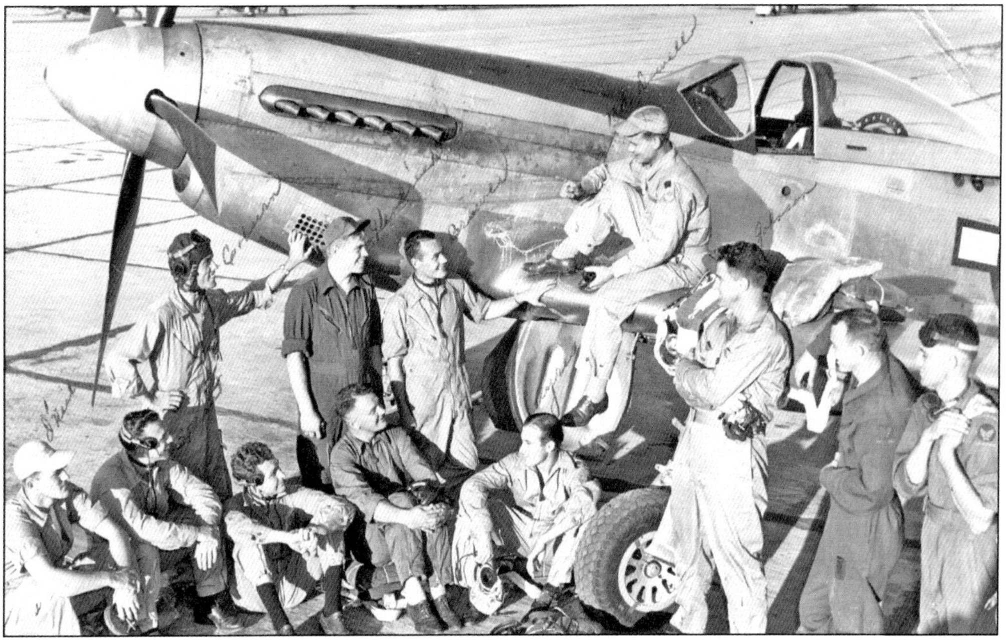

In 1947, members of the original aircrew sit on an F-51 and discuss the latest mission. The first Mustangs arrived at Gowen Field in November 1946, just three weeks after the military had activated the 190th Fighter Squadron. Idaho received a total of 25 aircraft, which the men referred to as P-51s until the defense department formed the air force. Afterward, the planes were designated as F-51s.

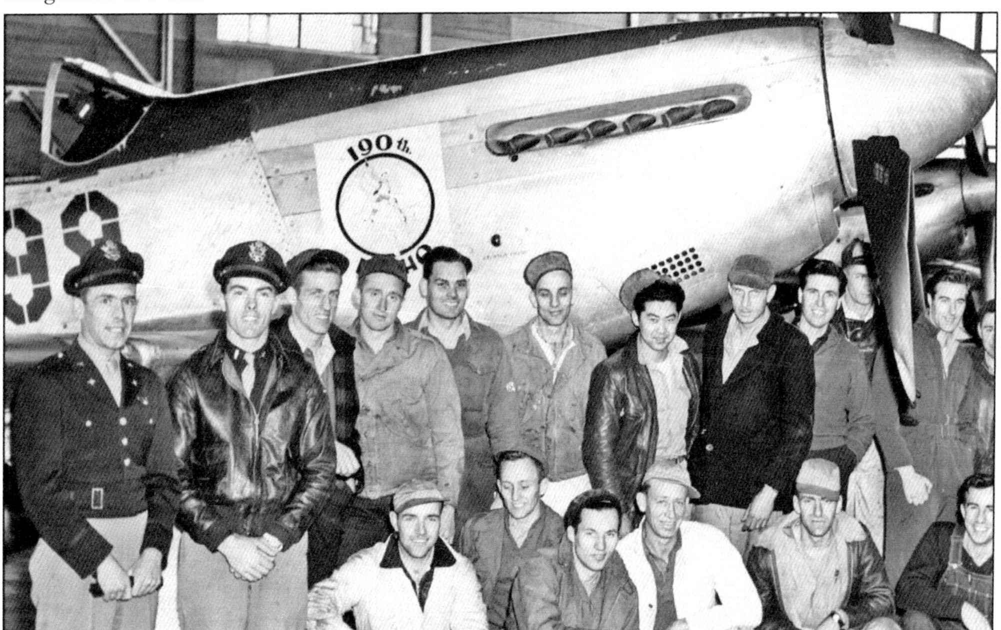

An assembly of the original technicians poses in front of an F-51, with Bill Bozman on the left and Bill Coburn on the right. Of particular interest is the emblem painted on the side of the aircraft. This insignia, used for a very short period, depicted a wild, winged mustang being tamed by a cowboy.

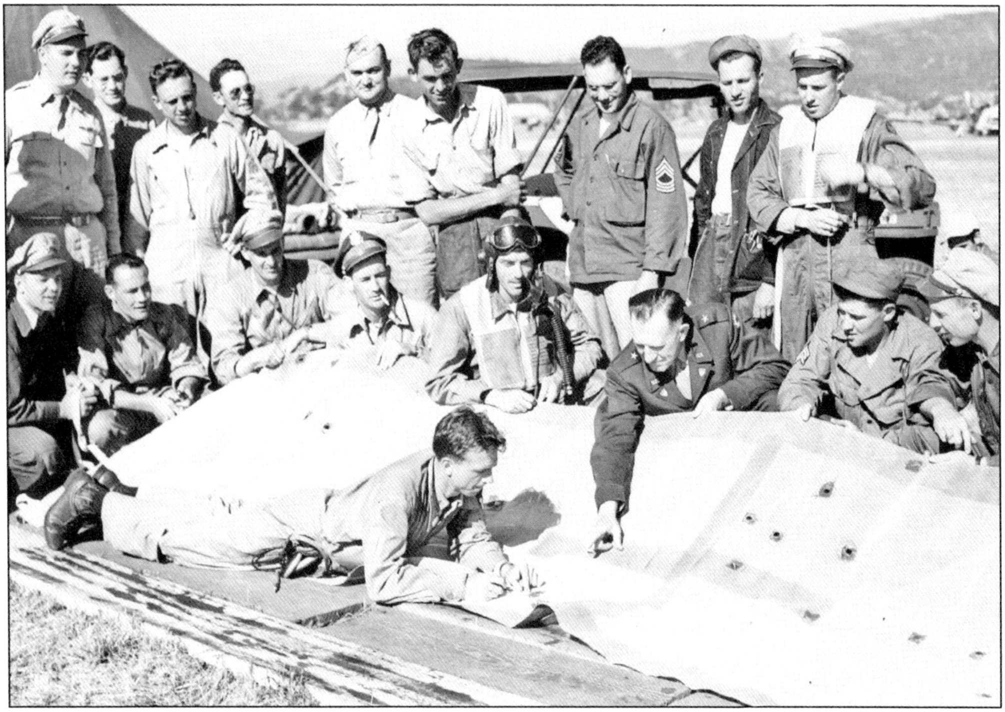

During the first summer camp held at Hamilton Field, California, the 190th pilots honed their skills for aerial dogfighting by firing their guns at a towed target. Here Ken Nordling (lying on the target) examines the bullet holes while General Walsh makes comments on his accuracy. To distinguish bullet holes, bullets were dipped in different color paint for each pilot.

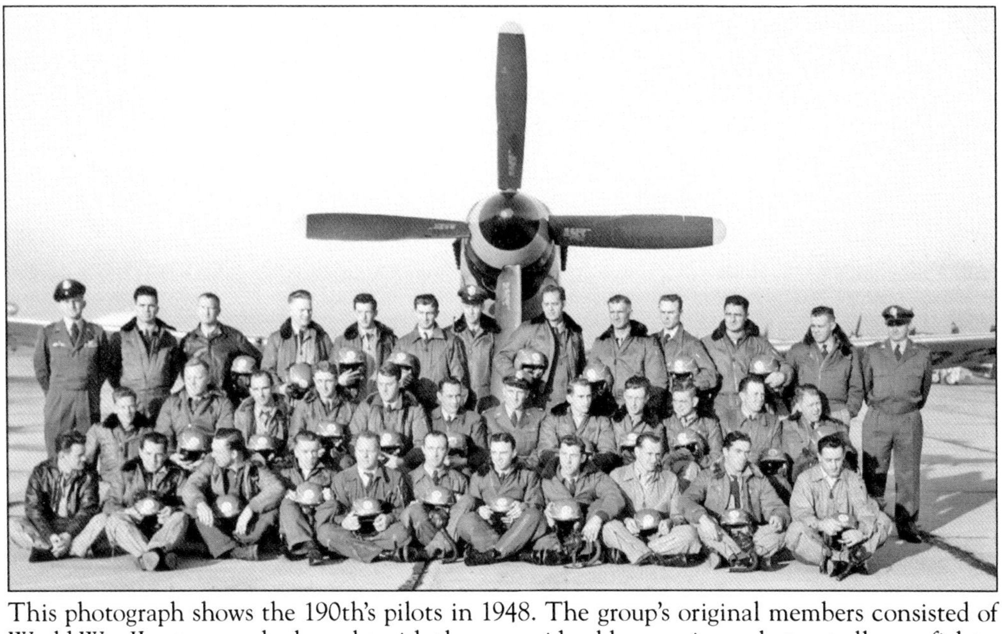

This photograph shows the 190th's pilots in 1948. The group's original members consisted of World War II veterans who brought with them considerable experience, but not all were fighter pilots. Some had served as bomber and cargo pilots during the war, but the allure of being a fighter pilot had drawn them into the ranks of the Idaho Air Guard.

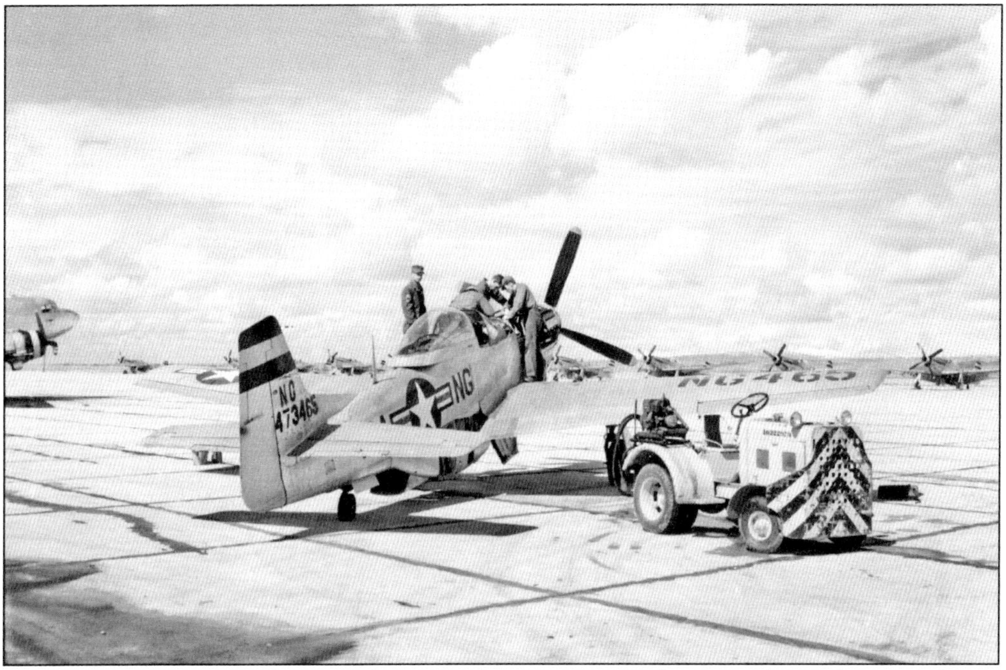

A maintenance crew readies an F-51 for another mission. At the time, the single-seat F-51 was recognized as the world's fastest single-engine propeller-driven aircraft. Armed with six .50-caliber machine guns as well as bombs, the Mustang was also a devastating weapon.

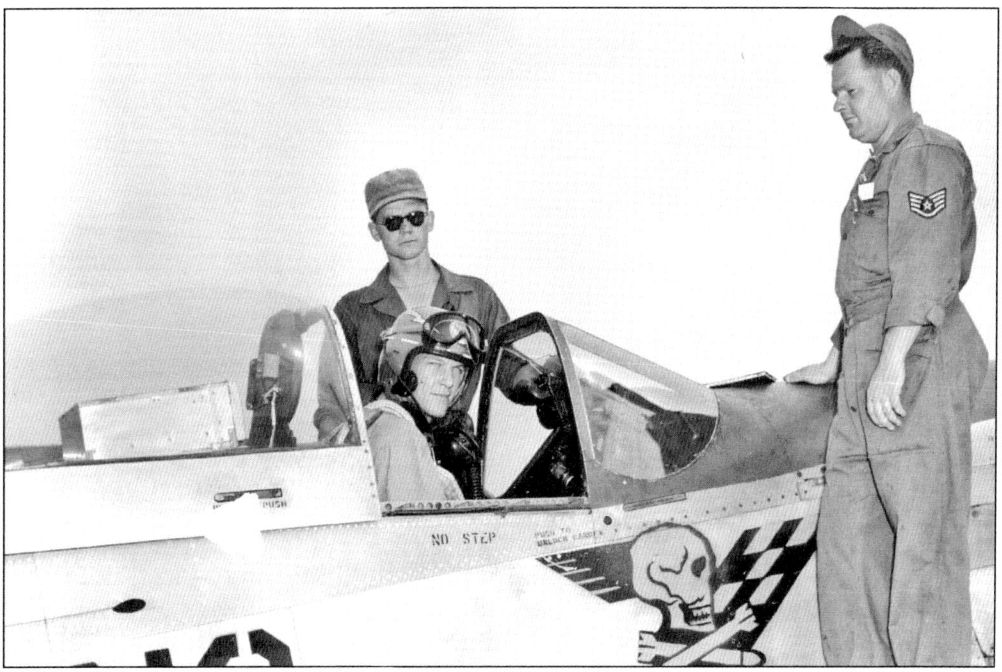

This hero's shot of Lt. Orlando Dalke (left), TSgt. Jay Gregory (center), and SSgt. Robert Hall was taken prior to takeoff. The redesigned emblem of the 190th is visible. The skull with crossed rockets became a very familiar site at Gowen Field, as it adorned pilots' helmets, aircraft, and, eventually, squadron patches.

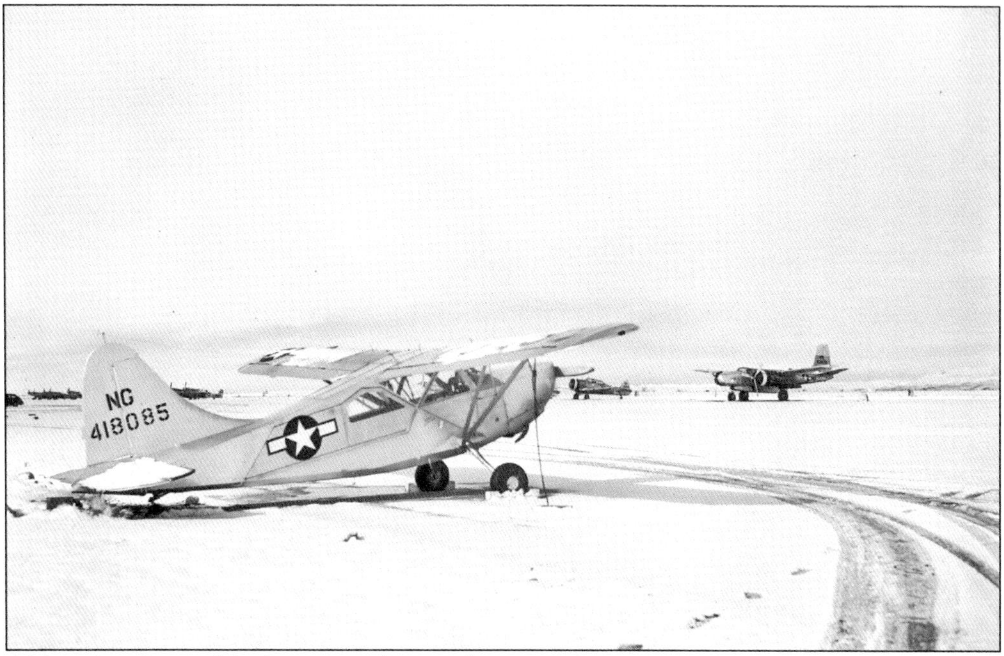

Although a fact widely forgotten, the 190th operated many support aircraft throughout the years. Here a Stinson L-5 sits on a snow-covered taxiway with a B-26 and T-6 in the background. The crews used these aircraft for various tasks such as cross-country trips, pilot proficiency, and tow-target duty.

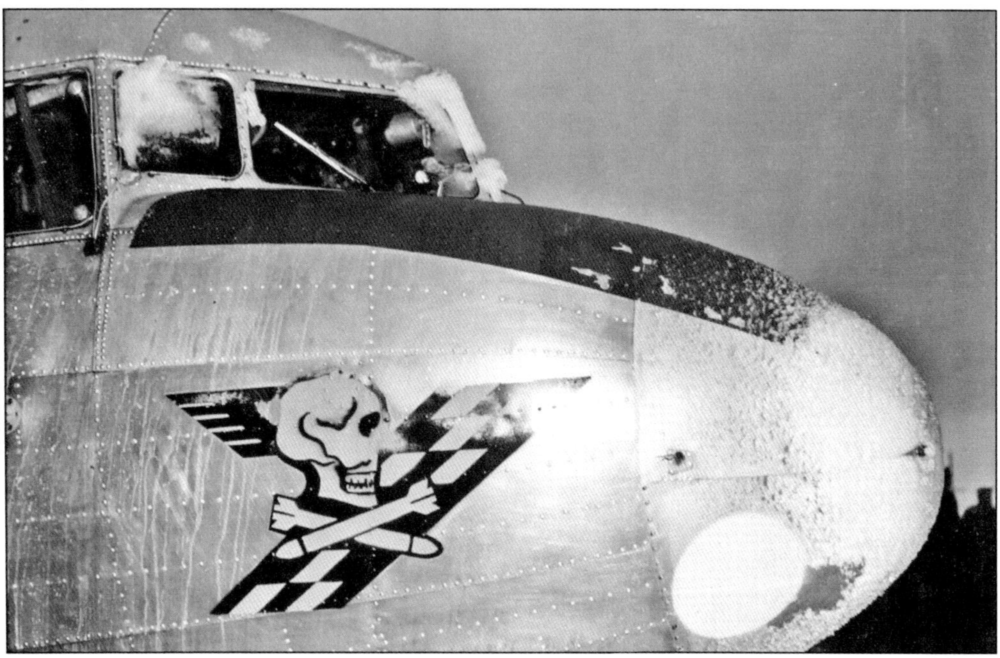

This C-47 bears the 190th skull emblem on its nose. The 190th utilized its C-47s for multiple tasks, for instance drawing on the aircrafts' ability to carry large amounts of cargo and troops when the group needed to attend summer camp. The troops would load into the aircraft, and the pilots would ferry the group to Walla Walla, Washington, or other fantastic locations.

Lt. Cliff Agenbroad props the engine prior to starting a Douglas A-26 Invader in 1948. The Douglas A-26 was designed as a medium attack bomber replacement for the B-25s and Martin B-26s of pre–World War II vintage. The United States used the Douglas A-26 in every theater of World War II, Korea, and Vietnam. The air force re-designated the aircraft as the Douglas B-26 in 1948, after the service retired all Martin B-26 Marauders.

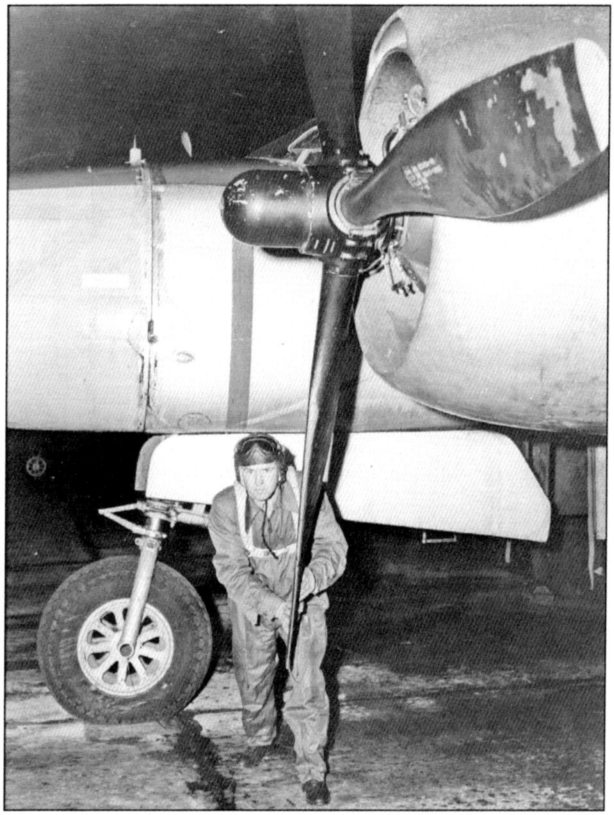

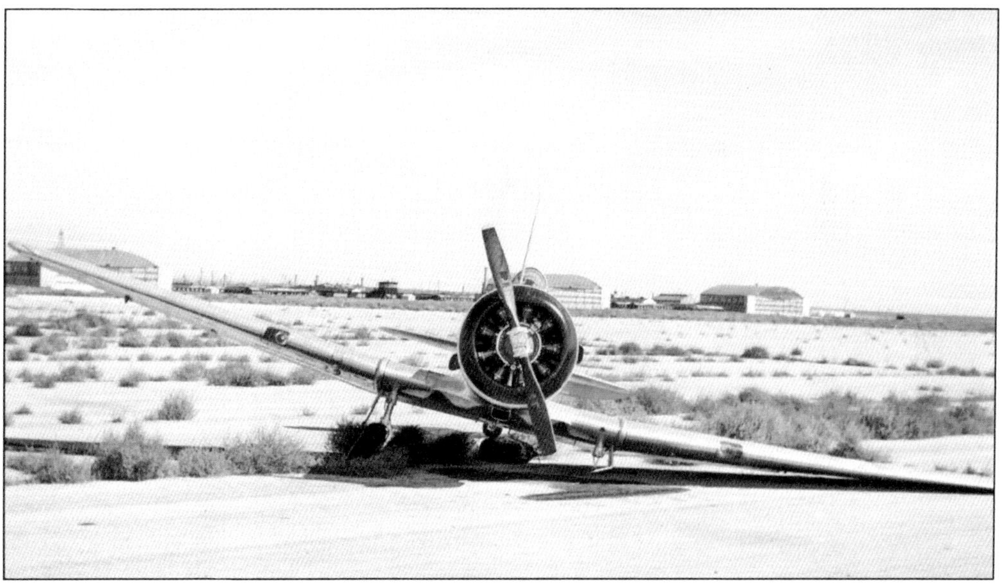

A T-6 Texan rests on the Mountain Home Air Base runway after one of its main gears collapsed. Following World War II, the air base closed, and the 190th used the space for training in order to save 44 miles' flight time to the Saylor Creek gunnery range. The ground crews would convoy their equipment and armament to Mountain Home, and then the pilots would fly from the abandoned runways.

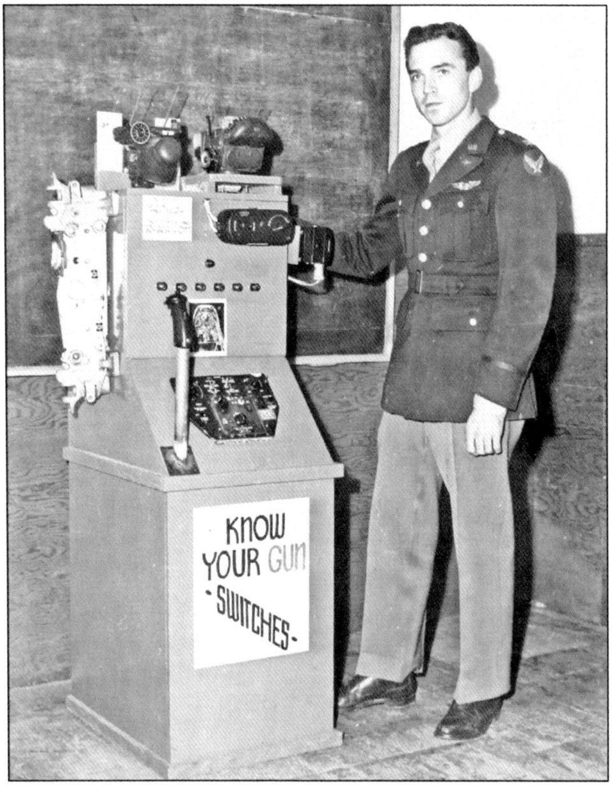

Capt. Ken Nordling poses with a "know your gun switches" contraption. This simulator of sorts assisted new pilots with general reference. The placard in the upper left instructs the pilot to press the trigger to fire the guns and push the red button on the stick to drop bombs or fire rockets. The two items at the top are the two types of gun sights. These projected information on glass so the pilot did not need to look down while flying.

David N. Johnson is pictured prior to a flight in his F-51. In early 1953, Major Johnson succeeded his brother Lt. Col. Martin Johnson as commander of the 190th. Major Johnson saw the 190th through its transition from a single-engine unit to an all-jet squadron when it received its first T-33 in November 1953.

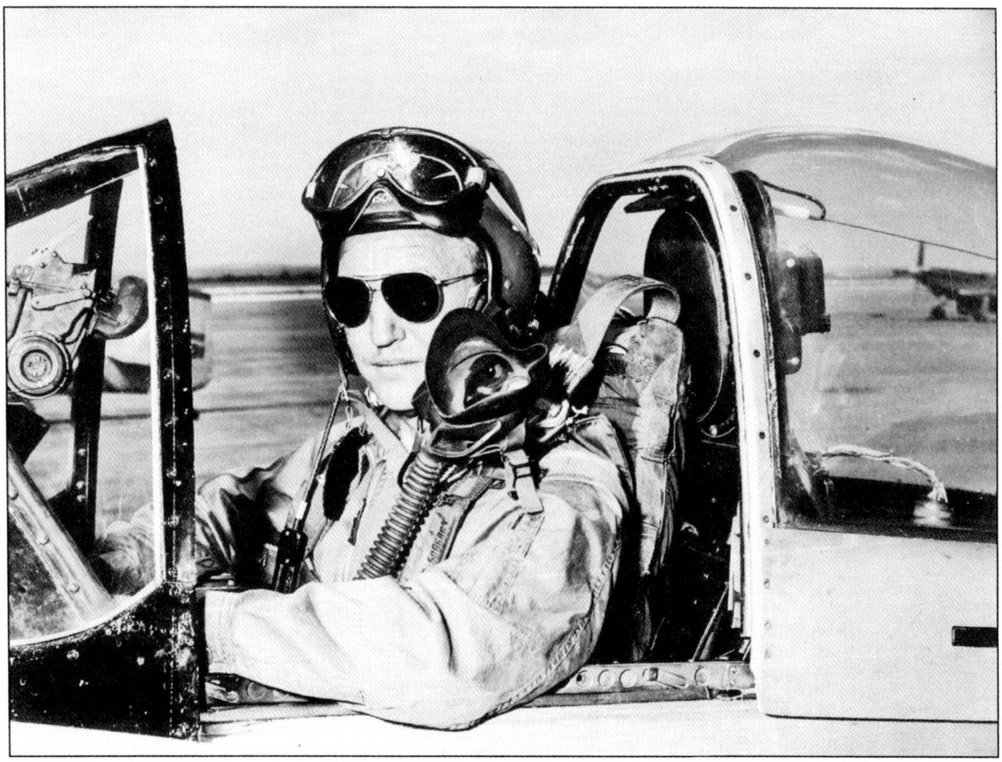

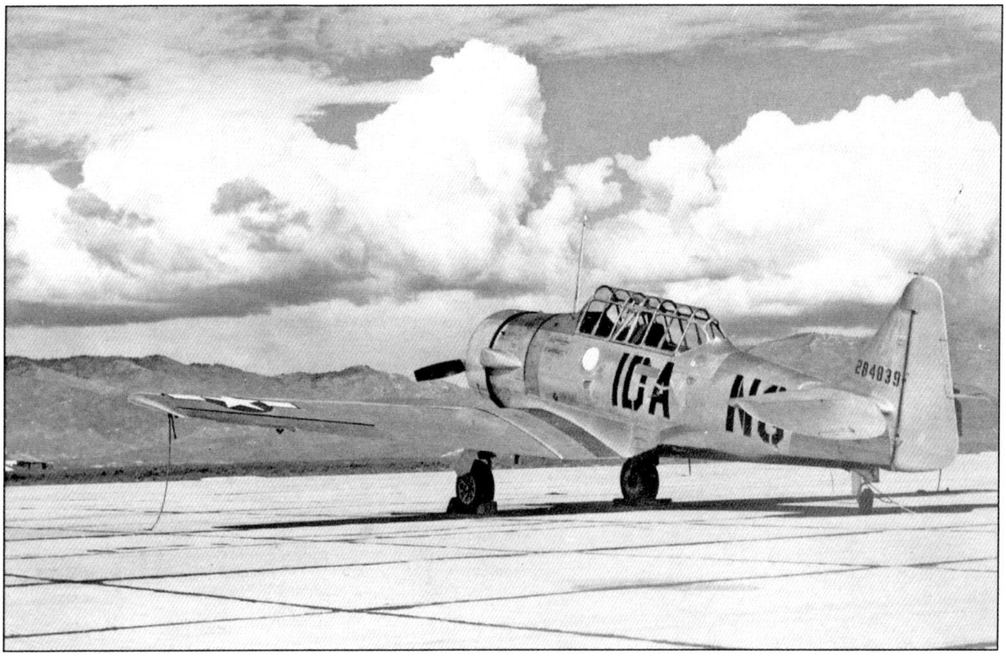

A T-6 Texan sits on the ramp at Gowen Field with the beautiful Boise foothills in the background. The 190th used the T-6 for various chores around the patch, including pilot proficiency and target spotting.

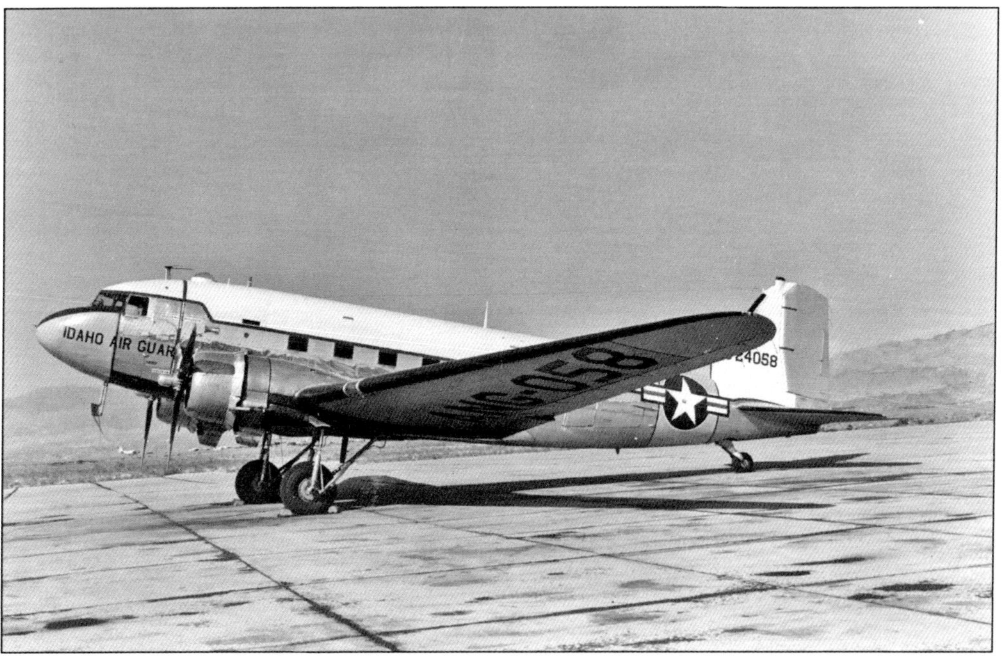

An Idaho Air National Guard C-47 Gooney Bird sits on the Gowen Field ramp. M. R. Smith crewed one of the two C-47s owned by the 190th, and while it was not one of the flashy F-51s or even an A-26, he was dedicated to his aircraft. One of the better-known C-47 efforts involved eight missions flown in 1947 when the 190th crews delivered iron lungs to help combat an outbreak of infantile paralysis. The crews flew nine more similar missions in 1948.

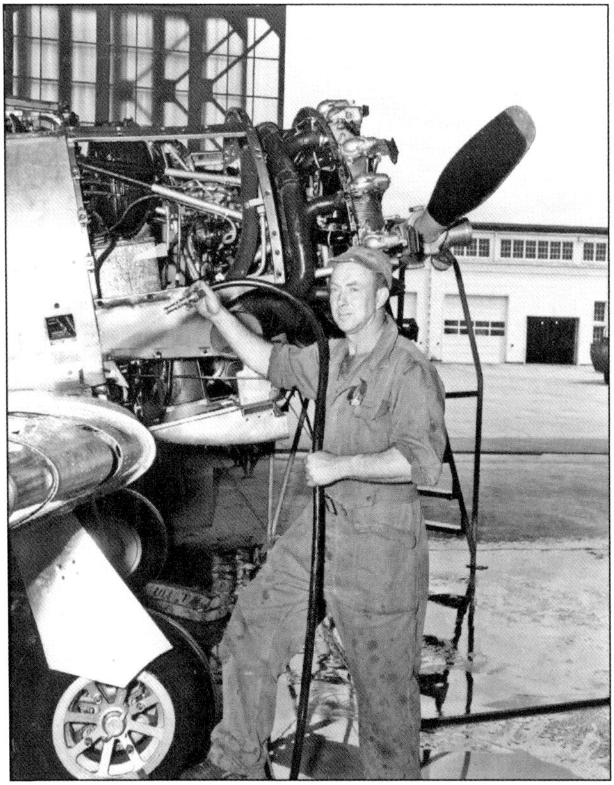

Jim Bates washes a T-6 Texan during preventive maintenance. Aviators referred to the North American T-6 Texan as "the Pilot Maker" because of its important role in preparing pilots for combat. Derived from the 1935 North American NA-16 prototype, a cantilever low-wing monoplane, the Texan filled the need for a basic combat trainer during World War II and into the early Cold War period.

Wes Lyons prepares an F-51 for a gunnery mission by loading and arming the rockets. In order to launch the rockets, the pilot put the F-51 in a slight dive while aiming at the target. He then pressed the pickle button, sending an electric current to the rocket motor that forced the munitions off the rail. In this photograph, Lyons attaches an electrical device to the back of the rocket.

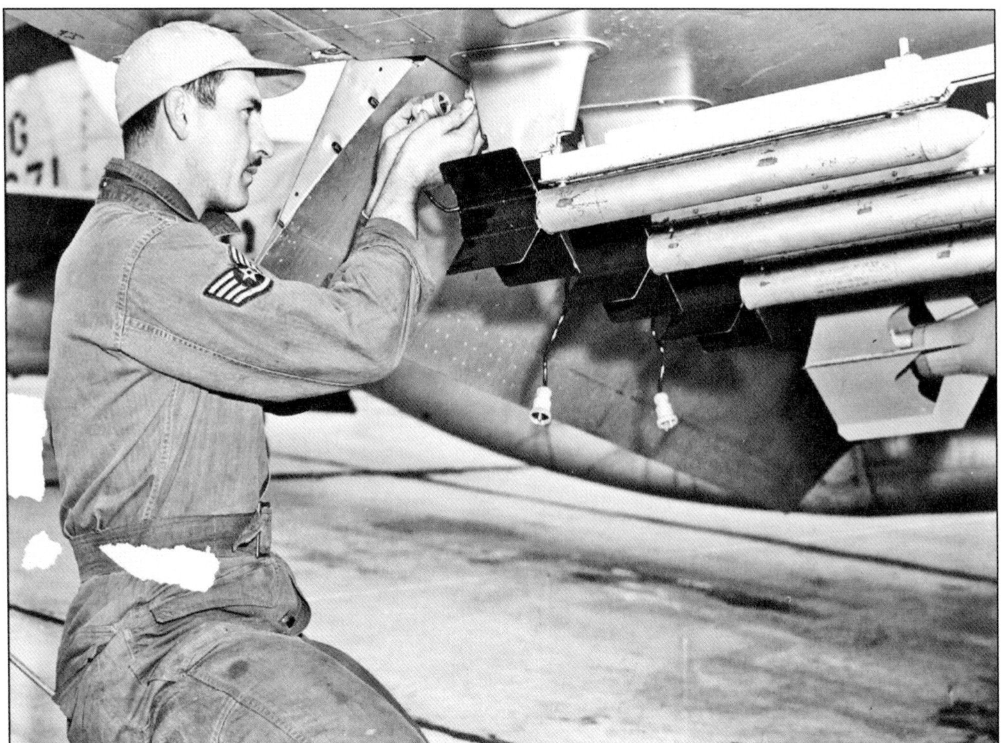

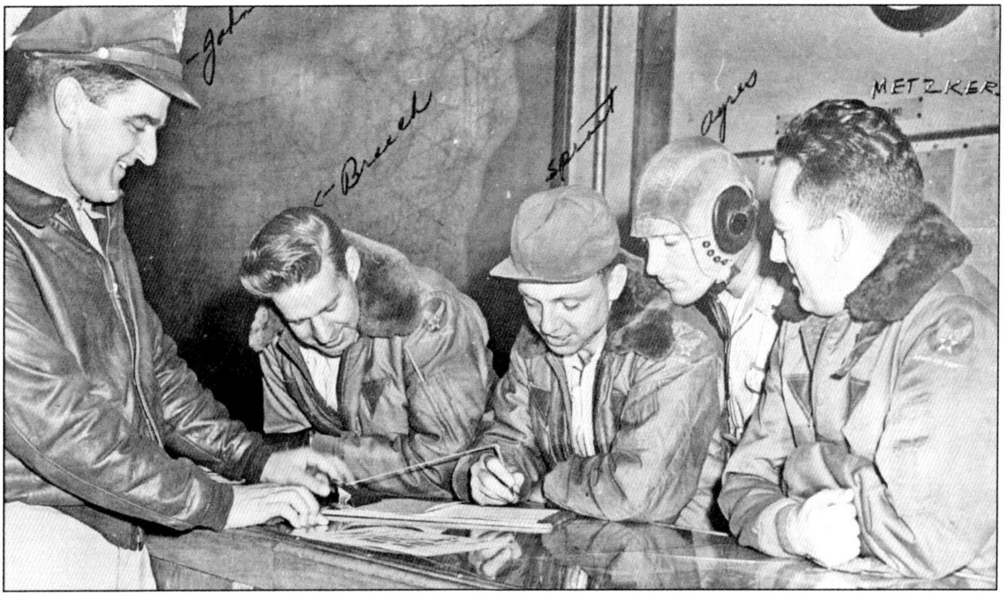

Looking over the flight roster are, from left to right, Martin Johnson, John Breach, Bill Sproat, F. Ayers, and J. Metzker. They are standing at a makeshift operations desk that more than likely doubled as a unit bar.

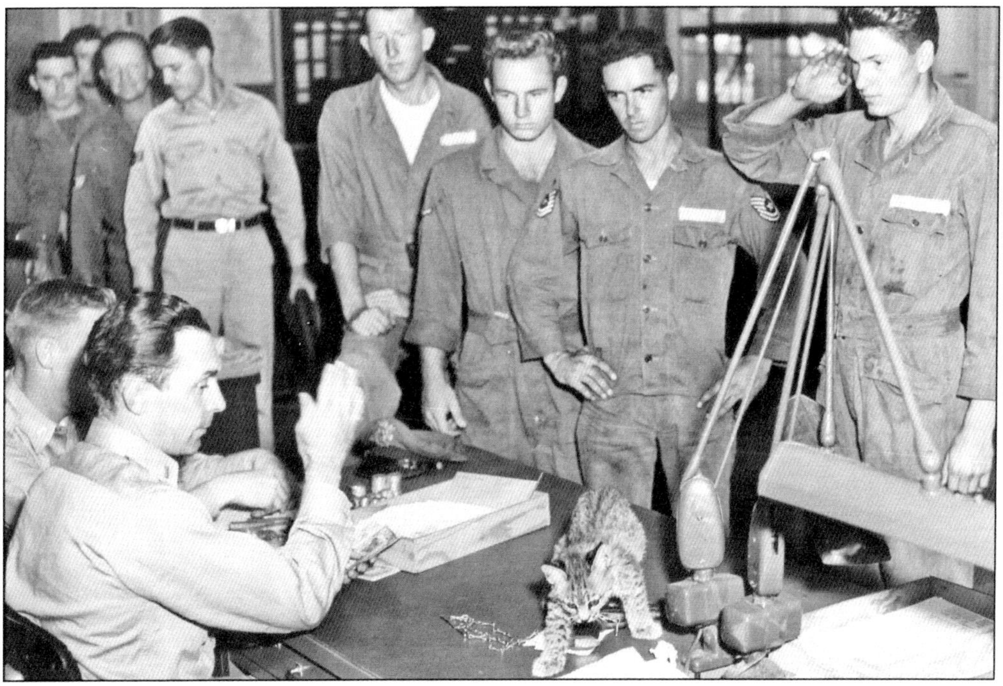

Enlisted men of the 190th line up and prepare to receive their pay. In order for the 190th to get paid, it had to have at least 90 people assigned to the squadron. Dale Hendry reminisced that Bill Bozman had once recruited a whole softball team in order to get everyone paid. At the time, the 190th was not too particular on whom they recruited, as the group needed the figures. As the story goes, a few days after all received their pay, many of the softball team got out of the Air National Guard.

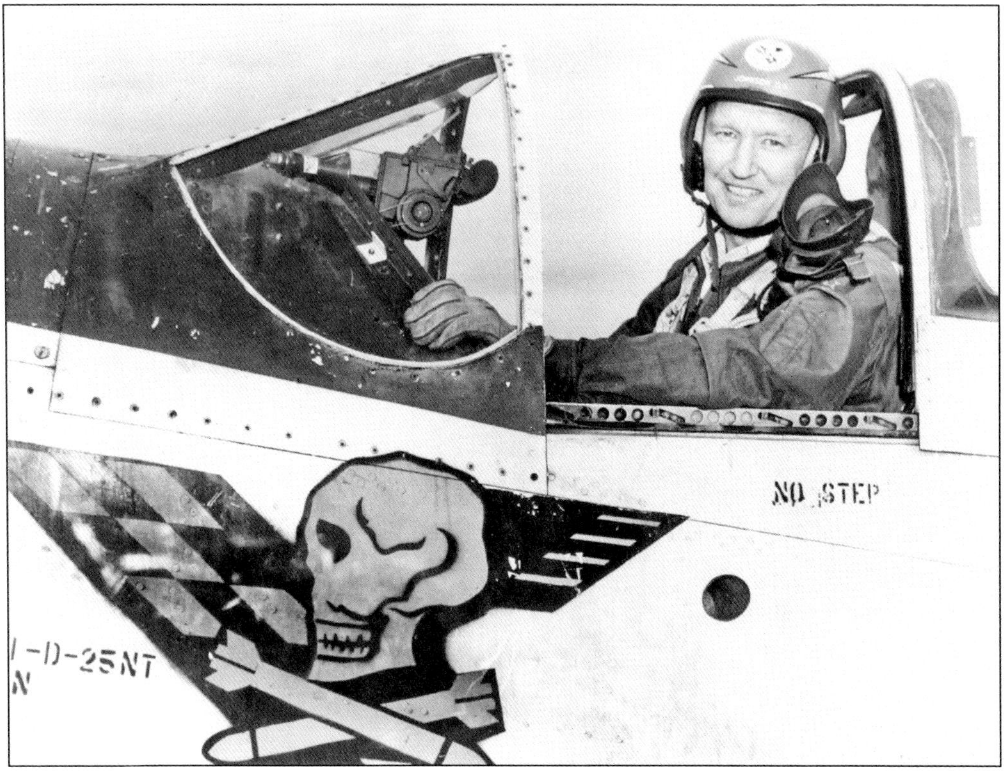

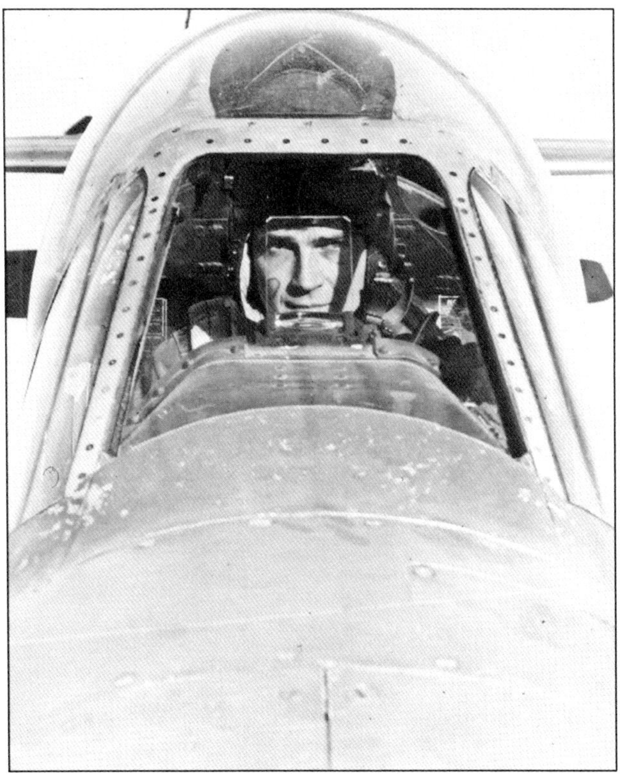

This photograph, another hero shot of David Johnson, clearly shows the skull insignia on not only Johnson's F-51 but also on his flight helmet. At the time, the flight helmet was nothing more than a glorified football helmet with radio headphones inside.

Ken Nordling looks through the N9 gun sight of his F-51D Mustang. During World War II, the British adapted their P-51s with fishbowl-shaped canopies called Malcolm Hoods. American manufacturers quickly followed suit, installing bubble canopies on the P-51D/K.

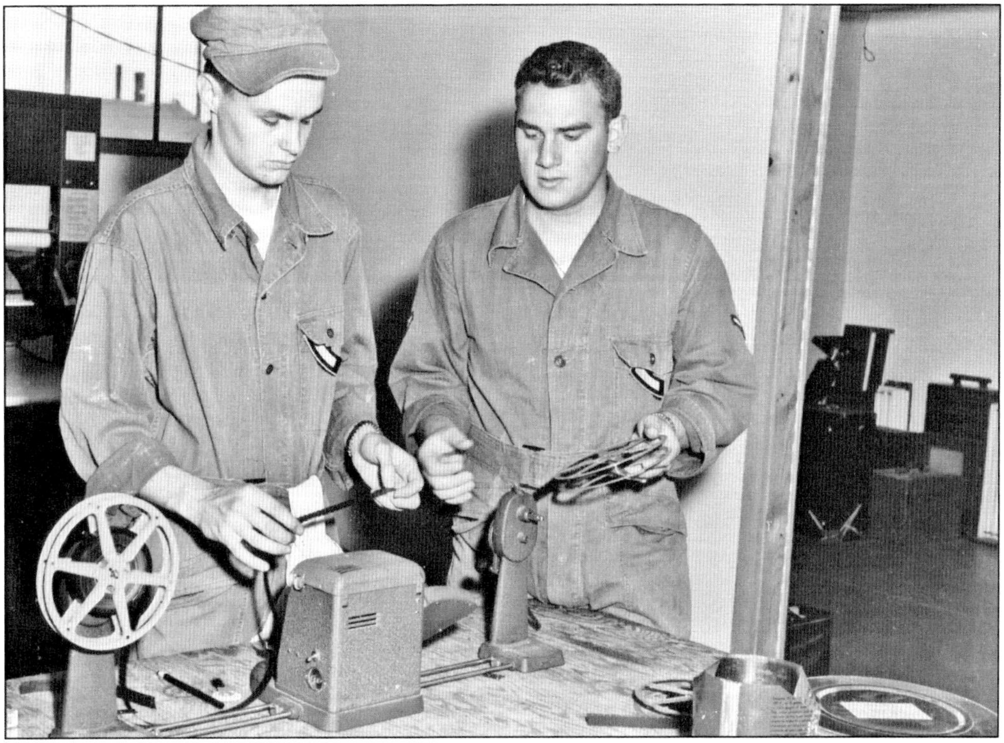

These two enlisted men cut and paste gun camera footage so pilots can review their mission accomplishments. The aircrews used the movies to verify their scoring from previous missions and as a tool on how to better attack the target, be it on the ground or in the air.

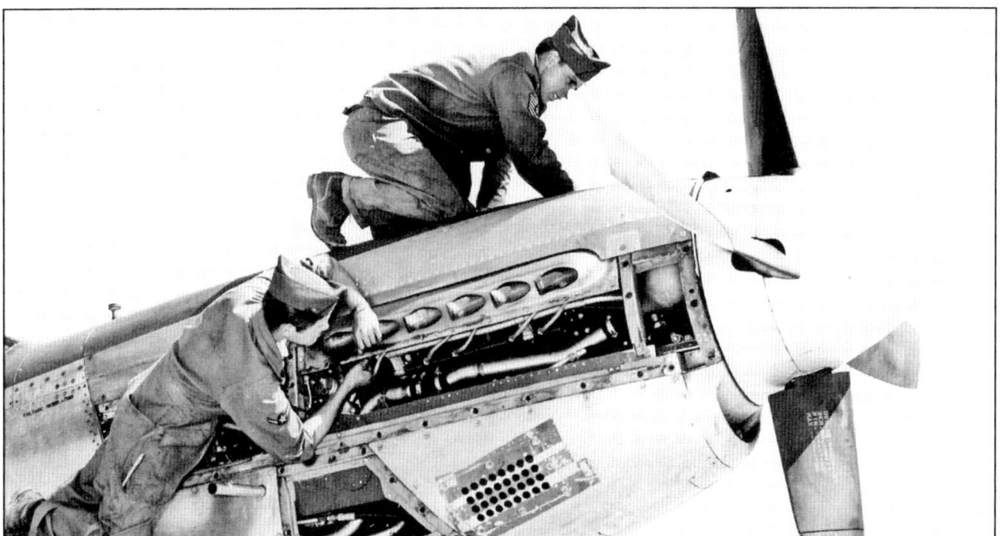

Enlisted technicians conduct a maintenance inspection on the Merlin engine of their F-51. The P-51 originally entered combat during World War II equipped with the supercharged Allison V-1710 engine, but the Allies quickly learned that the plane performed poorly at high altitudes. The British stepped in and modified the Mustang with the Packard-Merlin V-1650 engine, which allowed the aircraft to reach altitudes of 25,000 feet and speeds up to 440 miles per hour.

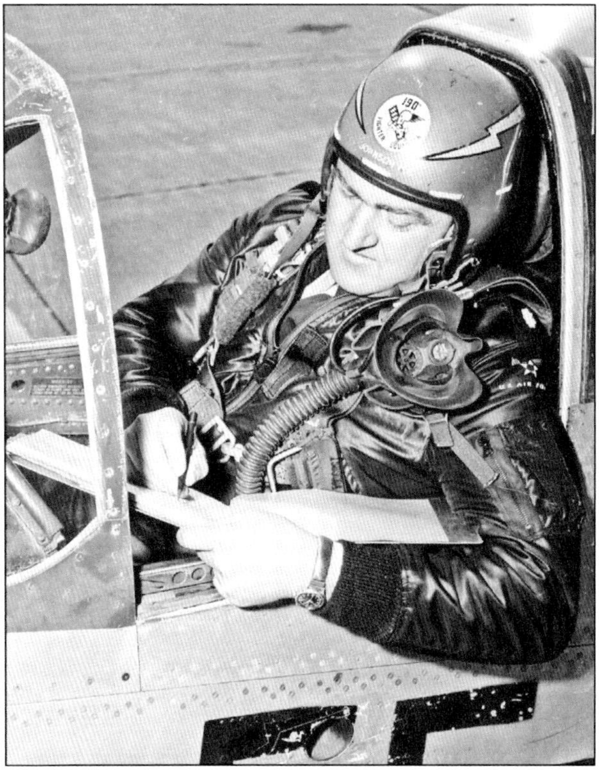

Maj. Martin H. Johnson signs his aircraft logbook after a flight. In January 1951, Major Johnson assumed command of the 190th Fighter Squadron. Later that year, on April 1st, he led 452 officers and enlisted men to active duty as they were activated for the Korean War.

Bernie Troutfetter (left), Harry O'Neal (center), and Waxy Wheeler look over a map of Washington State that includes the North-Pacific Ocean. In the background, the gunnery meet status board tells who the "Top Gun" is on that day. Maj. Martin Johnson led the field with 30.9 points in the air-to-air competition and 29.0 in the air-to-ground.

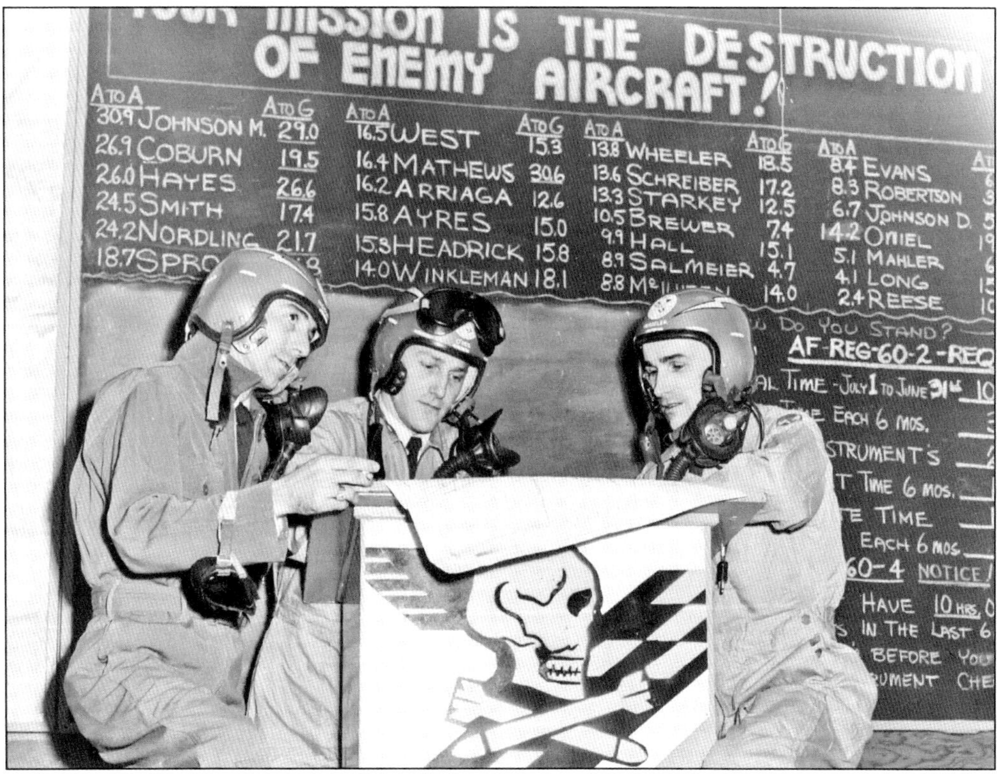

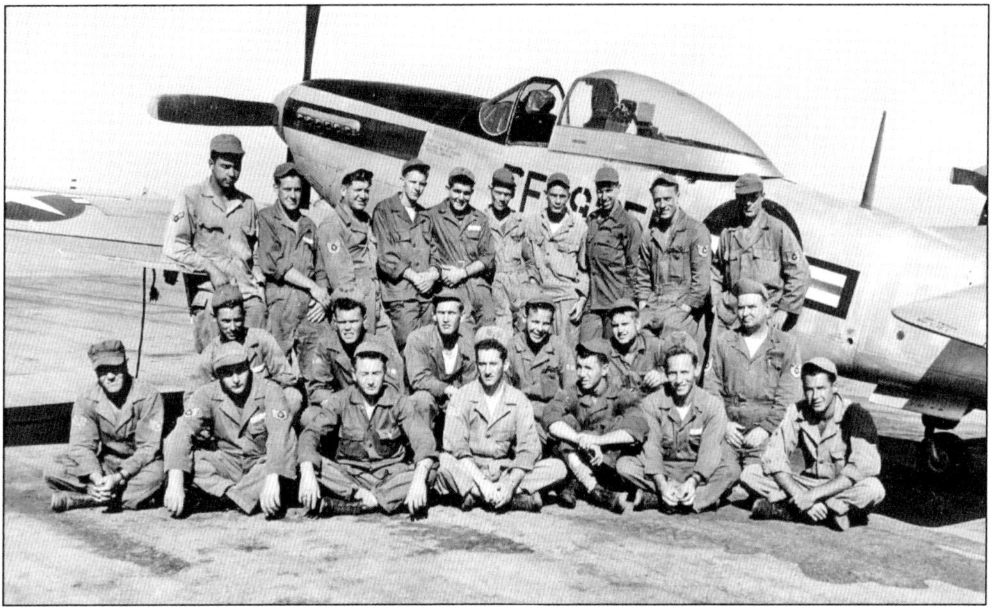

When the U.S. Air Force first activated the 190th for the Korean War, it deployed the unit to Moody Air Force Base at Valdosta, Georgia, but by November 1951, the whole unit had been transferred to George Air Force Base in California. While there, the pilots received extensive training in the art of close air support. Here the 190th's weapons section poses while stationed at George in 1952.

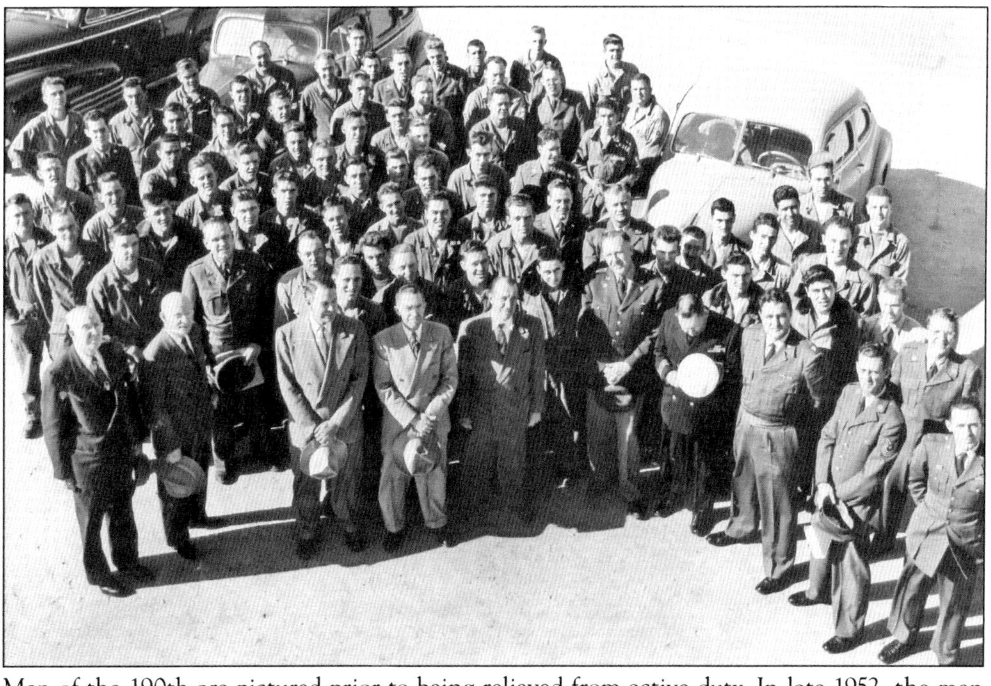

Men of the 190th are pictured prior to being relieved from active duty. In late 1952, the men began returning to Boise, and by January 1953, the 190th had returned to state control. The tour of duty had taken its toll on the 190th, and the group needed to fill ranks to assume its upcoming mission of transitioning to an all-jet force.

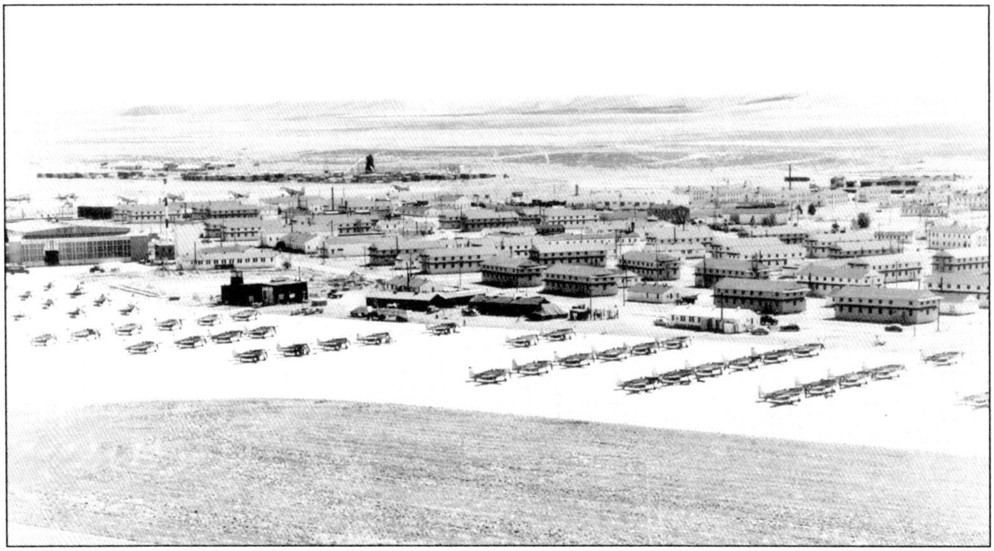

Because of the availability of housing, warehouses, and fuel storage, the excellent runway, and the proximity to Saylor Creek gunnery range, the Air National Guard Bureau chose Gowen Field as its primary site for aerial gunnery meets. Teams from all 48 states and the territories of Alaska and Hawaii descended on Boise to compete in this event. In 1953, the ramp is busting at its seams, full of F-51 Mustangs.

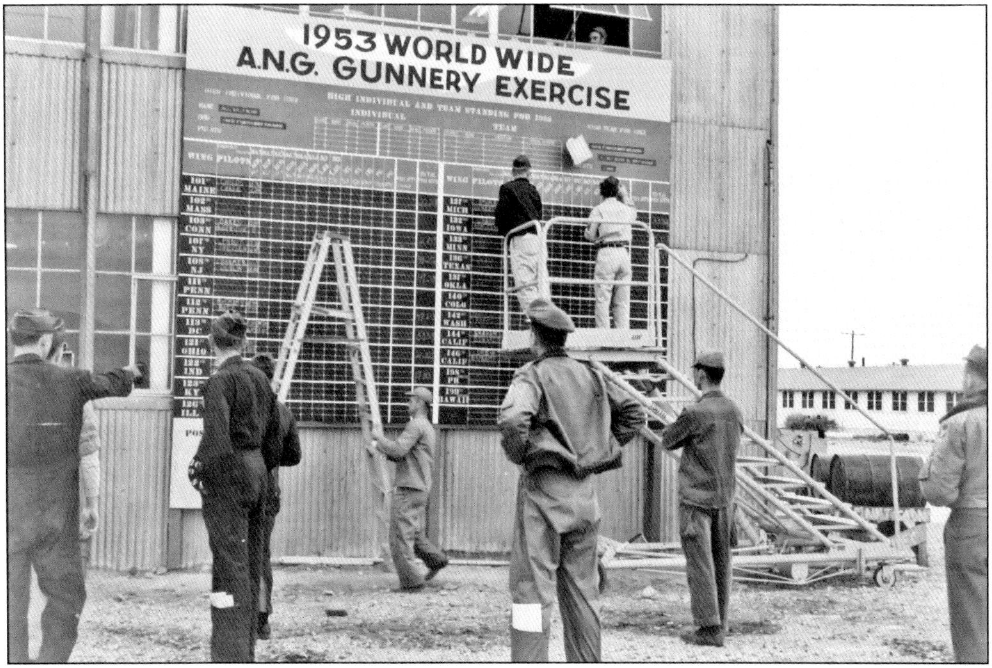

Enlisted men begin to chalk in the first day's results as inquisitive pilots look on. The division of accomplishment was not separated by individual squadron, but rather by wing. The 190th reported to the 142nd Wing of Spokane, Washington, which competed against 22 other wings from throughout the country. The only time a squadron was singled out was when it held the best score from the previous year. The pilot to be beat in 1953 was Maj. Billy Means of the 194th Fighter-Bomber Squadron.

Three

Jets, Jets, Jets

In November 1953, the first of three Lockheed T-33s touched down at Gowen Field, signaling the beginning of the Idaho Air National Guard jet age. A short time later, 25 F-86As arrived, allowing the 190th to build a stable of daytime alert aircraft. With the coming of the jets, 190th and the Idaho Air National Guard shed the stigma of a good ol' boys' flying club.

Over the next 10 years, the 190th operated multiple aircraft, including the T-33, F-86A, F-94B, F-89B, and various support planes. While the hardware aspect is the easiest portion of the history to relate, Gowen Field's change in mission is by far the most impacting to the Idaho Air Guard. Mere months before the first F-89 landed at Gowen, the air force activated the 124th Fighter Interceptor Group. This activation signaled a growth that had been eking along since the fighter jets arrived in Boise. With the establishment of the 124th and its three new subordinate squadrons, the Idaho Air Guard became a self-supporting organization able to deploy to any base in the world without the assistance of another unit.

Furthermore, since the entrance of the F-86 into the 190th's fold, the Idaho Air Guard had periodically maintained a 14-hour daylight alert commitment to supplement the regular air defense of the Pacific Northwest. With the arrival of the F-89 and later the F86L, the 190th (led by the 124th) began a 24-hour alert program in support of the nationwide defense against a Russian attack.

Although it was the men and machinery combined with the new mission at Gowen Field that attracted new recruits, the whole dynamic surrounding the base altered the way Boise viewed the military. Gowen Field leadership often encouraged the local community to come and see Gowen up close and personal while its military members recruited from the local population. This relationship formed a bond between Gowen and the locals that is romanticized in our memories.

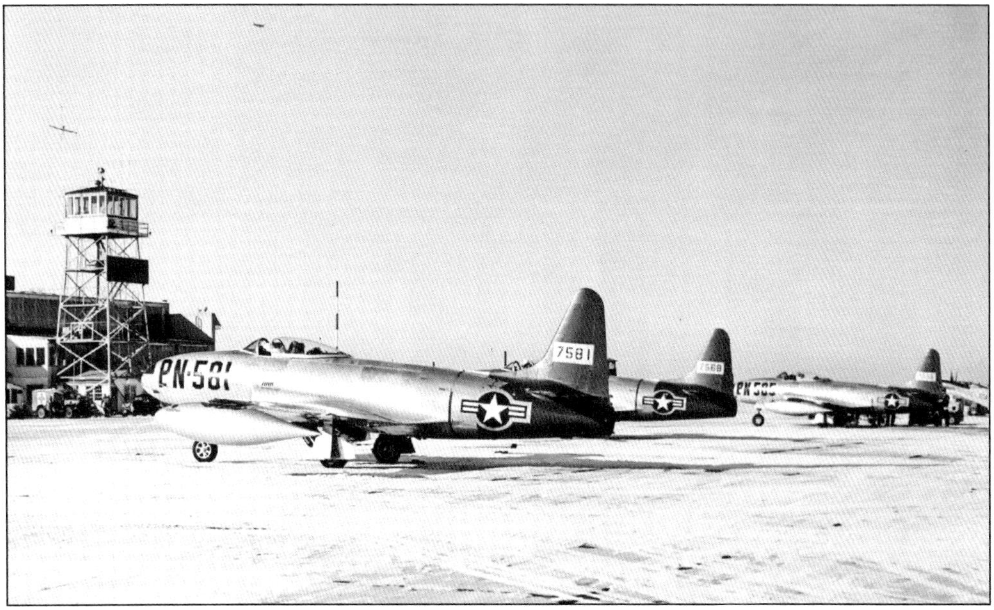

The first of three Lockheed T-33 Shooting Stars arrived at Gowen Field in November 1953. Originally designated as the TF-80C, the T-33 made its first flight on March 22, 1948. The two-place aircraft proved to be a suitable advanced trainer, and in addition to its primary use, the 190th utilized the new plane to tow targets for aerial gunnery. In the end, the 190th's T-33s were used as surrogate trainers for the much more sophisticated F-86 Sabres.

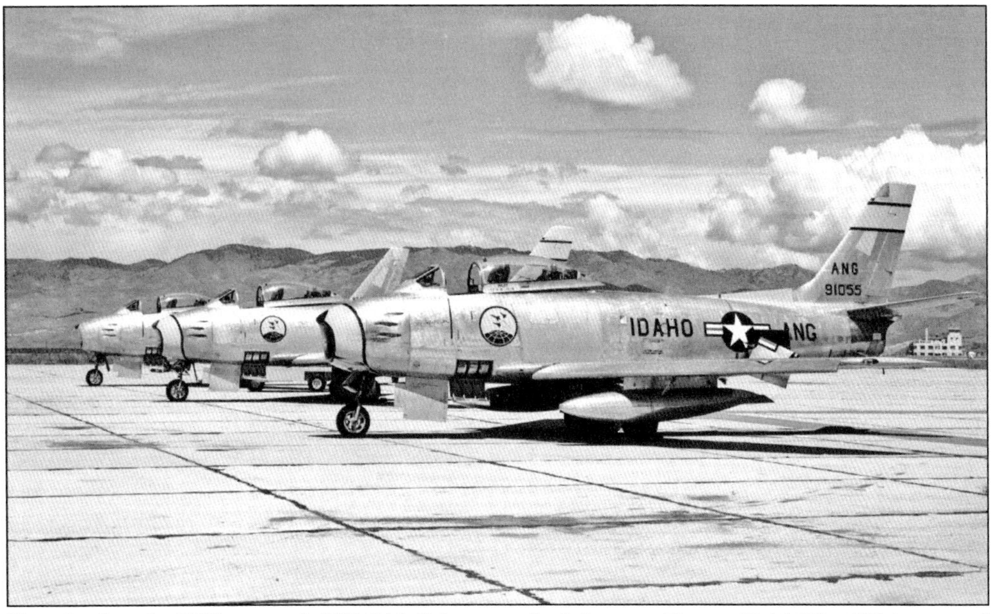

Shortly after the T-33s arrived, 25 F-86A Sabres touched down at Gowen Field. The 190th entered the Jet Age in style, as this new airplane could reach speeds up to 600 miles per hour and its six .50-caliber machine guns could shred an enemy airplane to bits. While the unit only operated the Sabre for close to two years, its arrival indicated a change in the Idaho Air Guard. No longer was Gowen Field considered just a local flying club, but now the base would play an active role in the nation's defense.

Maj. Kenneth Nordling (center) poses with two unidentified men from the 142nd Wing of Spokane, Washington. Major Nordling holds the second-place trophy for best team in the 1954 Air Guard Jet Fighter Gunnery Competition. This was a monumental accomplishment for the 190th, as the unit had just transitioned to the F-86 months before this gunnery meet.

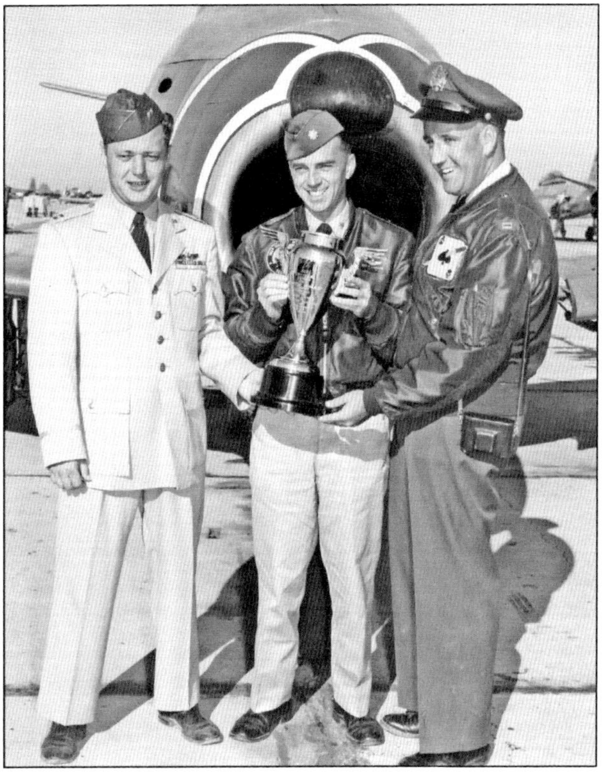

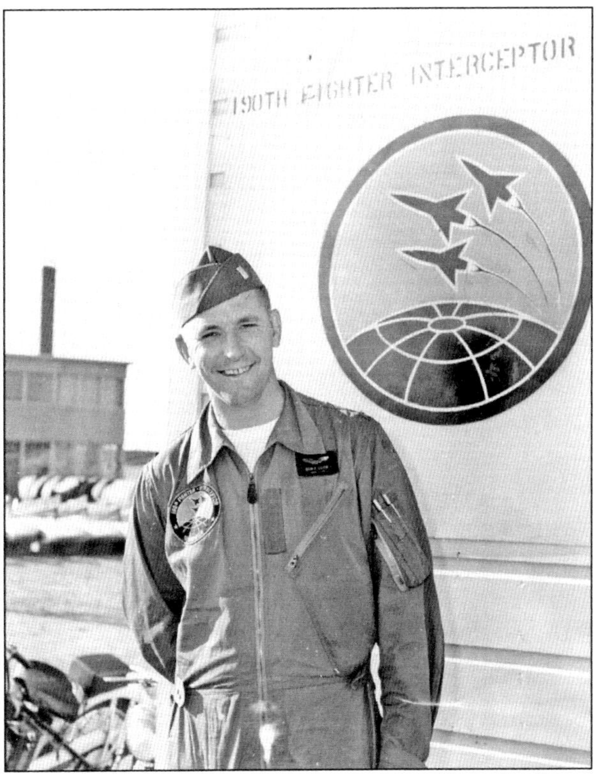

Lt. Sam Corn stands in front of the 190th squadron operations building. During the F-86 time period, the squadron became proficient in air-to-air gunnery using the Sabre's radar-ranging gun sight. Eventually seven 190th pilots achieved gunnery scores of over 50 percent, and Lt. Sam Corn scored an exceptional 87 percent on one mission. In the background, the newly designed 190th Fighter Interceptor emblem portrays the unit's mission of defending the northern hemisphere from the Russians.

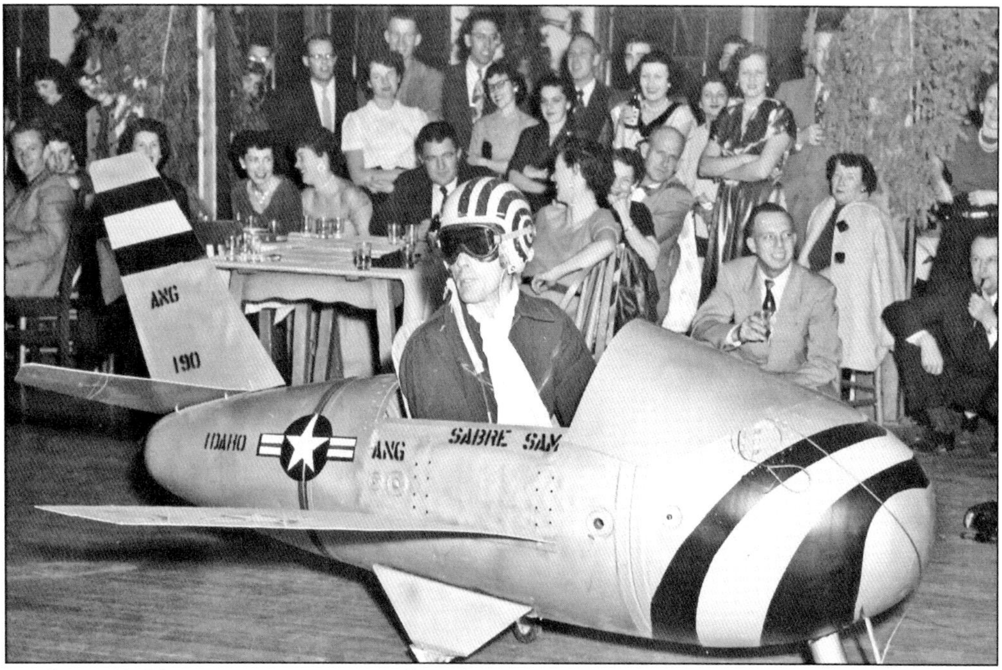

At the 1953 Christmas party, Maj. Bill Coburn entertains the crowd as "Sabre Sam" and his amazing F-86. During the skit, his airplane moved around the stage shooting sparks from its tailpipe. To give Major Coburn the effect he desired, two creative young men—airman 1st class Russell Chase and airman 3rd class Dean Peterson—welded together an old aircraft drop tank.

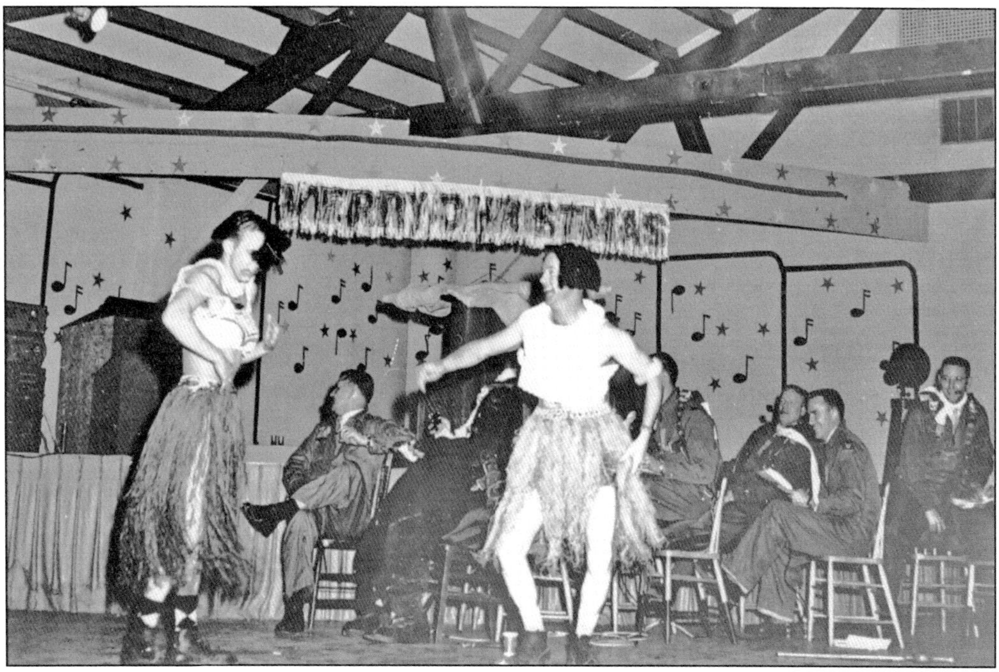

Ralph Wozniak (left) and Holly Moore (center) perform a skit wearing hula outfits at that same party. Moore, a charter member of the Idaho Air National Guard, served in various sections including gunnery scoring and simulator training.

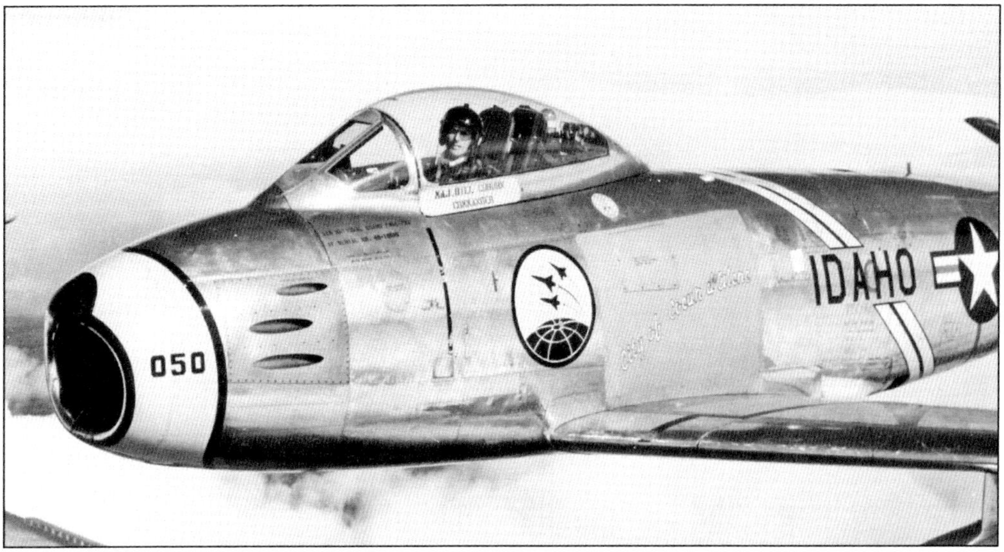

Maj. Bill Coburn pilots his F-86 in the skies over Boise. In June 1954, Major Johnson relinquished command of the 190th Fighter Inceptor Squadron to Coburn, who commanded the unit through its transition to the F-94B Starfire. A veteran pilot of the 190th, Major Coburn had set a speed record when he flew his F-51 between Boise and San Francisco in 1 hour, 16 minutes, and 51 seconds.

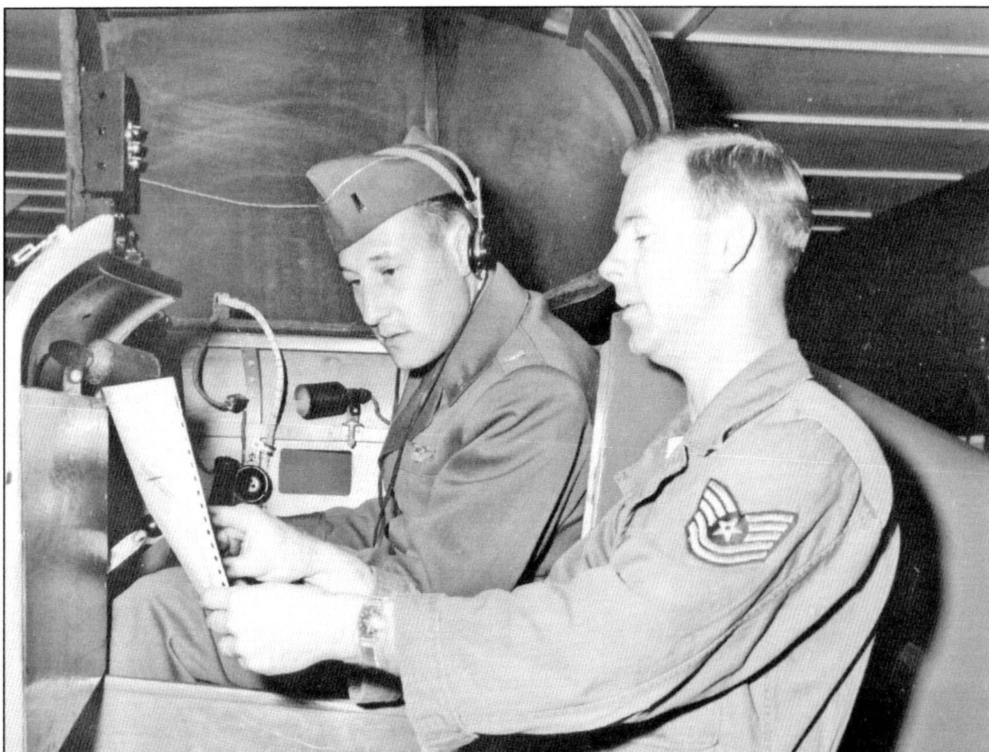

Sgt. Holly Moore (right) gives Lieutenant Lenhart (left) some basic instruction on the LINK trainer. Sergeant Moore went on to oversee the simulator training for all of the 190th and, later, the 124th Fighter Group.

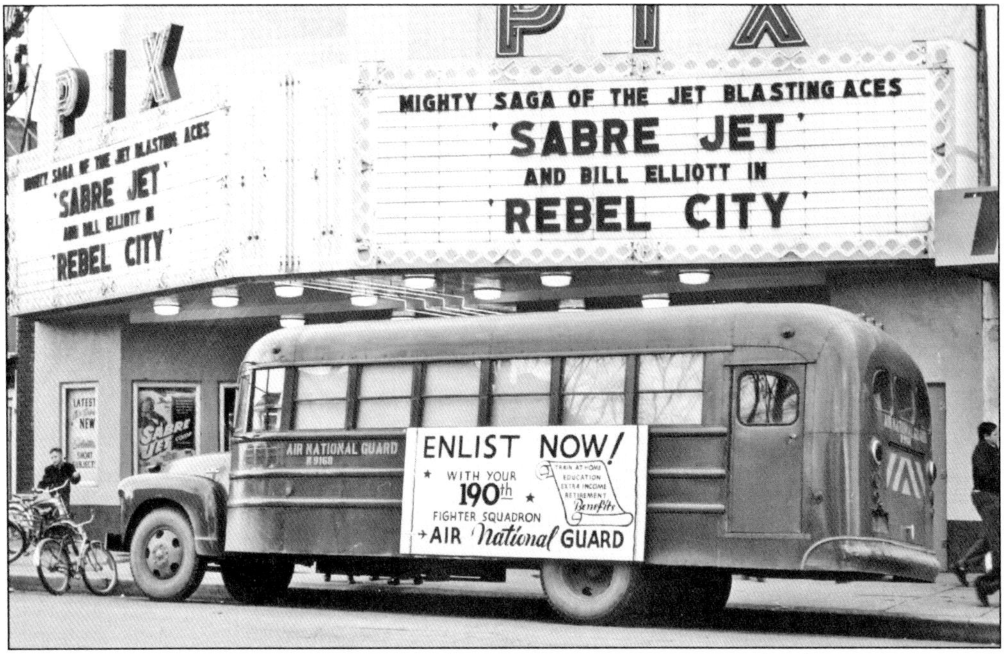

As with the post–World War II time period, recruitment was paramount for the 190th's survival. With the unit's conversion to the F-86, it was assigned to the Air Defense Command and began to sit on 14-hour daylight alert duty, supplementing the regular air defense of the Pacific Northwest. To meet this new mission, the 190th needed more men to fill its ranks, and some very clever airmen came up with these two recruitment attractions. The unit took a defunct F-86 (below) and clipped its wings short for passage down local streets, luring prospective recruits. The 190th recruiters used a dressed-up bus (above) for physicals and enlistment administration. Some recall that they could process a new recruit within a two-hour time period.

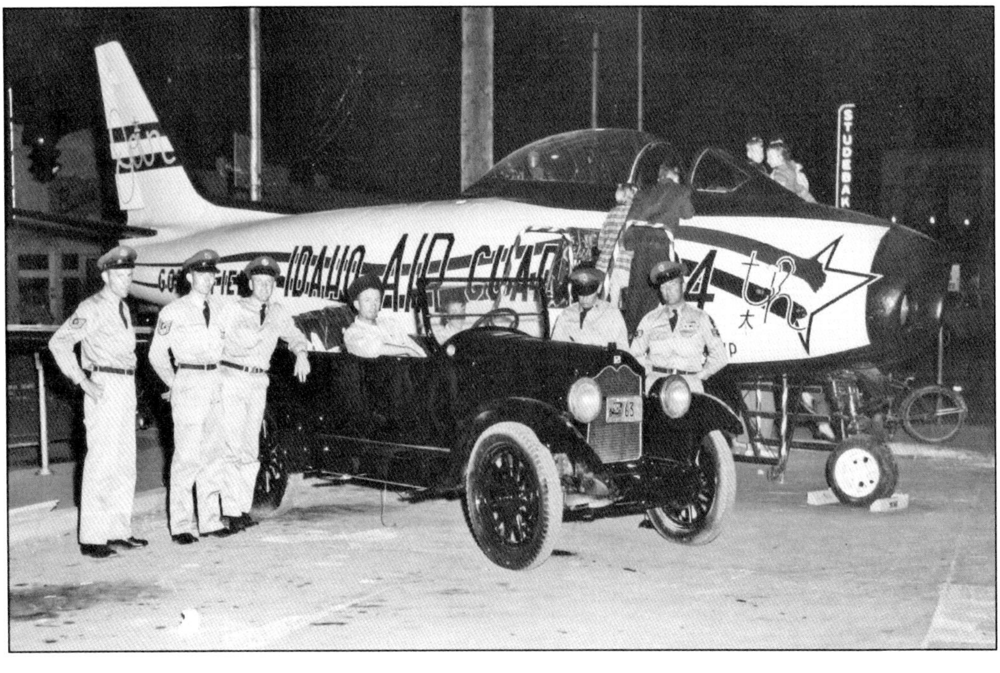

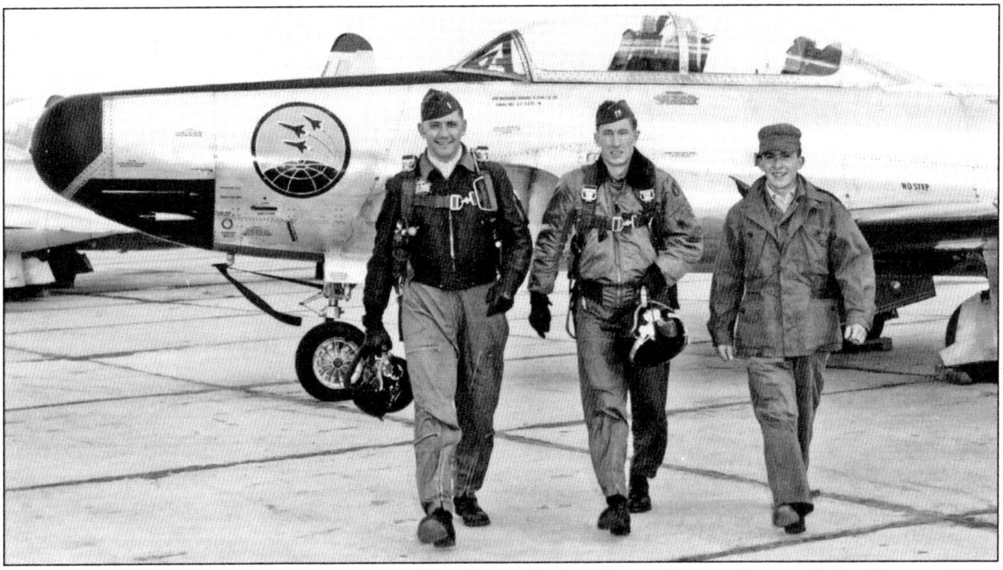

In September 1955, the first of 25 Lockheed F-94B Starfires, descendants of the famous F-80 Shooting Stars, arrived at Gowen Field. The radar-equipped airplane was the air force's first jet all-weather interceptor to become operational and was armed with four .50-caliber machine guns. With the addition of the second crewman operating the aircraft's radar, the 190th began a program to train radar observers. Here Lt. Sam Corn (left), Captain Bedford (center), and Curtis Smith walk away from an F-94B.

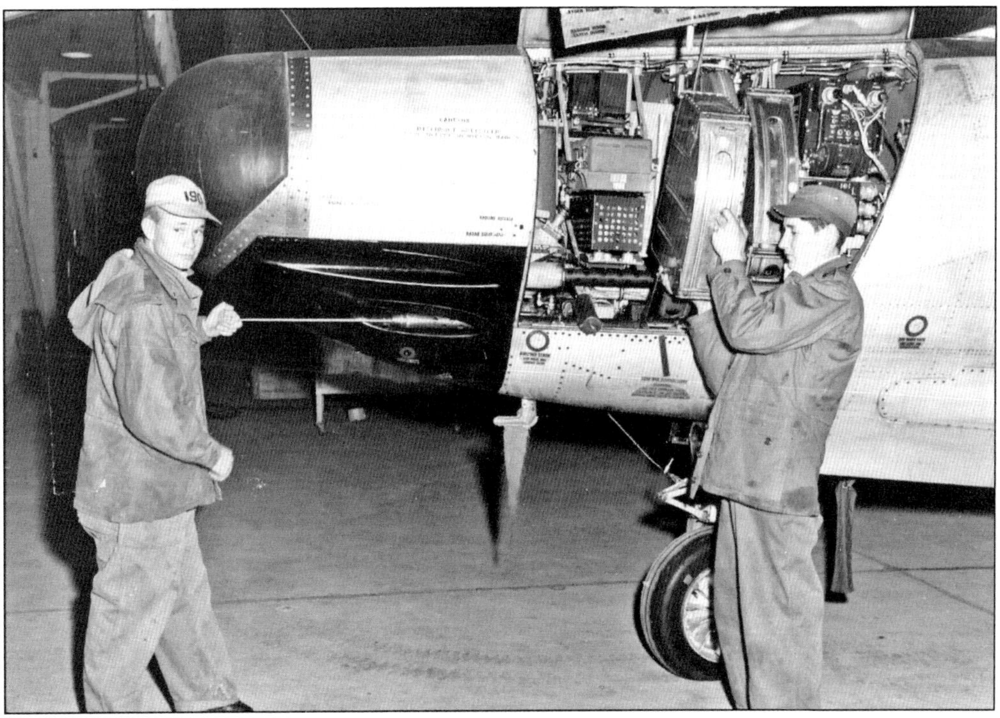

Alva Savage swabs an F-94 .50-caliber machine gun while his counterpart reloads the ammunition. The radar operator guided the pilot to the enemy via the F-94's radar dish housed inside the aircraft's nose. Once the target was acquired, the pilot fired the guns by pulling the trigger.

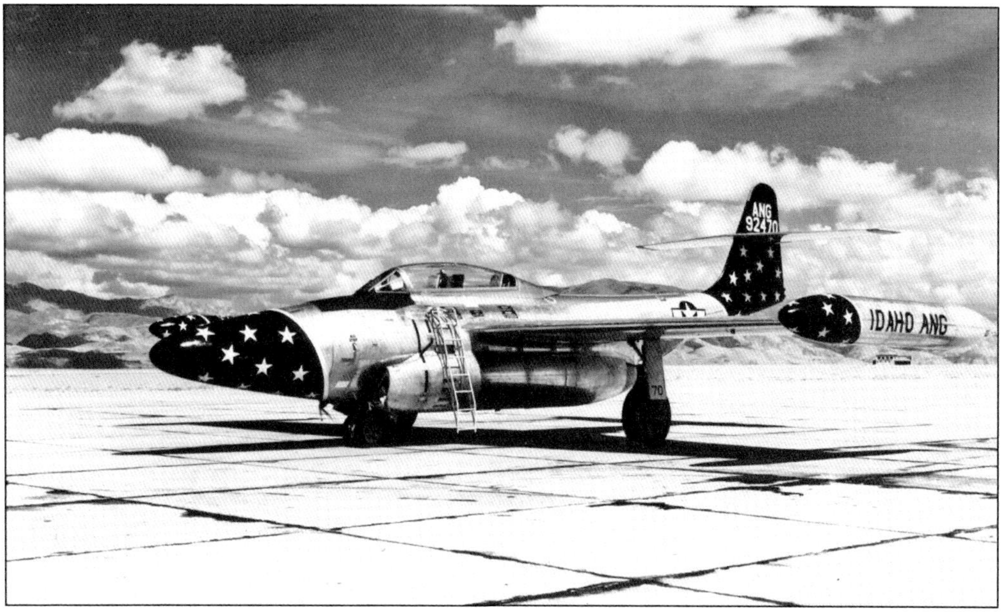

In June 1956, the Idaho Air Guard received 25 F-89B Scorpions—larger, more powerful two-seat all-weather jet inceptors armed with four nose-mounted 20-millimeter cannons. The F-89 was affectionately known as "the Ramp Sweeper" for its low intakes and its insatiable appetite to devour foreign objects lying on the flight line. Under the command of Lt. Col. Ken Nordling, the 190th operated the F-89 from June 1956 until 1959.

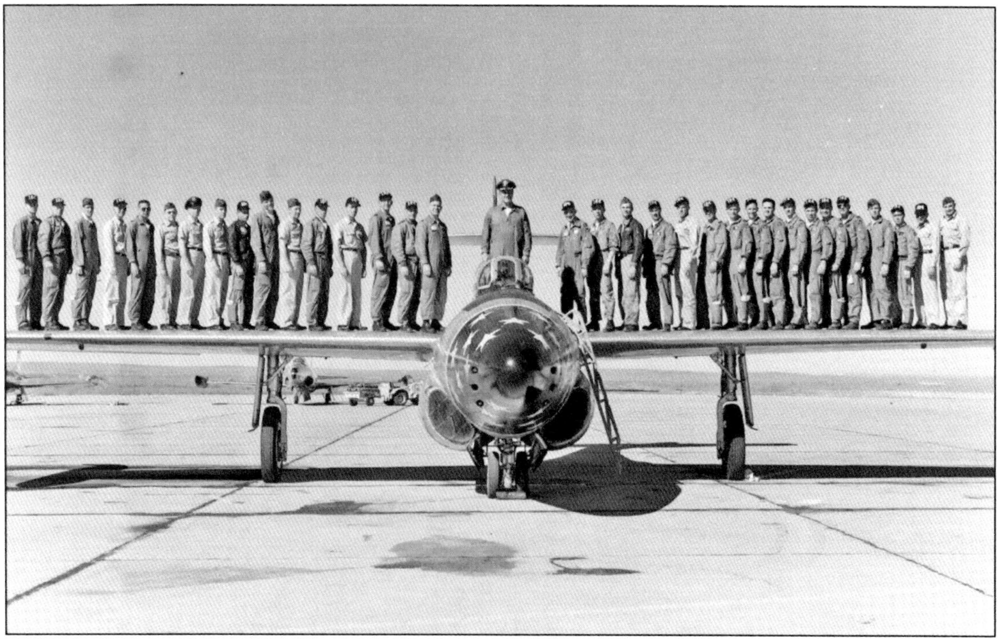

On April 14, 1956, the Idaho Air Guard expanded when the air force activated the 124th Fighter Interceptor Group and charged the previous 190th commander, Lt. Col. Martin Johnson, as its commanding officer. While at summer camp in Casper, Wyoming, Colonel Johnson (center) poses with pilots of the 190th. The 124th would become Gowen's parent organization and oversee the growth of the base from 1956 until the present day.

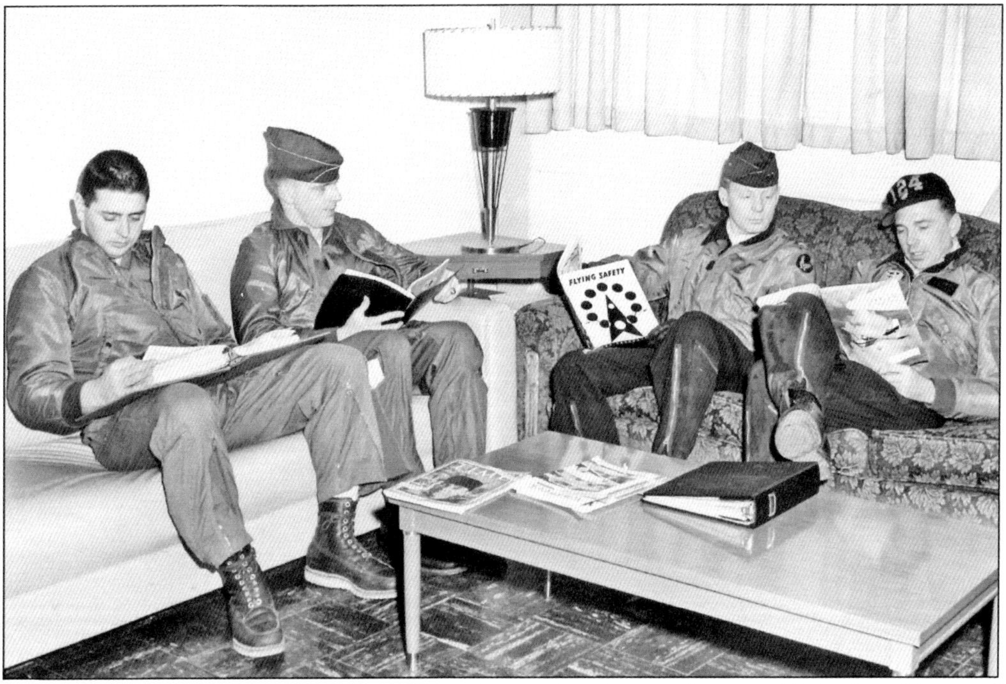

Ken Nordling (right) sits with three other pilots in the alert ready room. With the addition of the F-89, the 124th began participating in a sunrise-to-sunset alert duty to supplement the air defense of the Northwest. Colonel Johnson announced, "In case of a scramble signal from an air force radar site, the pilots—already garbed to go—have only to leap into their aircraft as the crew chief starts the engines."

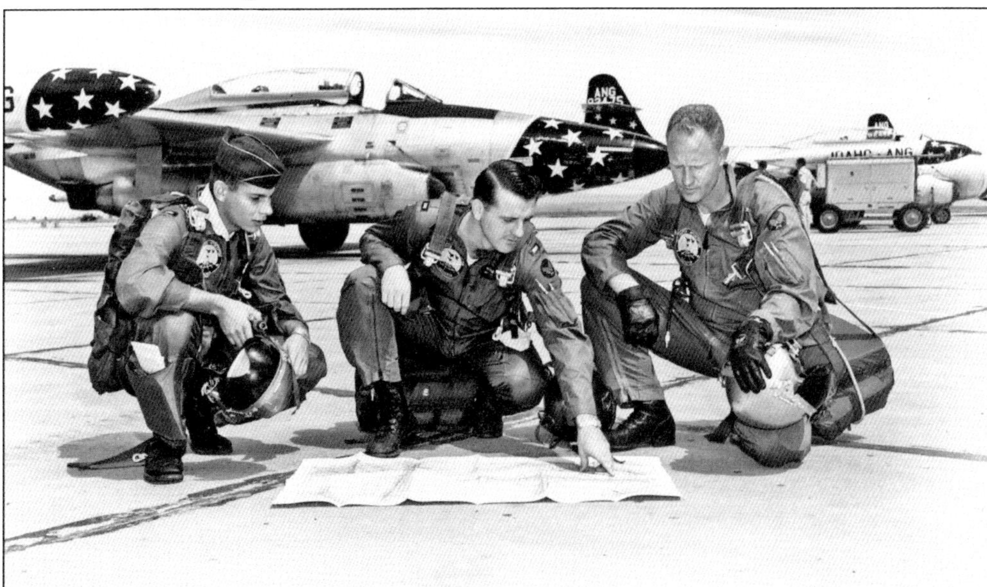

Don Hyatt (left), Jonathan L. Scott (center), and Dewey Bills review a map of the local range in preparation for an upcoming mission. The mission was more than likely flown either over the Craters of the Moon National Park or the Saylor Creek gunnery range.

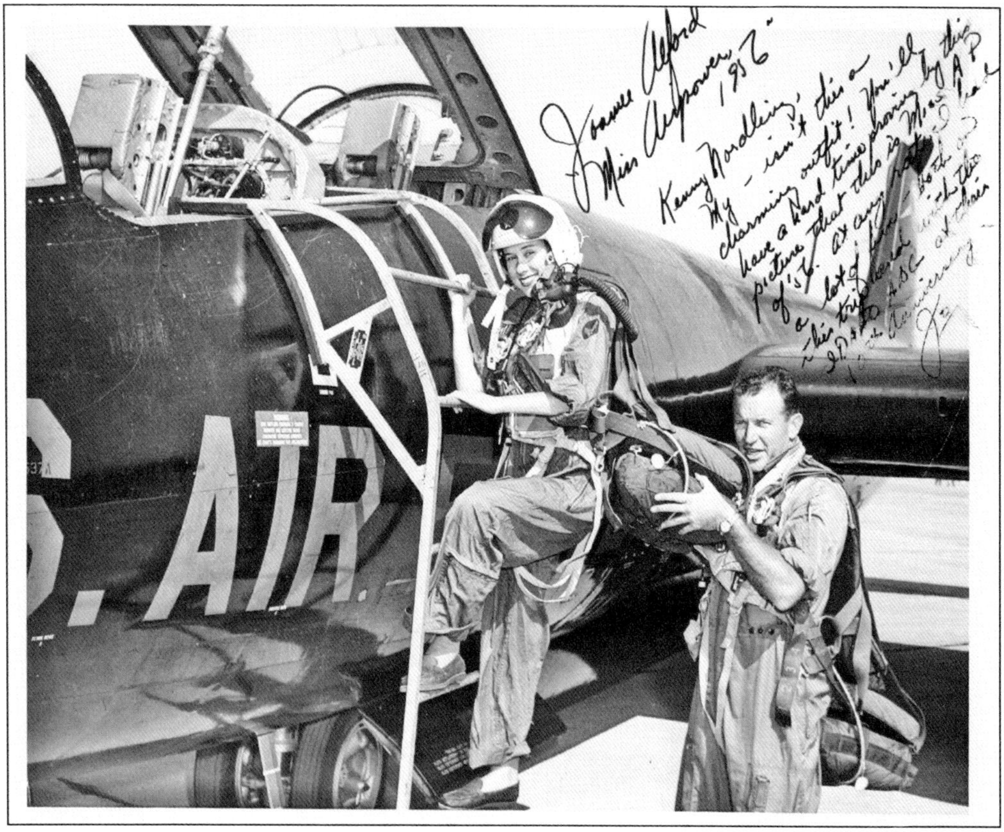

Joanne Alford, Miss Airpower 1956, is assisted into the cockpit of an F-89 by a 190th pilot in 1957. Her loving inscription says, "Kenny Nordling—My isn't this a charming outfit! You'll have a hard time proving by this picture that this is Miss AP of '56. At any rate I had a lot of fun—both on this trip and with the Idaho ANG at their 10th anniversary."

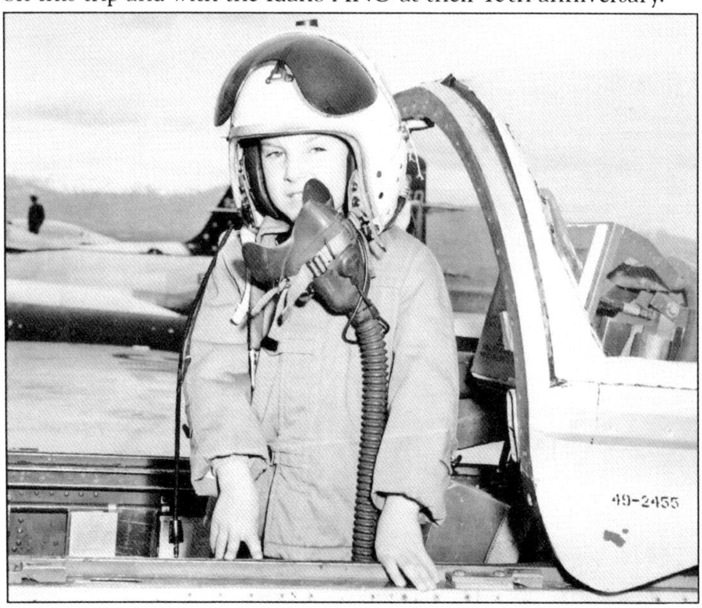

In February 1959, the 124th invited the 25th Idaho legislature to the base to inspect the facilities as well as the training. Among those attending were Sen. Vernon Daniel, his wife, and three children. Here his son Dean Daniel stands in the cockpit of an F-89 with a pilot's helmet on his head.

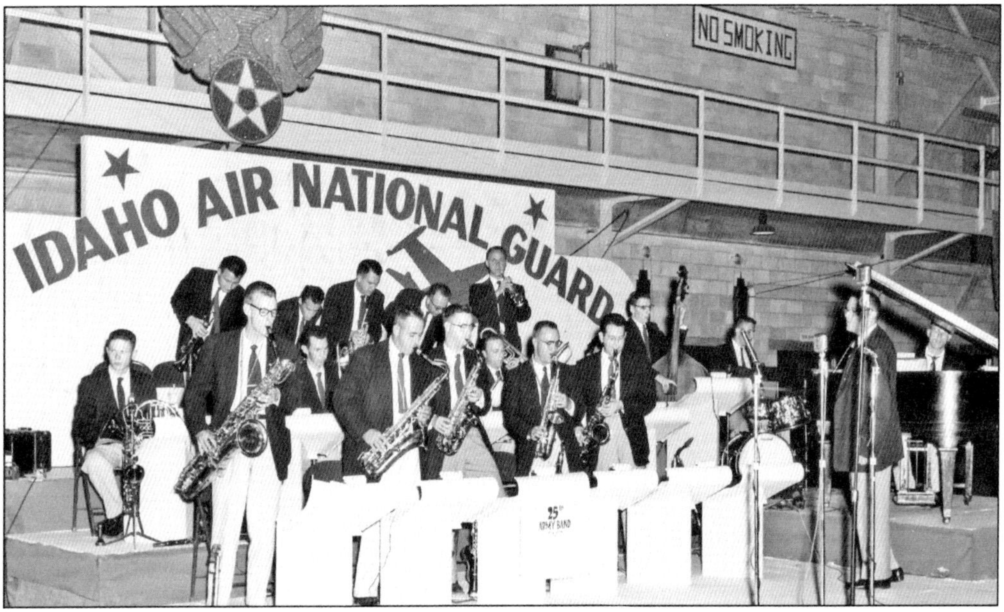

In November 1956, the 124th Fighter Interceptor Group celebrated the Idaho Air National Guard's 10th anniversary. In just 10 years, the fledgling unit had developed from a single-engine fighter squadron into an all-weather interceptor force defending the nation's northern tier. It had grown from a meager 44 airmen and 23 officers in 1946 to more than 1,000 men serving in regular drill formations in 1956. Here the 25th Army band performs at the large hangar celebration.

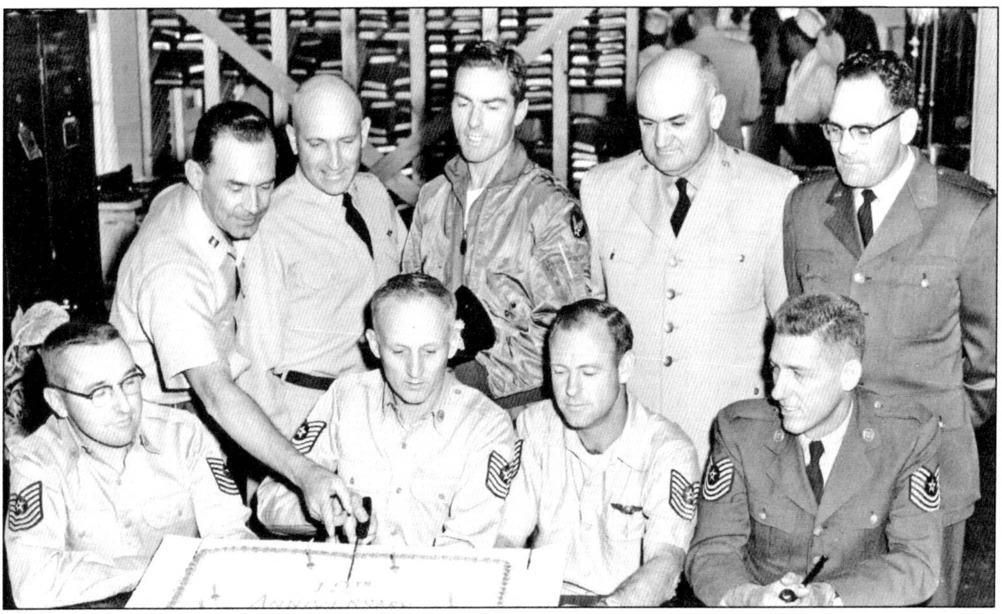

MSgt. William D. Fitzgerald makes the first cut in a cake commemorating the Idaho Air Guard's 12th anniversary of federal recognition. All personnel in this photograph served with the 190th since its inception in October 1946. Shown from left to right are the following: (first row) MSgt. Glen Carringer, MSgt. William Fitzgerald, MSgt. Holly B. Moore, and MSgt. Edward J. O'Donnell; (second row) Capt. Bill Bozman, Col. James M. Trail, Maj. Bill Coburn, Maj. Frank B. Bobbitt, and Capt. John Flaherty.

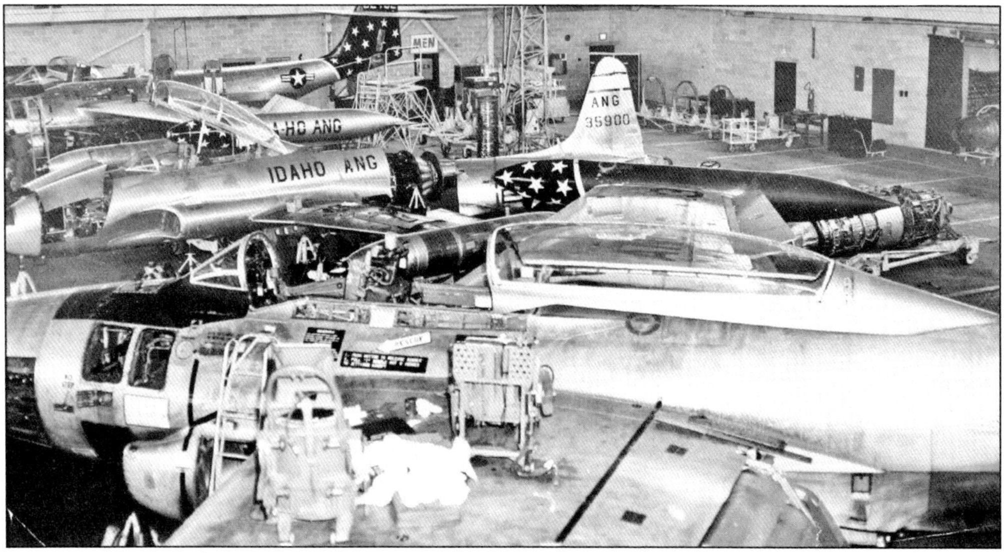

In a maintenance hangar located on the Gowen Field flight line, personnel have removed the ejection seats from an F-89 in the foreground, while the aft section of a T-33 has been disassembled for engine inspection. To accommodate the maintenance of the sophisticated aircraft, Gowen Field leadership began a program to build several large hangars.

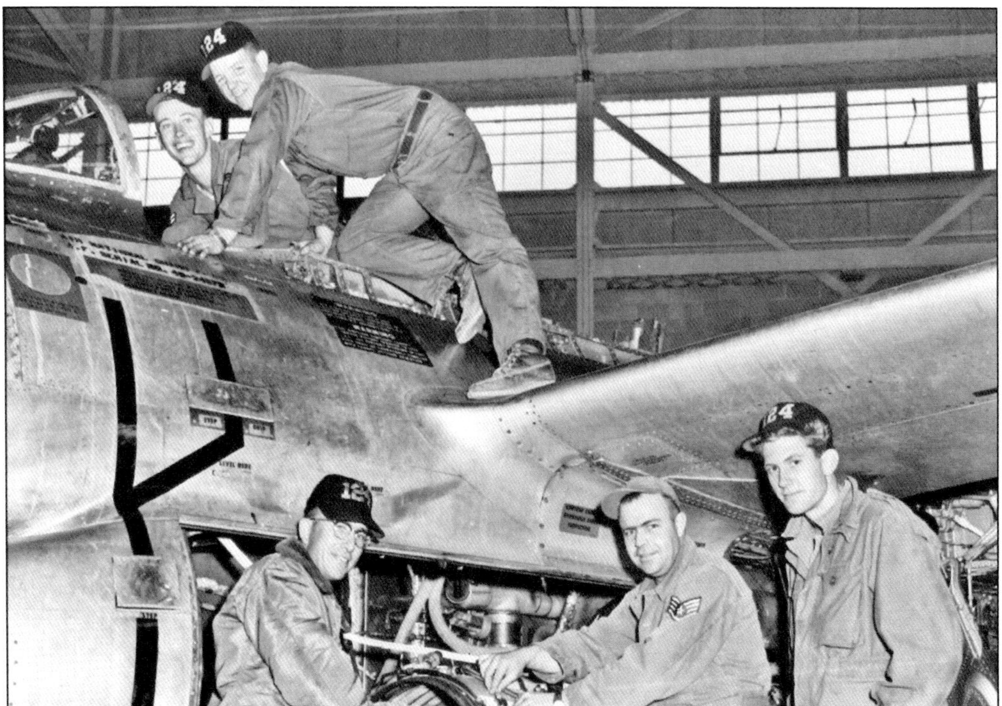

Harry Croy (left) and Herb Tongate (center) stop to pose with several unidentified 190th maintainers. These two old hands never attended basic training while working for the Guard; however, by 1959, the pictured new recruits had indeed traveled to basic training for a "proper" orientation into the military. Prior to this, air guardsmen had learned all of their basic military etiquette from the gray beards within the unit.

SSgt. Omar Fricke (right) of Gooding demonstrates to airman trainee Naylor the importance of care when loading gun camera film into an F-89B. Gunnery film was used as a training aid to improve the fighter pilot's marksmanship by allowing him to assess his air-to-air firing missions.

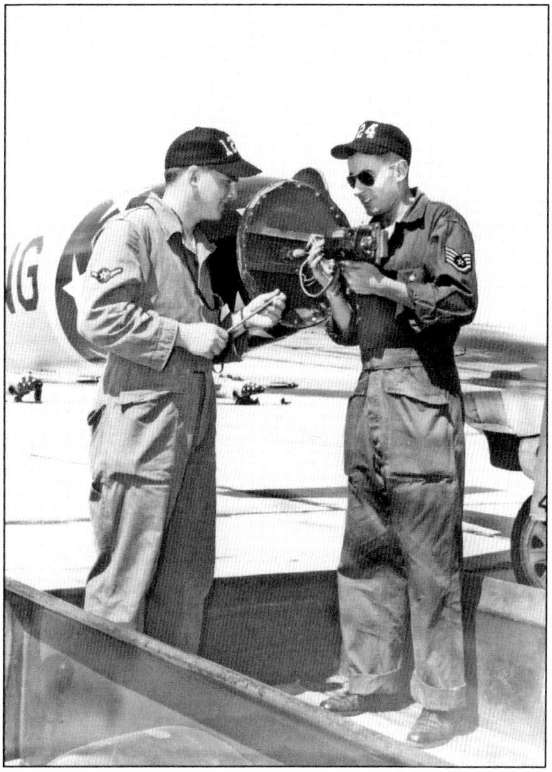

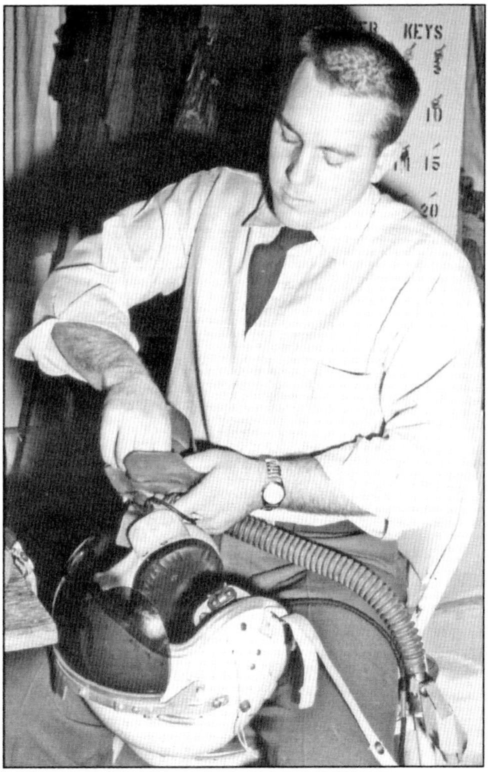

While working in the personal equipment room, airman 3rd class Gary Rogstad of Boise replaces a valve on a pilot's oxygen mask.

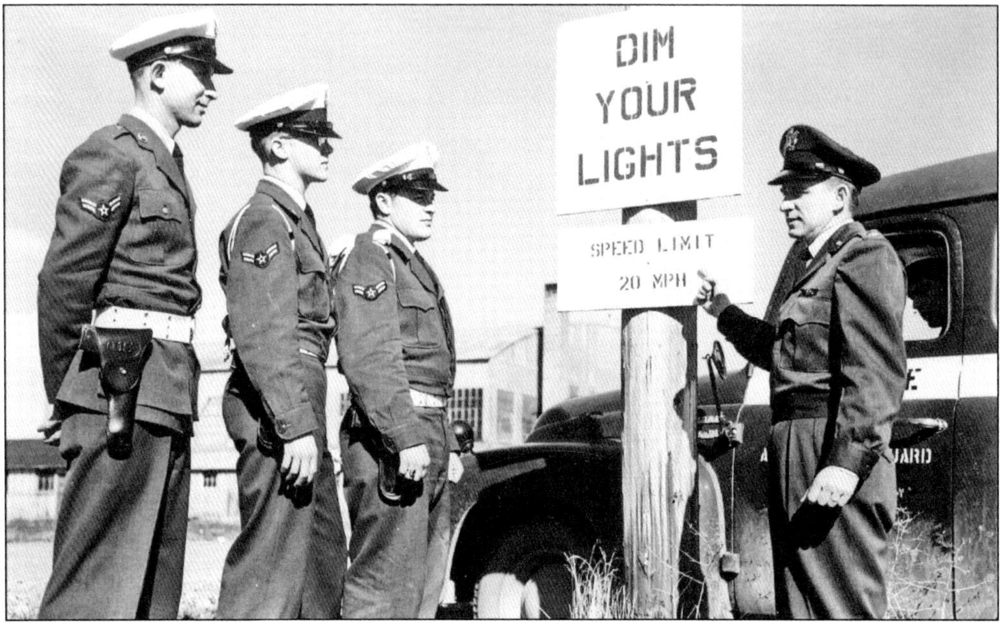

Three young air policemen listen as their officer in charge discusses the new speed limit on Gowen Field. As the 124th Fighter Interceptor Group formed its new subordinate units, Gowen Field began to resemble an active-duty base with all of the necessary support agencies.

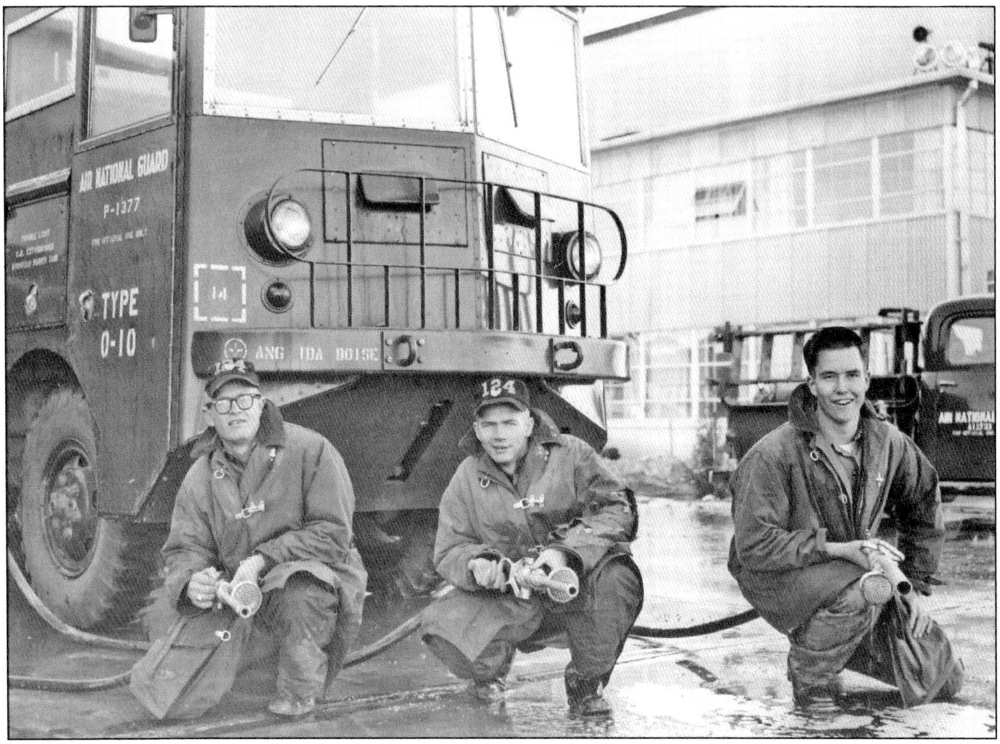

An Idaho Air National Guard crash recovery crew consisting of airman 3rd class Jack Blevins of Ontario, Oregon (left), airman 3rd class Carl A. Miller of Payette (center), and airman 2nd class Dorm Gilmore of Parma practice a rescue pattern known as the "V."

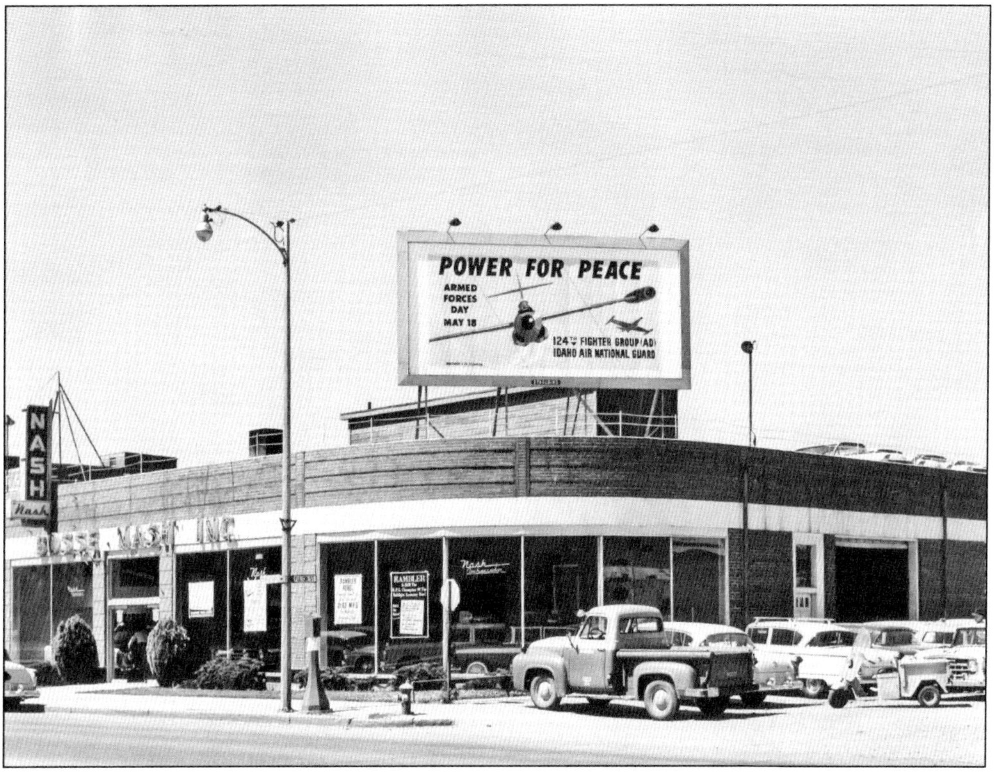

In support of the Idaho Air National Guard, Al Spaulding, owner of the Outdoor Display Company, donated the space above the Boise Nash dealership for this advertisement. Located at the corner of Capital Boulevard, the advertisement ran for one week in 1957 in honor of Armed Forces Day.

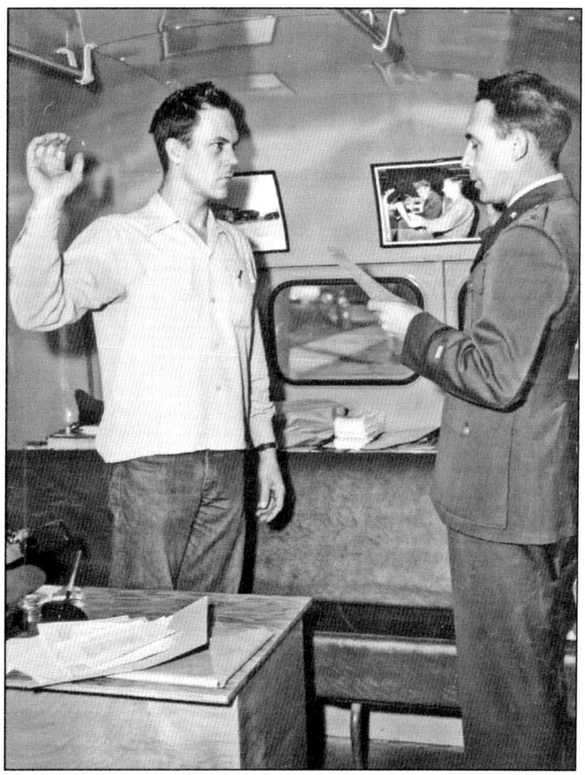

Another victim of the recruitment bus is sworn in by a captain of the 190th.

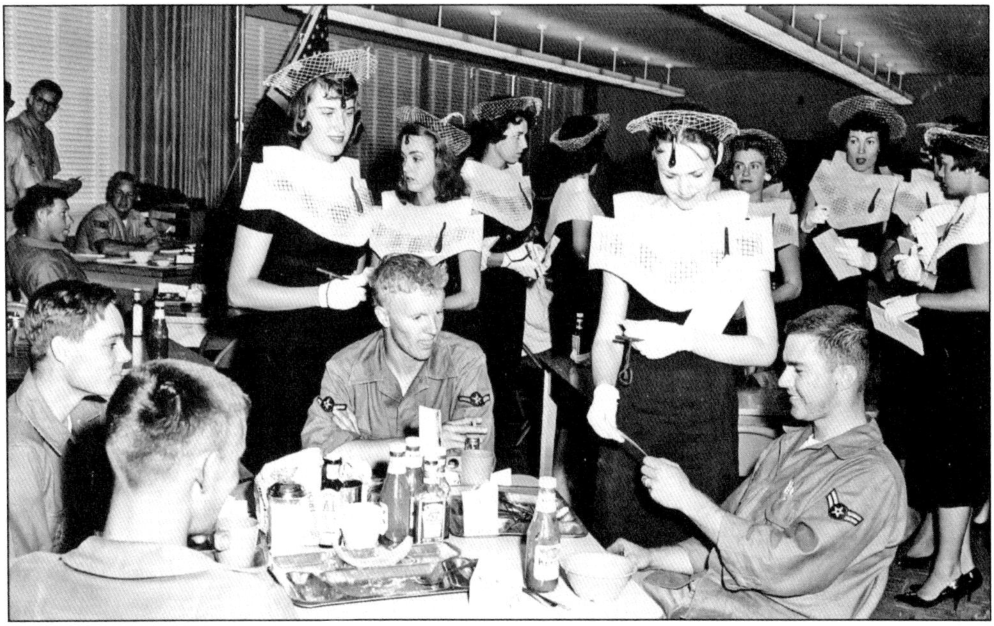

During summer camp in 1959, airman 2nd class Bill Lee (seated, right) returns a completed blood donor card to Shirley Mendiola (center) of Life Lines as airman 3rd class Lyale Herrera (left) and Sandra Jefferson look on. Life Lines was a volunteer group that visited the base in conjunction with the American Red Cross blood-drawing program that operated from Boise.

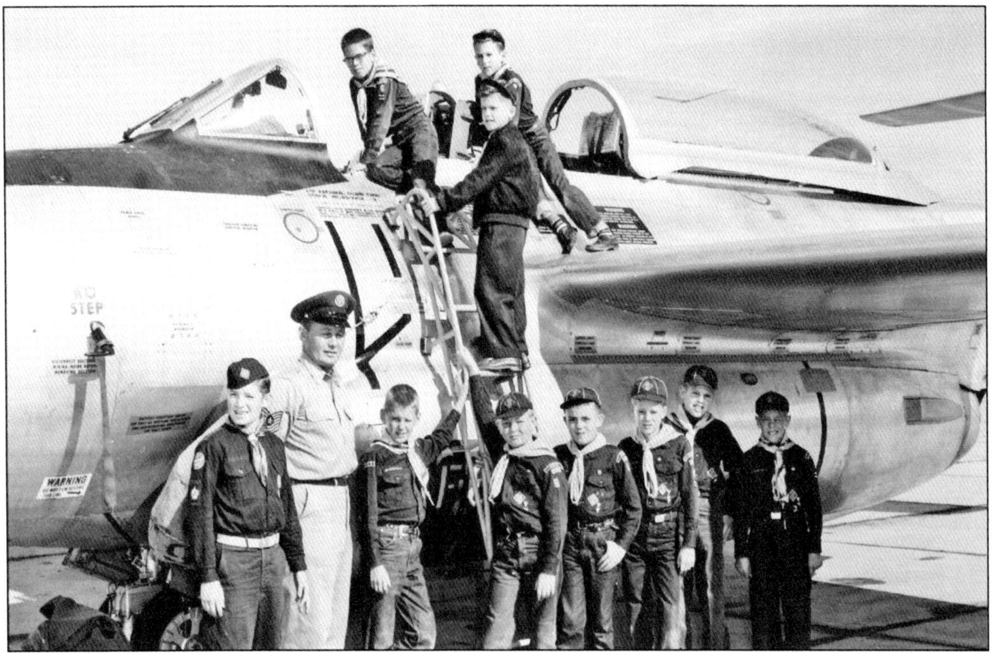

MSgt. David L. Cochran of the 124th Fighter Group hosts a group of Cub Scouts from Boise in October 1956. The young men won a tour of the Air National Guard base by raising funds for the treasury of the Roosevelt School pack. Pictured from left to right are the following: (first row) Pat Edwards, Sergeant Cochran, John Little, Mike Boegeman, Jedd Jones, Mike Glenn, John Schmelzer, and Bill Simonton; (second row) George Weick, John Milliner, and Bert Bowler.

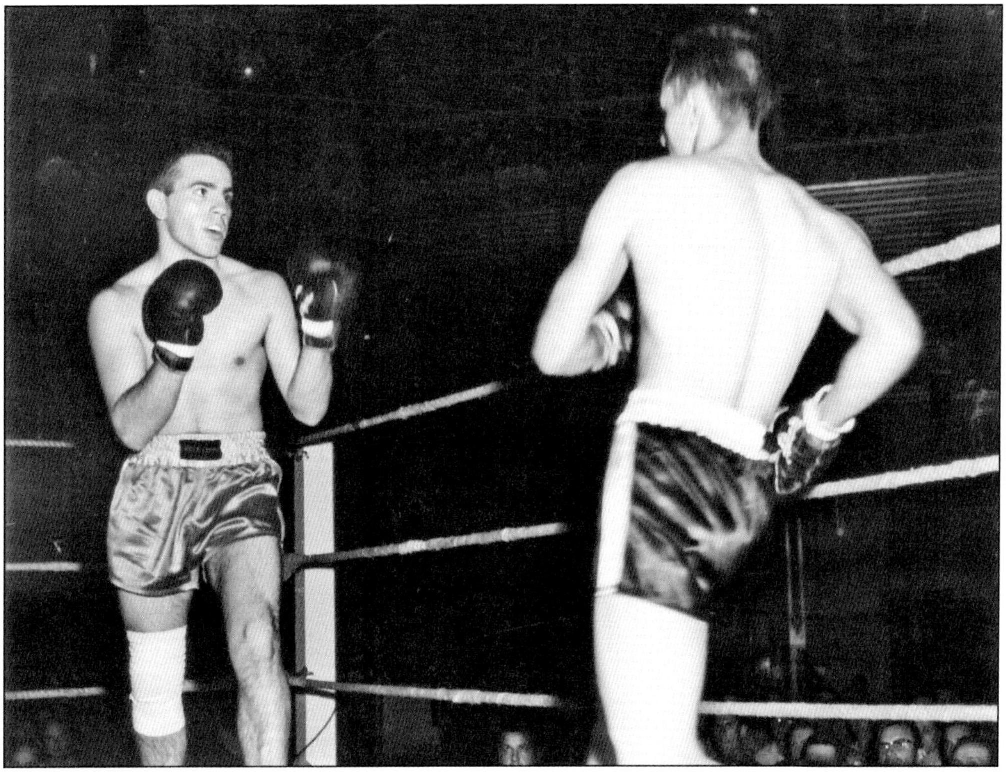

Two men take part in the time-honored military tradition of boxing while at summer camp in Casper, Wyoming. Unfortunately for the reader, the authors were unable to learn who won the fight.

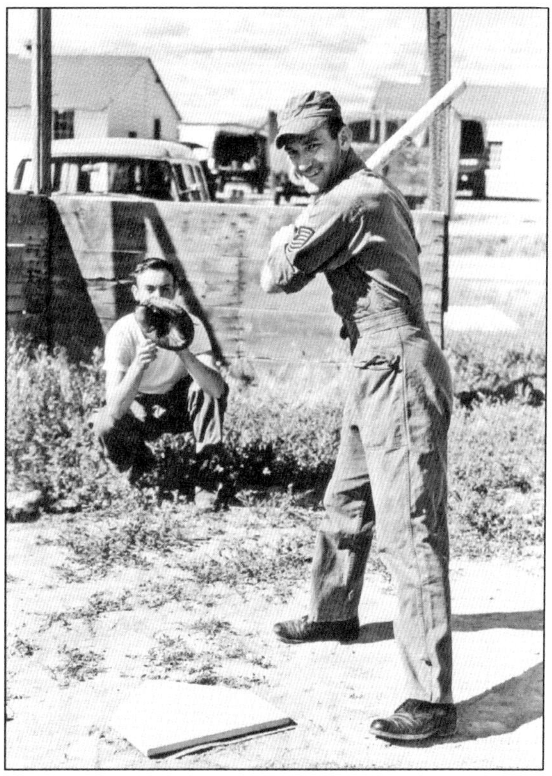

MSgt. Marion Carpenter of Boise is at bat while airman 3rd class David Schultz of Ola, Idaho, catches. The game occurred between the headquarters and maintenance units of the 124th Group. The headquarters section won with an impressive score of 26-69.

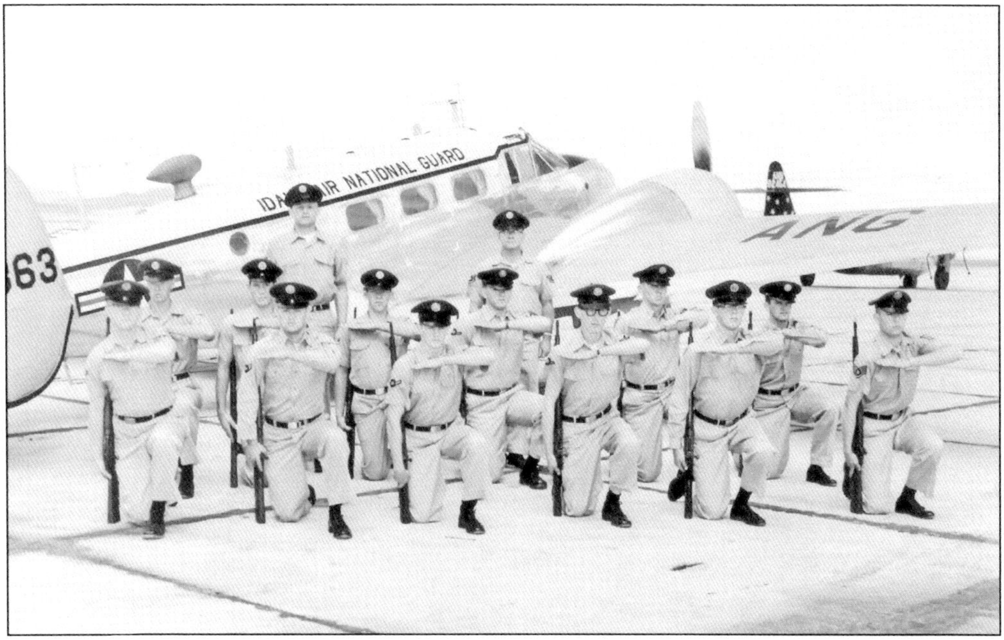

The Idaho Air National Guard Drill Team executes the "Queen Ann" salute for the camera during preparations for the 1958 Governor's Day Parade. Shown from left to right are the following: (first row) John W. Johnson, James F. Nevin, Donald I. Hutchinson, Richard R. Hesse, Gary L. Drown, and Vernon N. Davis; (second row) Vernon S. Dowdle, Charles S. Gross, Ernest W. Chandler, James M. Davis, Robert R. Korb, and Harold J. Nevin; (third row) coaches Steve E. Nielson and Donald Lowry.

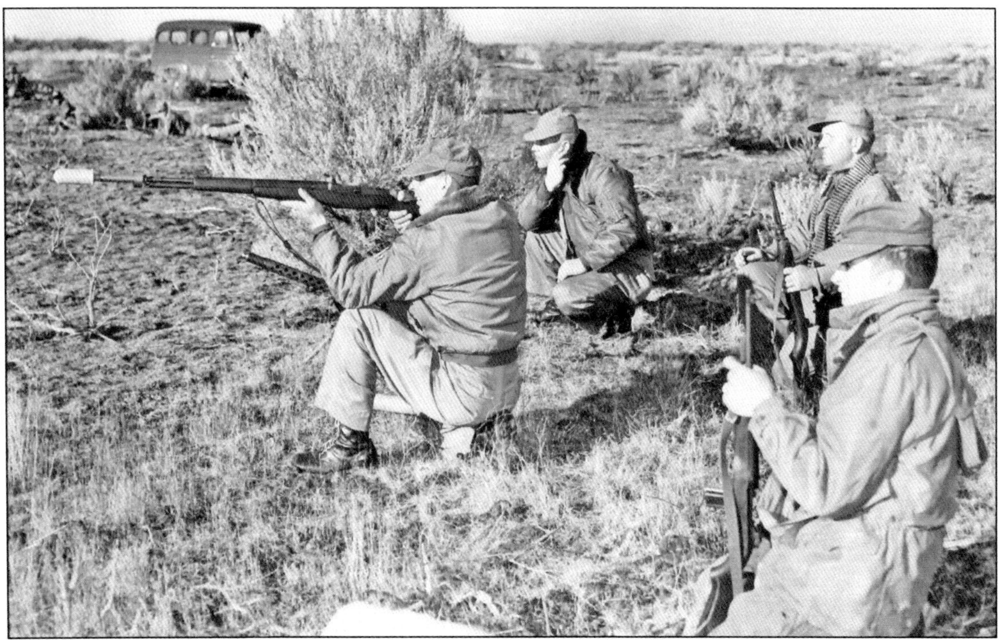
Three air base defense airmen look on as one of their own prepares to fire a rifle grenade from an M1 rifle, nicknamed "the Garand" after its inventor. This is a smoke grenade used for marking a position or creating a smoke screen.

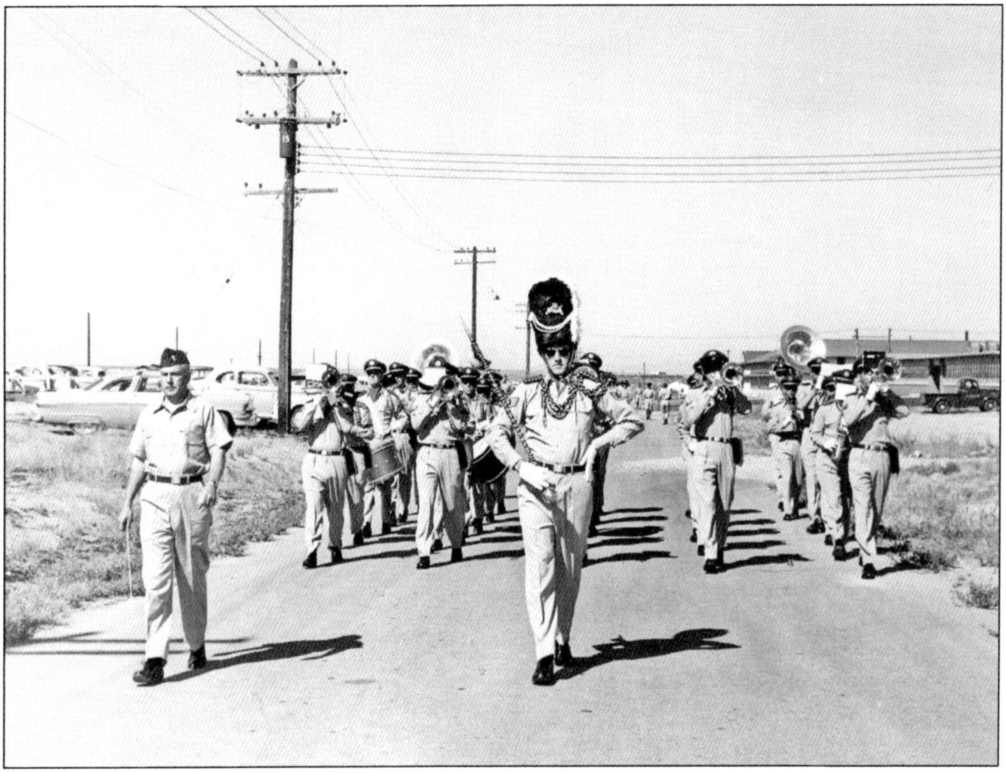

Prior to a 1959 retreat ceremony held at Gowen Field, the Air National Guard band moves into position. Bands in one form or another had been an integral part of the base's history since its inception in World War II. While the band was not used nearly as much as it had been in the past, it still provided basic functions at military ceremonies.

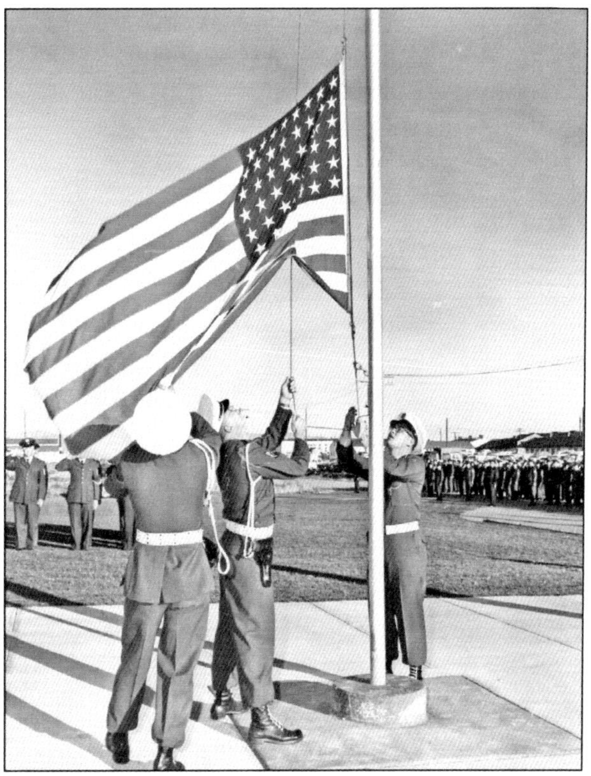

Three Gowen Field air policemen lower the U.S. flag during a retreat ceremony while the retreat formation renders the proper salute. Of particular interest is that everyone, including the air police, is wearing the new U.S. Air Force blue uniform instead of the World War II–vintage, U.S. Army–issued Class A.

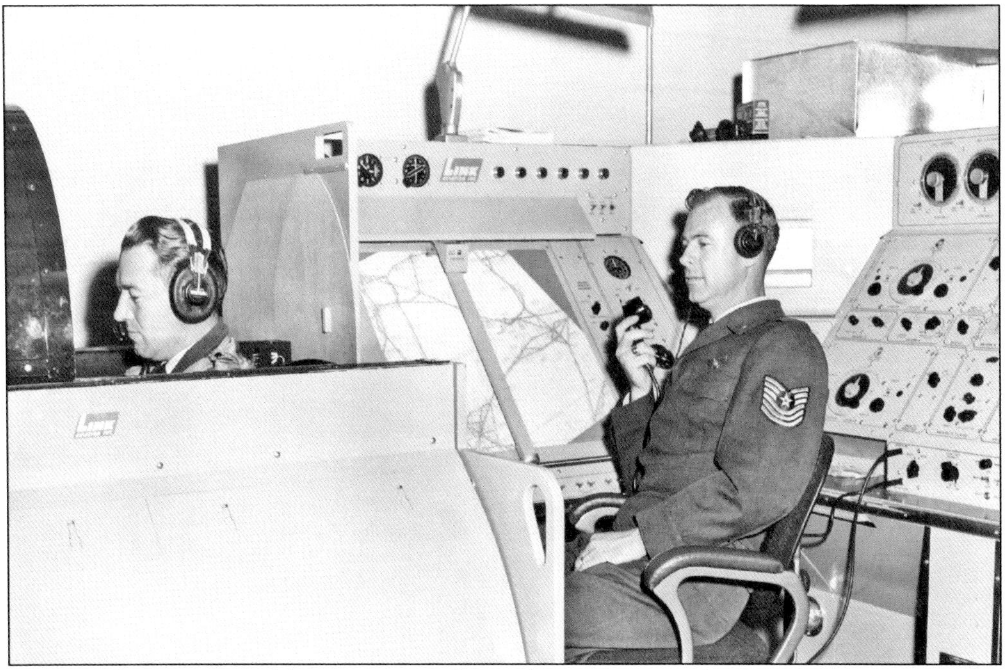

MSgt. Holly B. Moore, Idaho Air National Guard instrument and radio navigation instructor, guides Capt. F. T. Briggs through a simulated blind-flying exercise. After this workout, the captain will be better able to fly his F-89 without visual references and with the aid of navigation instruments only.

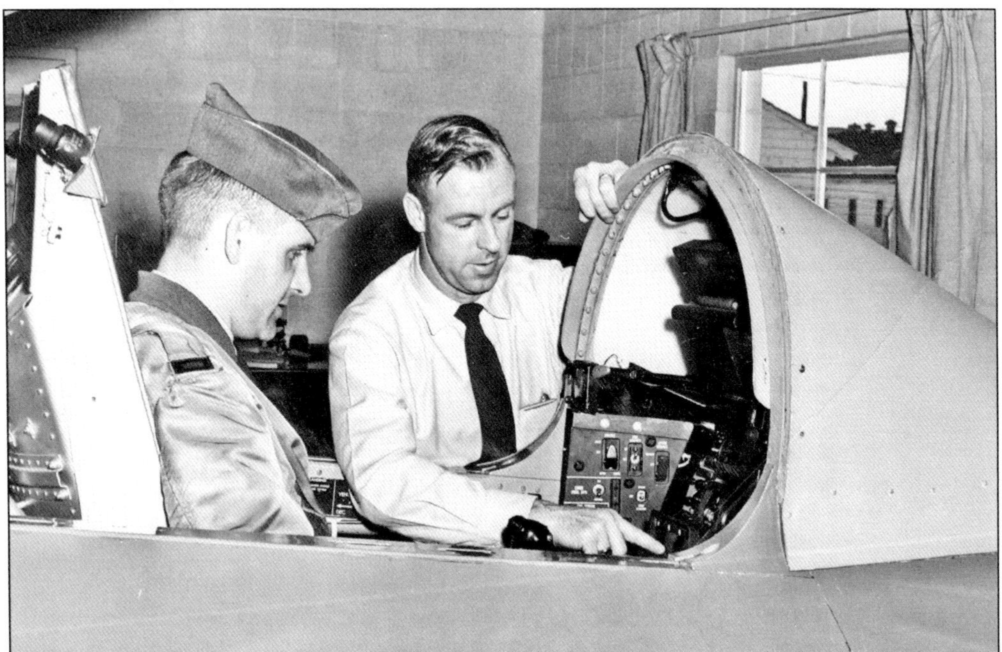

Now with a new simulator, Master Sergeant Moore puts yet another pilot through the paces. In 1959, the 124th received the North American F-86L and operated this platform for almost five years. As expected, the unit received a new simulator, and Holly Moore continued as instructor.

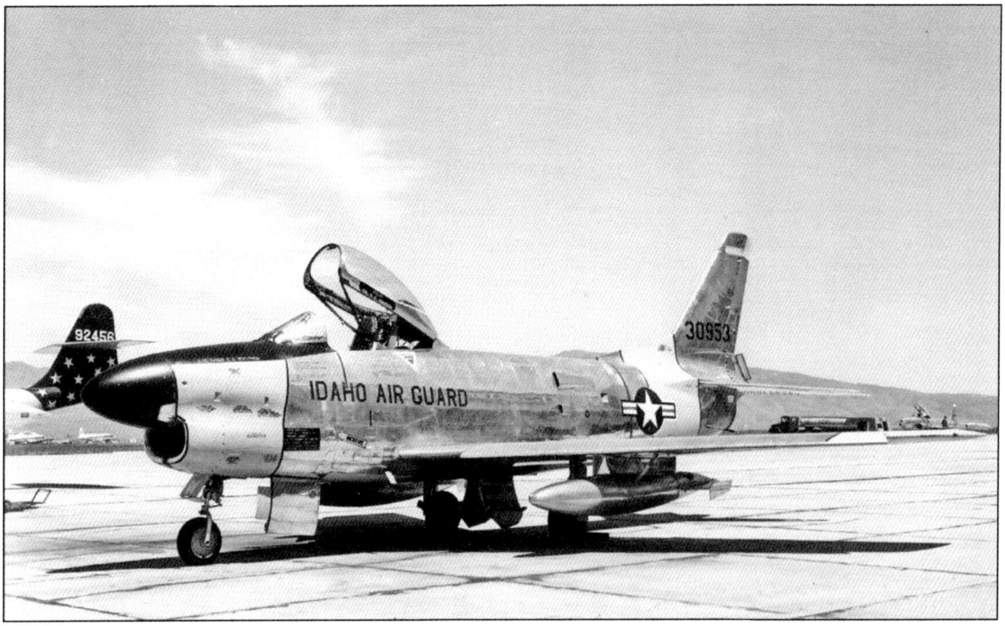

The 124th Fighter Interceptor Group received 25 F-86L Sabre jets, one of which is shown here in a beautiful side shot. The airplane contained radar in its nose, and due to advancements in technology, the need for a radar operator was eliminated. Beginning in 1961, the air force placed the 124th's F-86Ls on 24-hour alert duty as part of the nationwide air defense system.

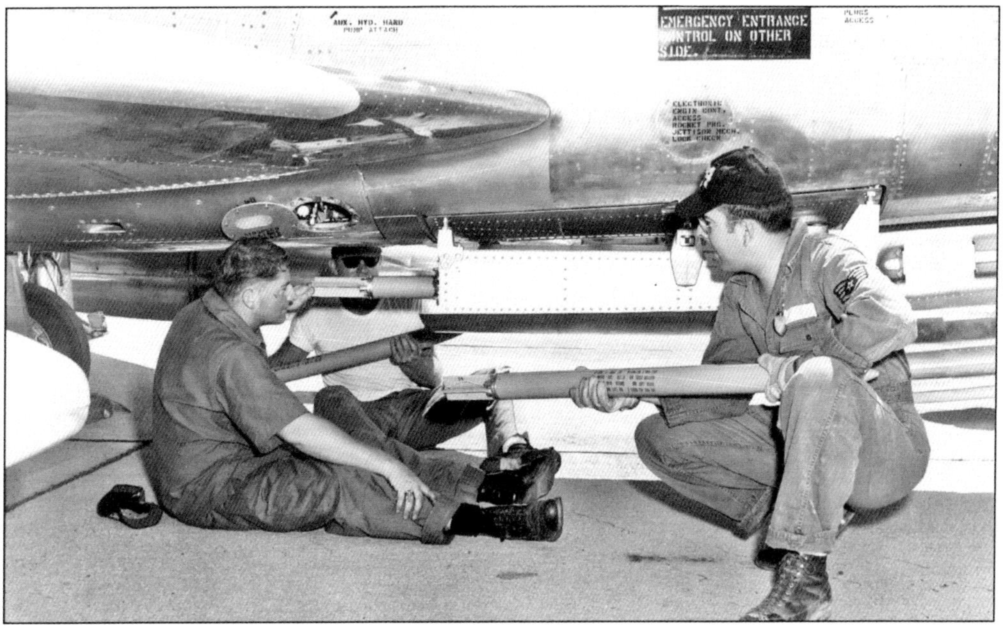

Dale Zollman (left) and David Payne load 2.75 rockets into a drop-down compartment in the F-86L. While the armament seemed meager, the real power of the F-86L was the data link system that communicated with the Semi-Automatic Ground Environment (SAGE) data link system. After gathering ground-based data, the SAGE system beamed the information to the F-86L. From there, the F-86L pilot could intercept enemy aircraft and down the opponent with the 2.75-inch rockets.

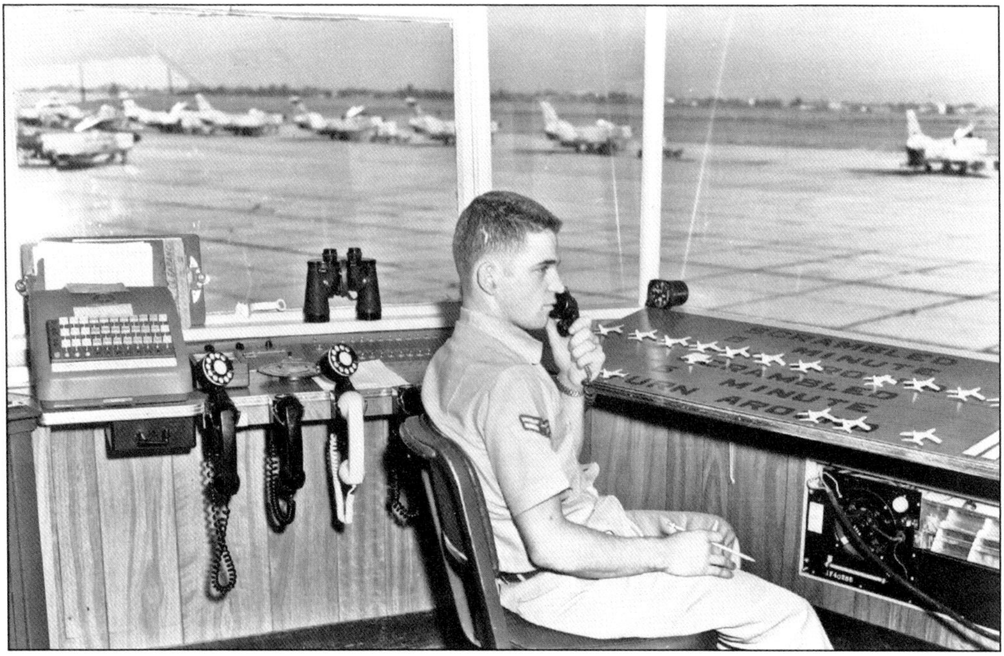

Airman 2nd class Ed Schrader communicates with pilots readying for an alert practice. He is seated in the flight operations center, where he can observe all aircraft inbound to Gowen Field as well as monitor ready status and maintenance activities on the flight line.

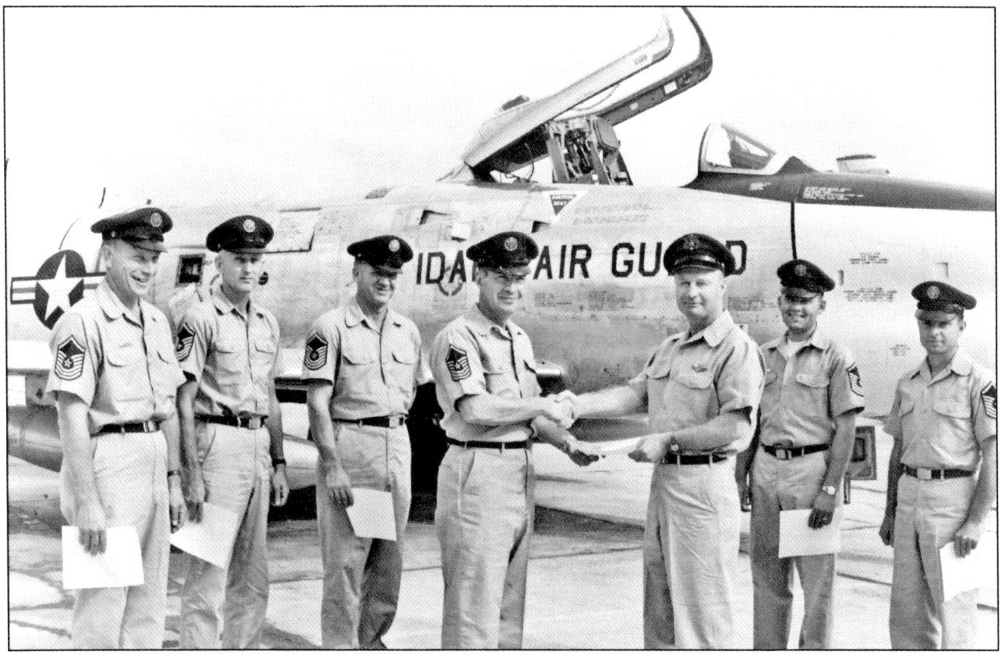

Lt. Col. Clancey Hall presents E-8 stripes (senior master sergeant) to, from left to right, Clint Gregory, Bill Fitzgerald, Lloyd "Red Dog" Martindale, Dick Gasparotti, Don Shutz, and Bob Johnston. Up until 1958, the air force enlisted corps topped out at the rank of master sergeant. To remedy this, in 1959 the service added two additional ranks: E-8 senior master sergeant and E-9 chief master sergeant.

Four

THE DEUCE

The 124th Fighter Interceptor Group proved capable of handling the air defense mission with its F-86L by meeting the demands of the 24-hour-a-day runway alerts. As new aircraft came into service with the active-duty U.S. Air Force, it began replacing the older Air National Guard aircraft with more technologically advanced interceptors. To this end, the 190th was selected to receive the F-102 Delta Dagger, a supersonic fighter capable of high-altitude flight with an advanced fire-control system and guided missiles. The 190th's mission did not change, but the ability to carry it out improved. The Idaho Air National Guardsmen demonstrated a high degree of proficiency during their years with "the Deuce."

In November 1964, the 124th's first F-102s arrived at Gowen Field, including the two-seat TF-102 trainer version that helped speed the transition process. From 1967 to 1969, the Guard commissioned additional pilots into the ranks of the 190th, full-timers as well as the traditional part-timers. From 1965 to 1975, the F-102s of the 190th stood 24-hour runway alert to defend the Pacific Northwest. Although this was a tremendous responsibility for an Air National Guard unit, the 124th proved capable.

After achieving proficiency with the F-102, the 124th received much recognition for its outstanding service, including the Aerospace Defense Command's A Award and two Air Force Outstanding Unit Awards two years in a row (the first Air Guard unit to accomplish this feat). Additionally, the 124th received two Flight Safety Awards from higher commands such as the National Guard Bureau.

Due to the 124th's reputation, it was invited to several William Tell Fighter Interceptor Weapons Meets. During these meets, Air National Guard and active-duty U.S. Air Force units competed against each other and were evaluated on their skills, flying, and maintenance. The 190th teams always placed high in the rankings.

In the early 1970s, when the air force determined that there was less of a threat from Soviet bombers, the F-102 was retired. The 124th's Delta Daggers departed in the fall of 1975.

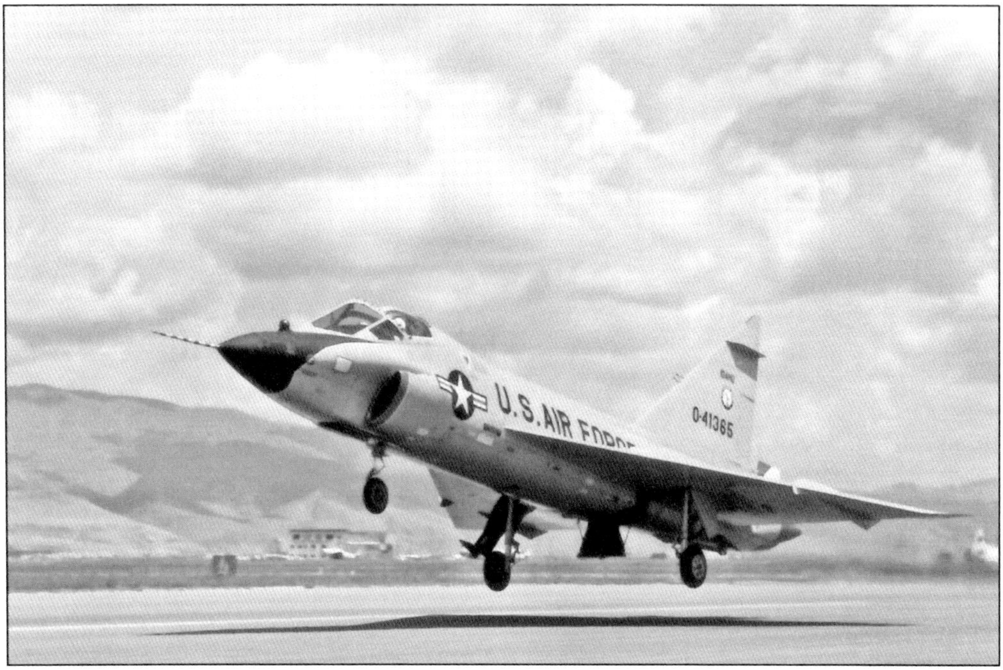

One of the 190th Fighter Interceptor Squadron's TF-102s is seen at takeoff from Gowen Field. The two-seat TF-102, fully mission capable, carried the same weapons load as single-seat "Deuce."

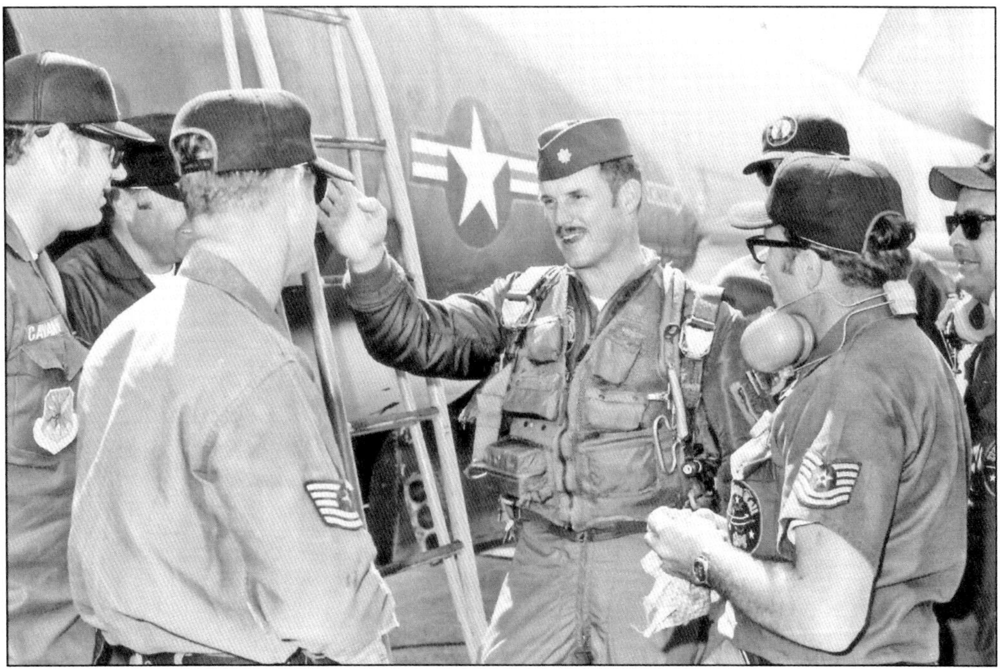

At the 1974 William Tell Fighter Interceptor Weapons Meet, Maj. Ralph Townsend (center) took the title of Top Gun as the highest score and the only pilot who shot down a target drone. Considering the size of potential wartime targets for the F-102s—large Soviet bombers—the small, nimble target drones were a challenge to hit. Major Townsend is pictured with 190th maintainers after a mission during William Tell 1974.

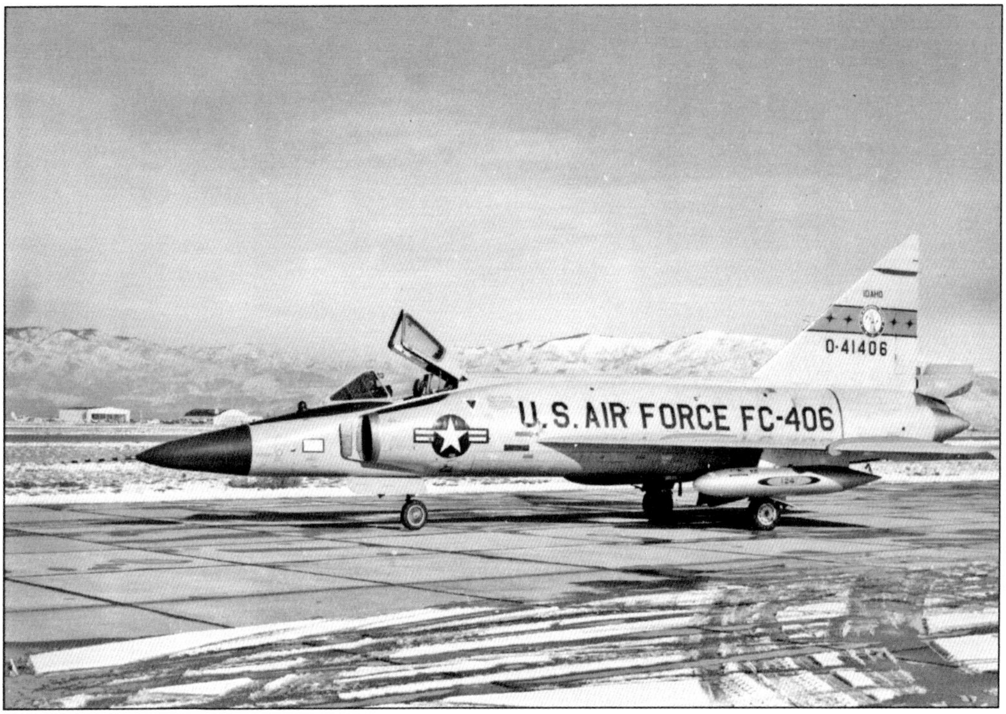

Entering a new age, the Idaho Air National Guard received its first F-102 Delta Daggers in 1964. The F-102 accomplished supersonic speeds and used guided missiles—a first for the Idaho Air National Guard. With these new missiles came the demand for more specialized training.

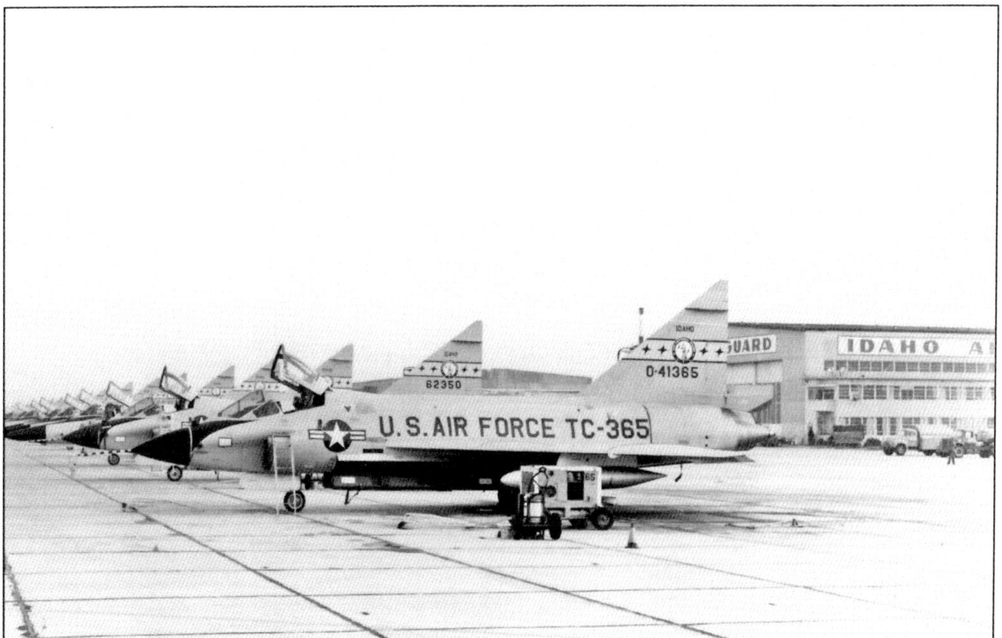

The Idaho Air National Guard operated two TF-102 trainers for the evaluation and training of pilots. The two crewmembers sat side by side, which required a wider cockpit area and fuselage. Due to their wider appearance and seating arrangement, the TF-102s were referred to as "Tubs."

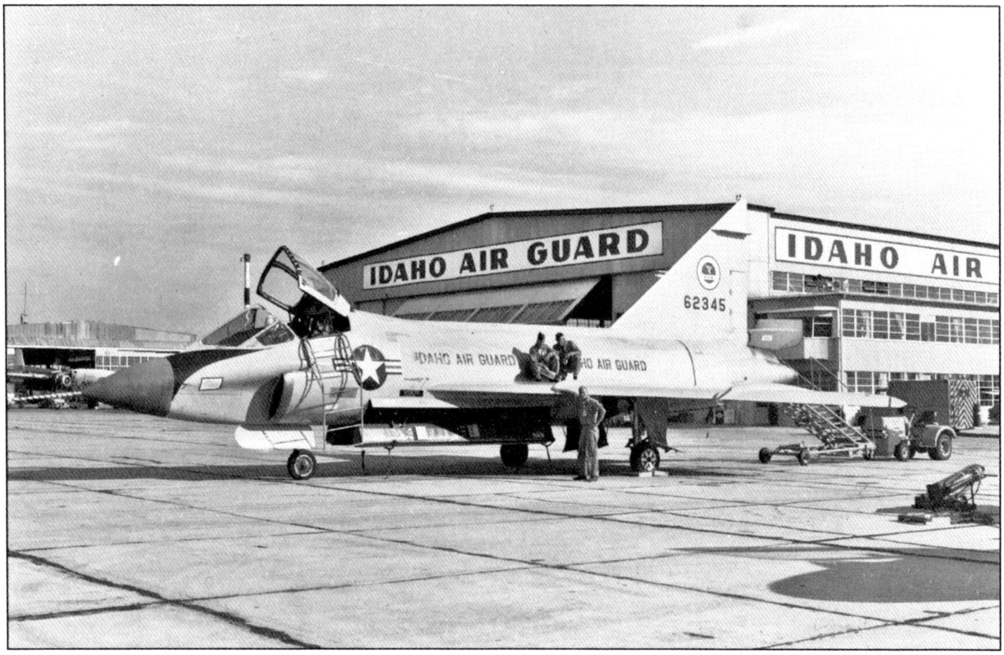

While the TF-102 provided the opportunity for the training and assessment of new pilots' skills, it was not as well liked by the more experienced pilots. Its maneuverability and speed were not quite the same as the single-seat F-102. Range was also a bit shorter, limiting the ability for cross-country flights. The F-102 series of aircraft did not have an in-flight refueling capability.

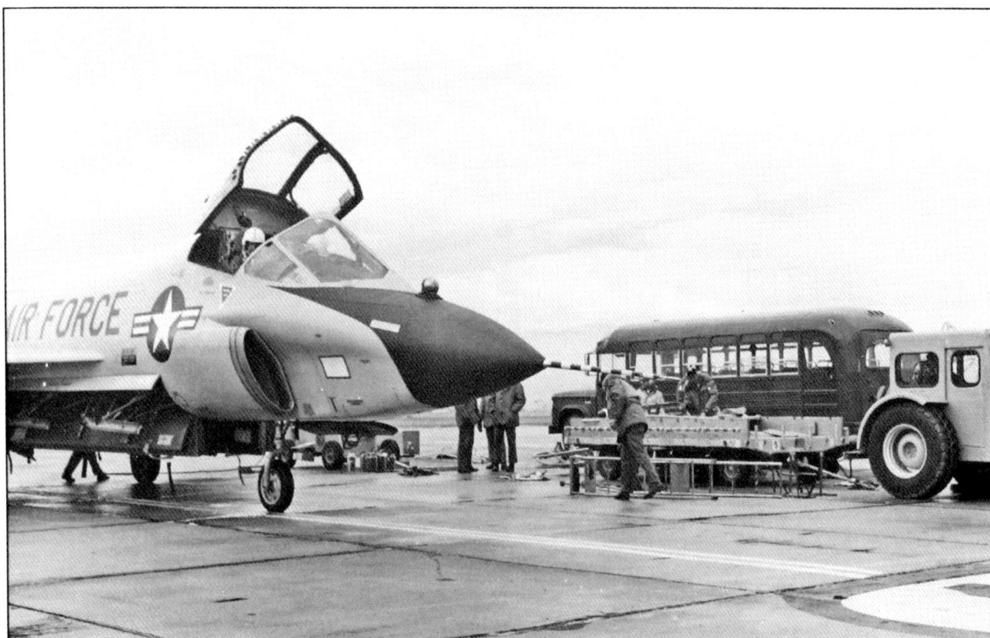

Two 190th pilots are in the "Tub," ready for a training flight, as maintainers move around to make last-minute preparations. The weapons bay doors show the missile rails that carried the AIM-4 Falcon missile. The rails dropped down so the missile's heat-seeking head could acquire the target's heat signature.

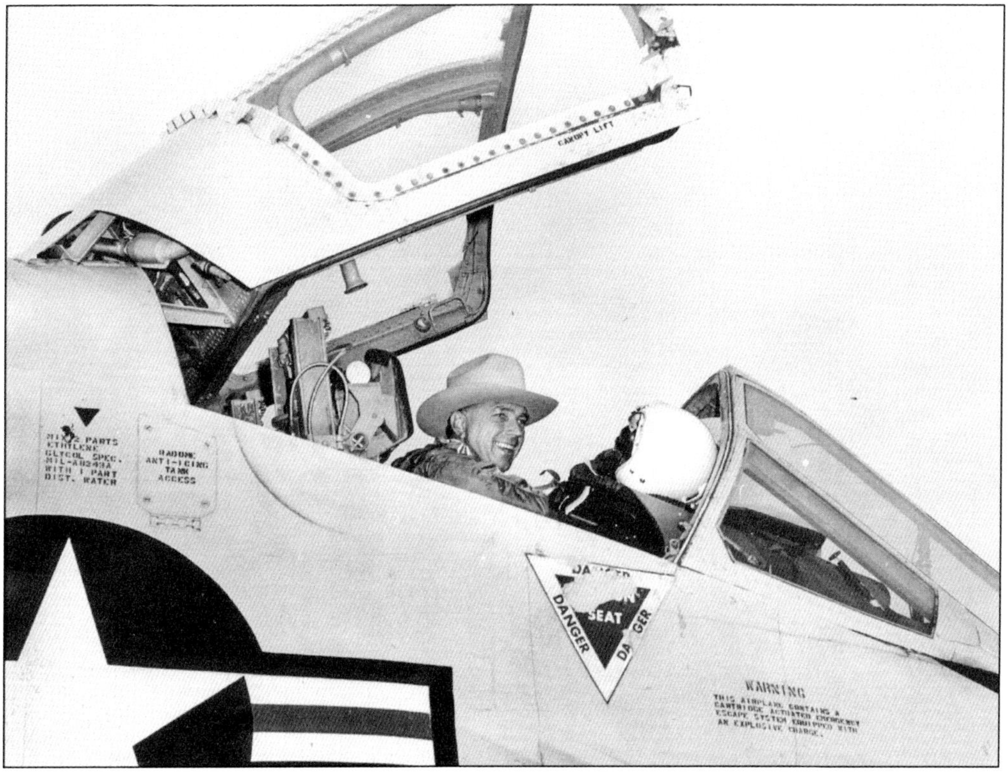

Colonel Nordling was known for fostering a very military bearing in the 124th Fighter Interceptor Group, but he also tried to bring a sense of humor with his leadership. Here "Nord," as he was called, has just landed with one of the 124th's first F-102s. He is credited as being the one who introduced the 124th's motto: "First class or not at all."

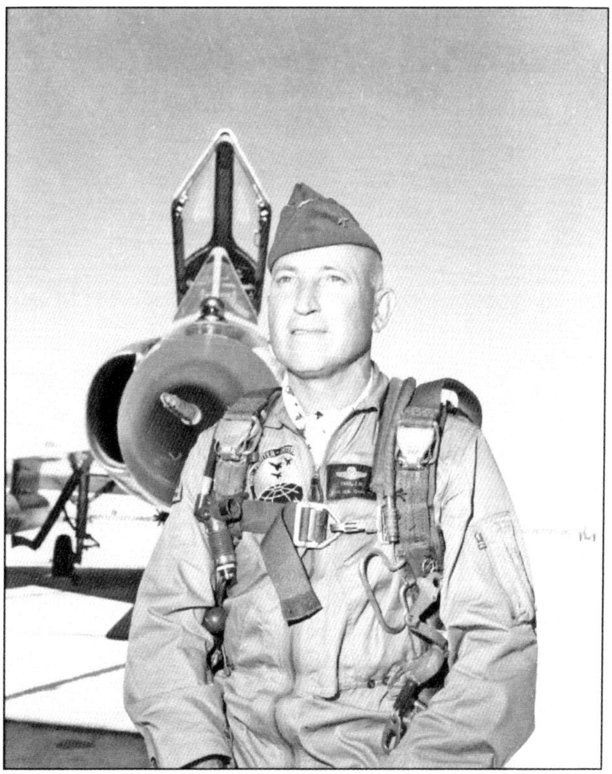

Brig. Gen. James Trail was one of the original members of the Idaho Air National Guard. He became Idaho's assistant adjutant general for air in 1960 and served in that capacity until 1978.

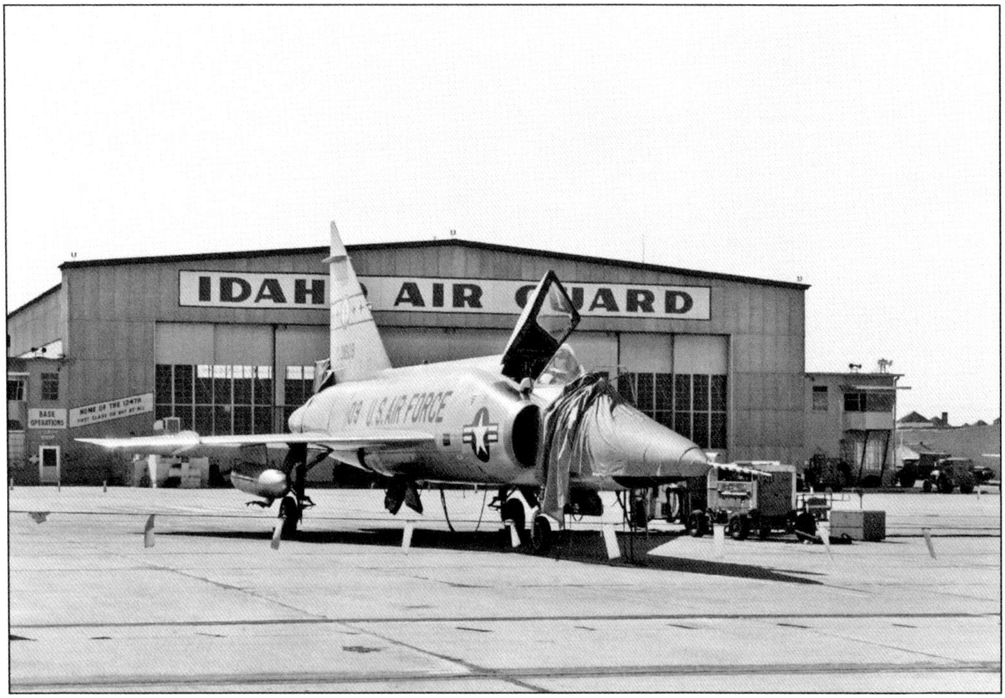

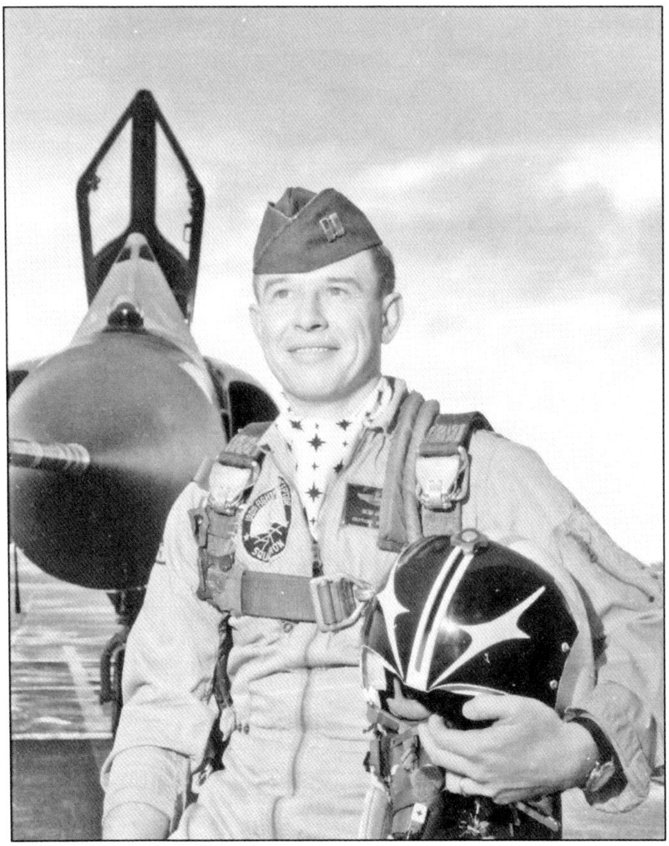

Just outside the maintenance hangar, this F-102 has a cover over its nose to protect the radar, possibly from the heat of an Idaho summer. Most maintenance took place in the hangar, but this F-102 may have been waiting for replacement parts to arrive.

Capt. Bob Bones of the 190th Fighter Interceptor Squadron is pictured with one of the unit's F-102s. Captain Bones is wearing his day-glow-orange flight suit, common among Air Defense Command crews. This bright color provided high visibility in case of ejection and aided search and rescue forces in locating the flier.

Capt. Don Troyer posed for a less-than-formal portrait with an F-102 at Gowen Field. He was once caught buzzing the docks at nearby McCall's Payette Lake by none other than Brigadier General Trail, the Idaho assistant adjutant general, who was boating that weekend. Despite his unmilitary appearance for this fun photograph, Captain Troyer was highly regarded by his fellow Idaho Air National Guardsmen.

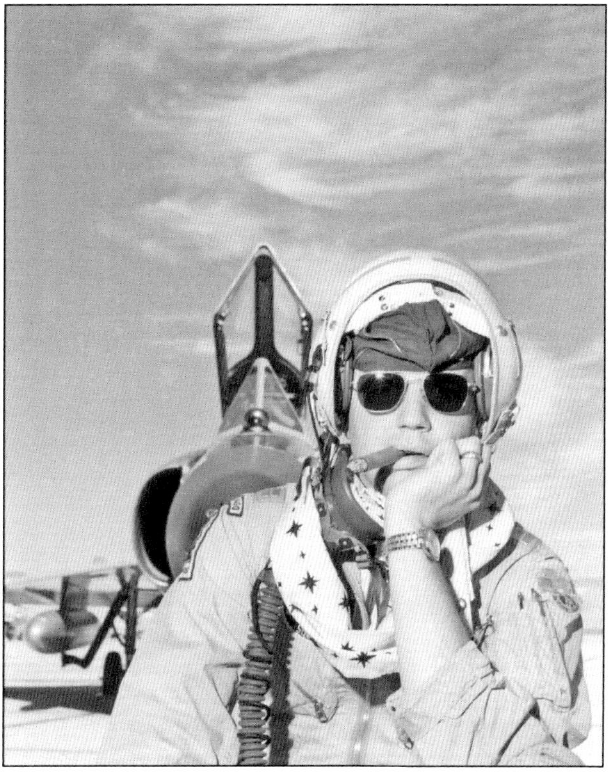

Members of the base defense team were instructed on how to fire a chemical grenade from an M1 rifle. The World War II–vintage rifle was still in the inventory of many Guard units into the 1960s and was used as seen here, to fire either smoke or tear gas grenades. For base defense and/or riot duty, tear gas grenades would have been a useful item.

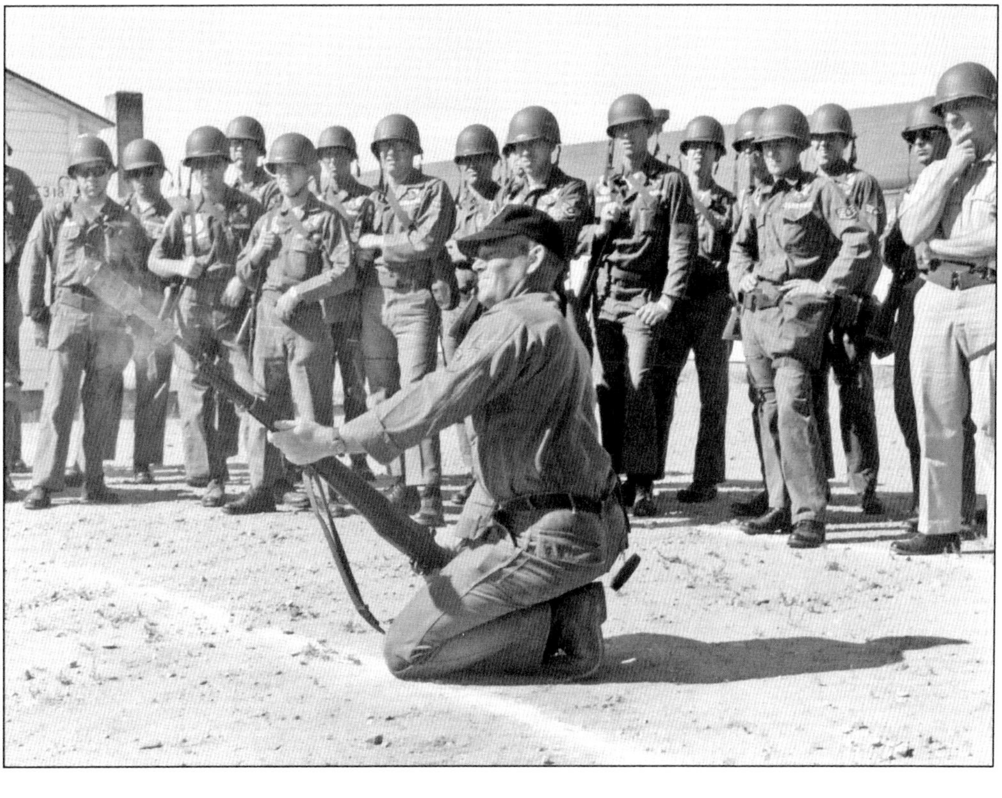

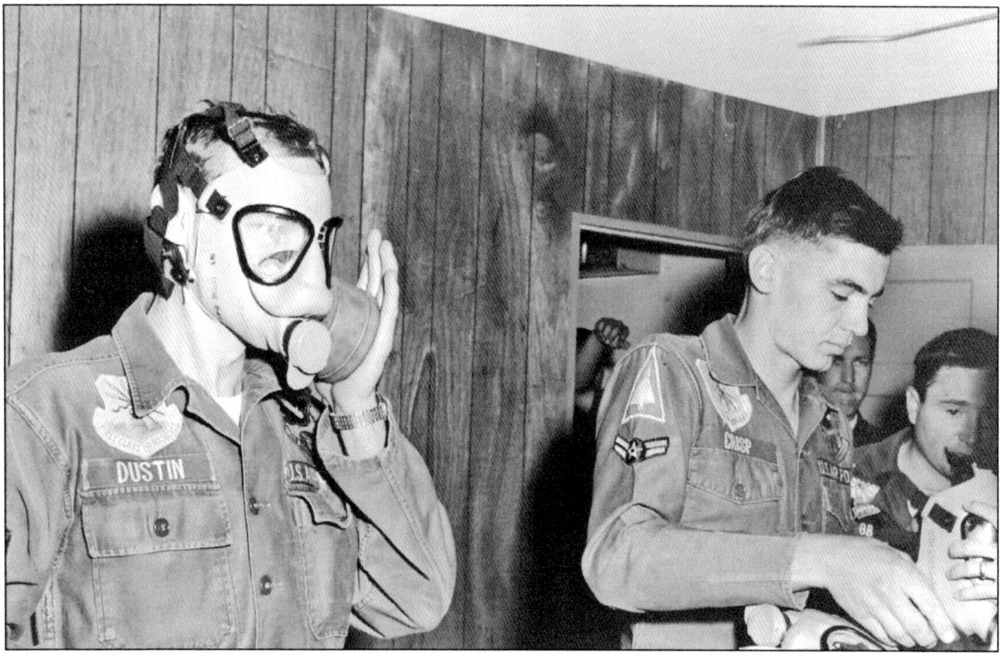

Chemical warfare training took place at Gowen Field well after World War II. These members of the 124th are checking gas masks for fit. Gas masks were standard items for troops on riot duty who might use tear gas. On several occasions, Idaho Air National Guardsmen responded as security augmenters to riots at the Idaho State Penitentiary.

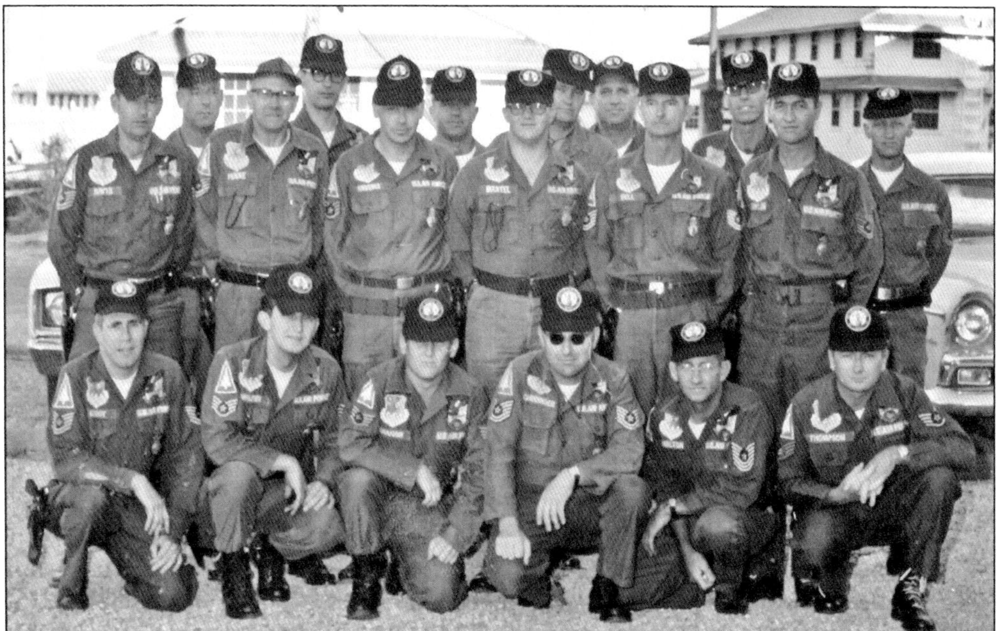

The base defense team evolved from a group of augmenters who performed a secondary duty to a more organized unit such as that seen here. With the more technologically advanced F-102 came the need for more security. TSgt. Glenn Carringer, kneeling fourth from left, was one of the original members of the Idaho Air National Guard, joining in 1946–1947.

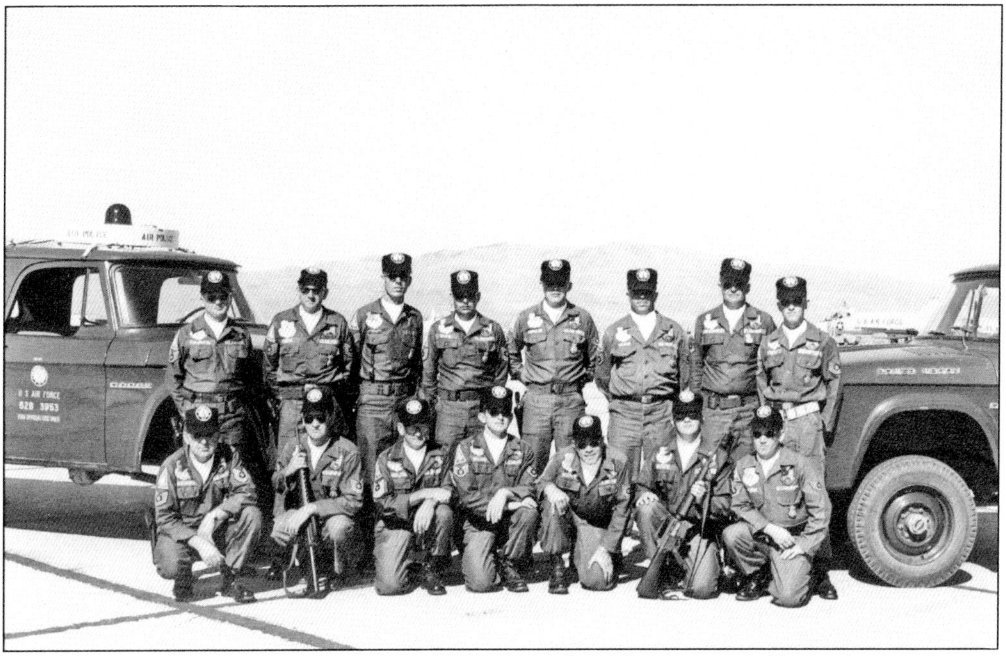

Members of the 124th's strike team pose with their brand-new M-16 rifles and white ascots. Previous base defense teams were not always armed with the latest weaponry. Thanks to Lt. Gen. Curtis LeMay, the U.S. Air Force was the first to adopt the M-16 for the defense of Strategic Air Command's bomber bases.

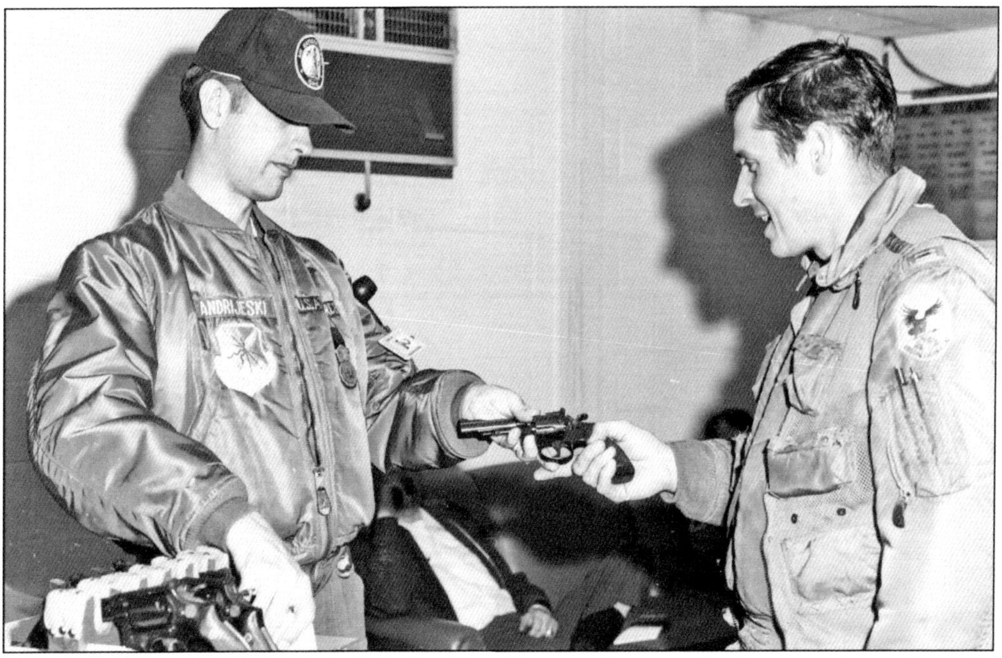

Part of the pilot's survival gear included a .38-caliber revolver, standard issue in the air force. In addition to self-defense, the pistol could be used with tracer bullets for signaling a downed flier's location. In this photograph, Harlan Andrijeski presents F-102 pilot Bruce Whittig with a revolver for carry in a holster on his survival vest.

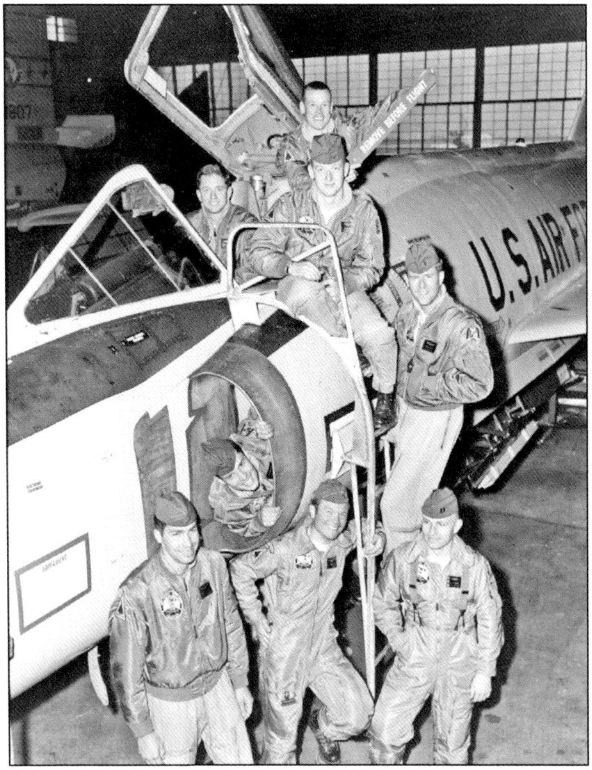

Pilots of the 190th stood alert 24 hours a day as part of the Air Defense Command. These are some of the pilots who waited in the "alert barns." Pictured are Joe Bunderson (left), Ben Zimmerman (center), Larry Leach (right), Bruce Whittig (in the intake), Wally Glass, Jim Ahrens (on the ladder), and Bill Miller (holding the "Remove before Flight" flag). Gary Brewington is in the cockpit.

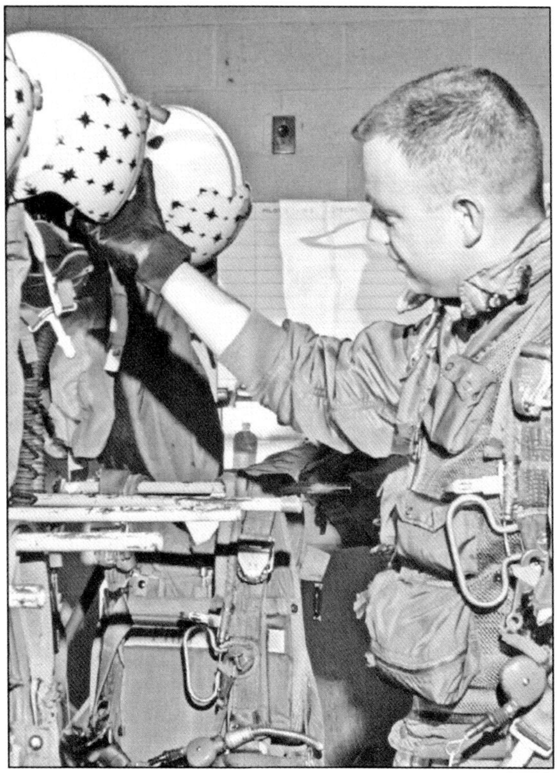

All suited up to fly, 190th pilot Dave Ahrens waits in the squadron ready room, prepared to head out and board his F-102. His survival vest is packed with items such as a small radio, water bottles, survival knife, signal flares, signal mirror, first aid supplies, and chocolate bars.

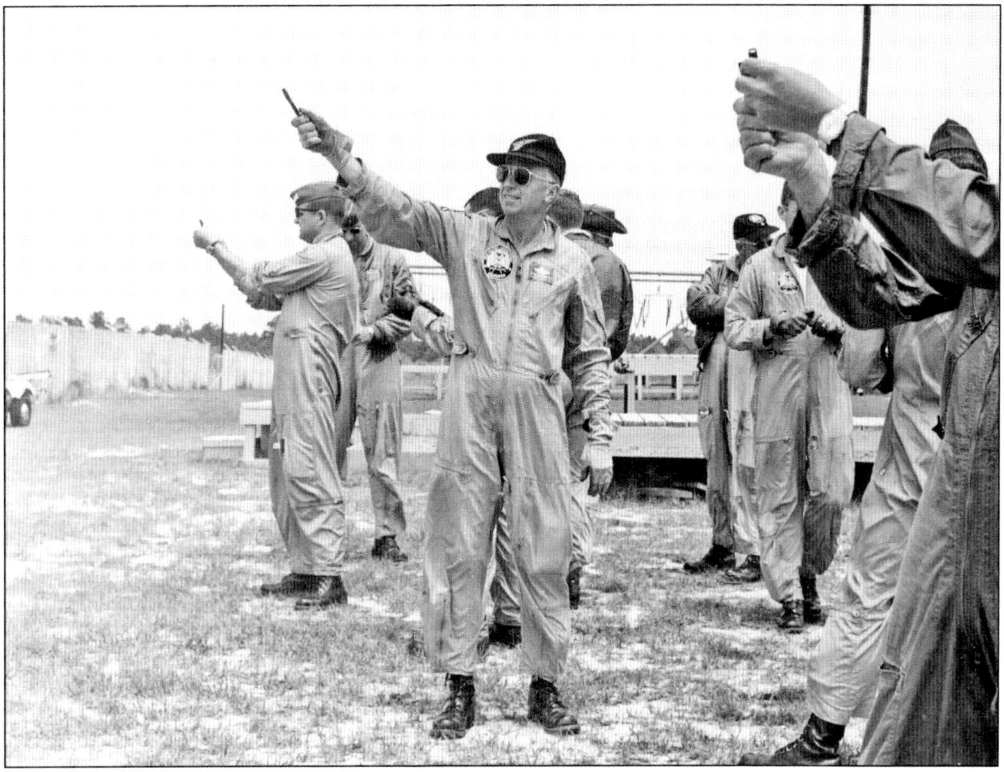

About twenty 124th pilots attended survival school training at Tyndall Air Force Base. Instruction covered a variety of skills, from water survival to parachute landings. Here Colonel Nordling fires a flare as part of the training.

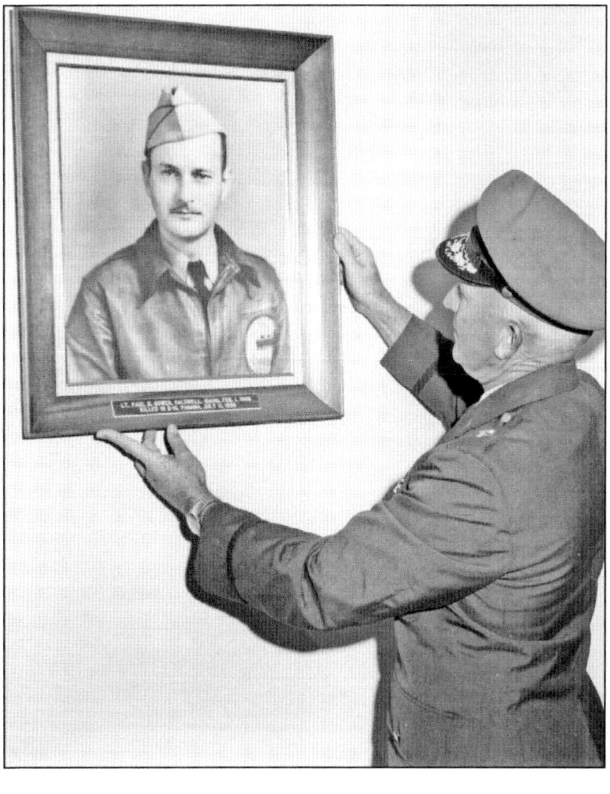

Brigadier General Trail hangs a photograph of Lt. Paul Gowen in the base headquarters building. Even after the hurried construction and naming of the base during World War II, aviators still remembered for whom it was named.

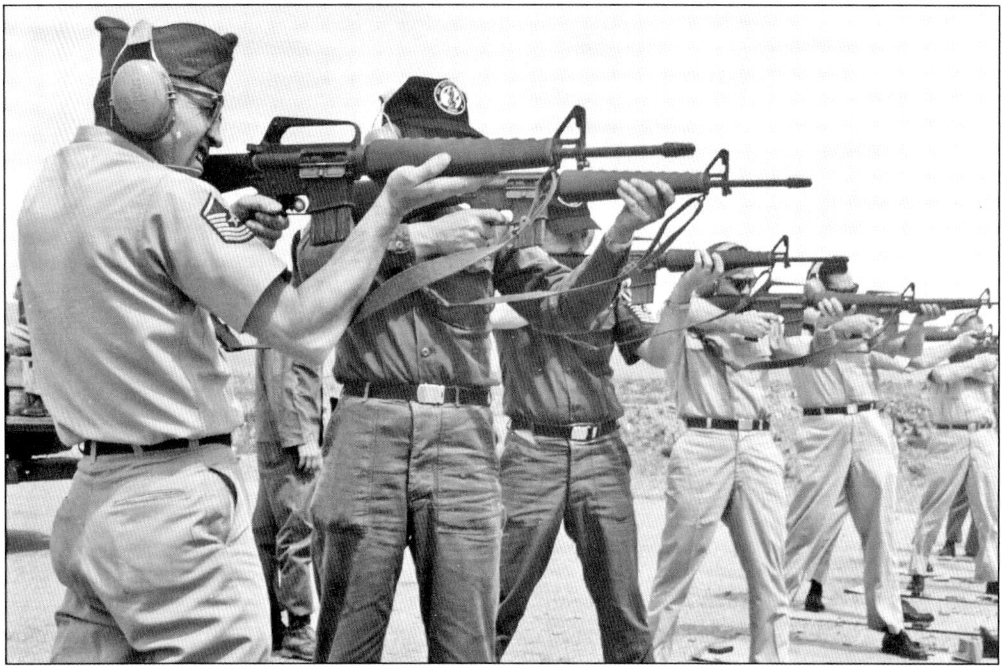

Idaho Air National Guardsmen are shown at the range where they would qualify on the M-16 rifle. It was unusual to see an Air National Guard unit with a new rifle that had barely reached active-duty units. The F-102 had nuclear missile capability, hence the increased emphasis on base security.

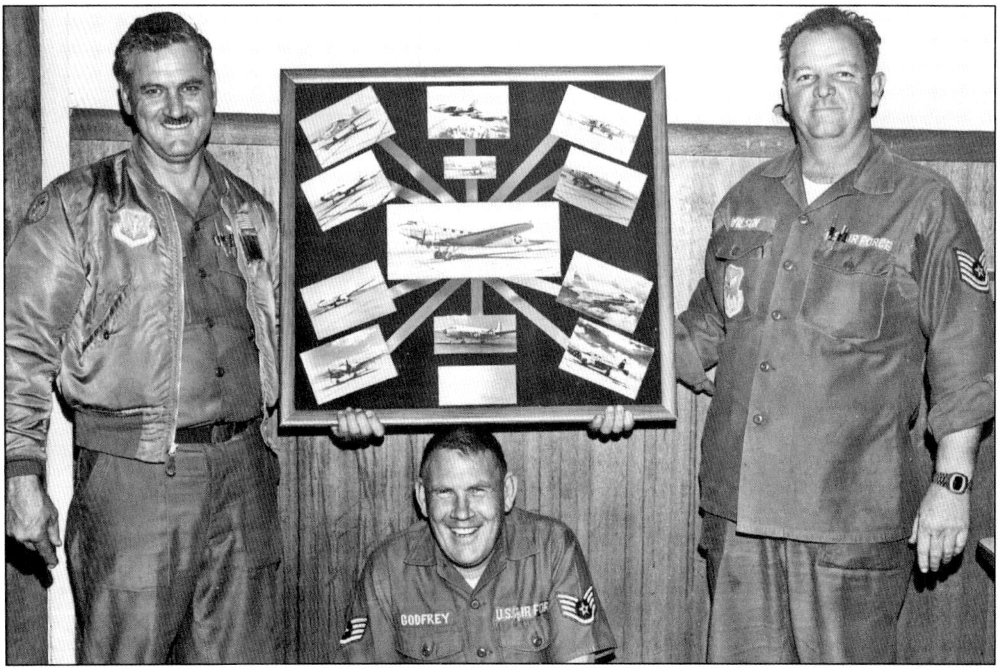

From left to right, MSgt. Melvin "Smitty" Smith, SSgt. Ben Godfrey, and Abe Wilson pose with a framed collage of the aircraft Smitty worked on during his career with the Idaho Air National Guard. The collage was created in recognition of 10,000 hours of service at Gowen Field.

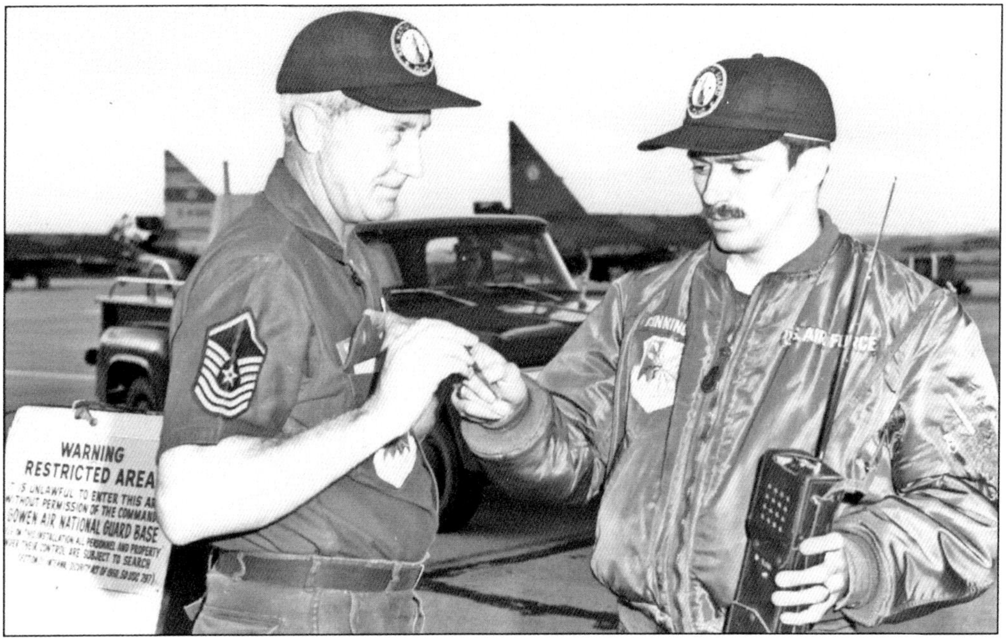

As part of security procedures, airman Frank Cunningham checks SMSgt. Don Noteboom's identification for entry onto the flight line, a restricted area. The base defense team and later the strike team used pickups like the one in the background to patrol the flight line and base perimeter; the teams also used the radio for communications with base operations.

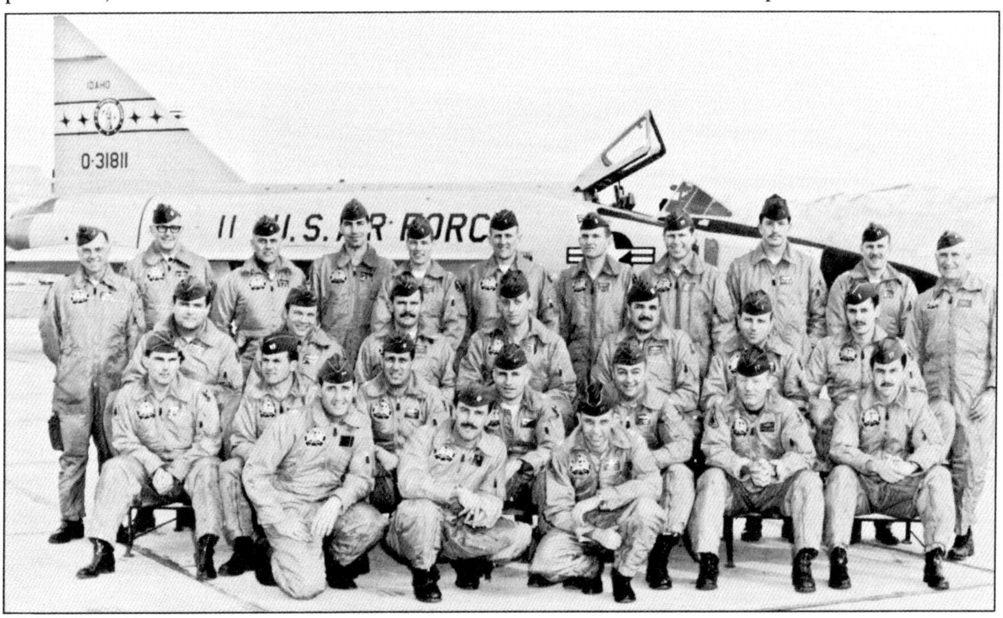

Pilots of the 190th in 1968–1969 included the following, from left to right: (first row) Don Troyer, Ron Weinert, and Lee Bernasconi; (second row) Bill Free, Gene Winchester, Jim O'Neal, Larry Leach, Ed Parsons, Mac McCormick, and Jack Newland; (third row) Len Johnson, Ben Zimmerman, Alvie Johnson, Jim Ahrens, Arnie Beaudreau, Jerre Kauffman, and Bruce Whittig; (fourth row) Ken Nordling, Sam Corn, Dick Weber, Joe Bunderson, Bill Miller, Jim Hunt, Ted Byrd, Wilbur Wortham, Gary Brewington, Bill Cooper, and Jim Trail.

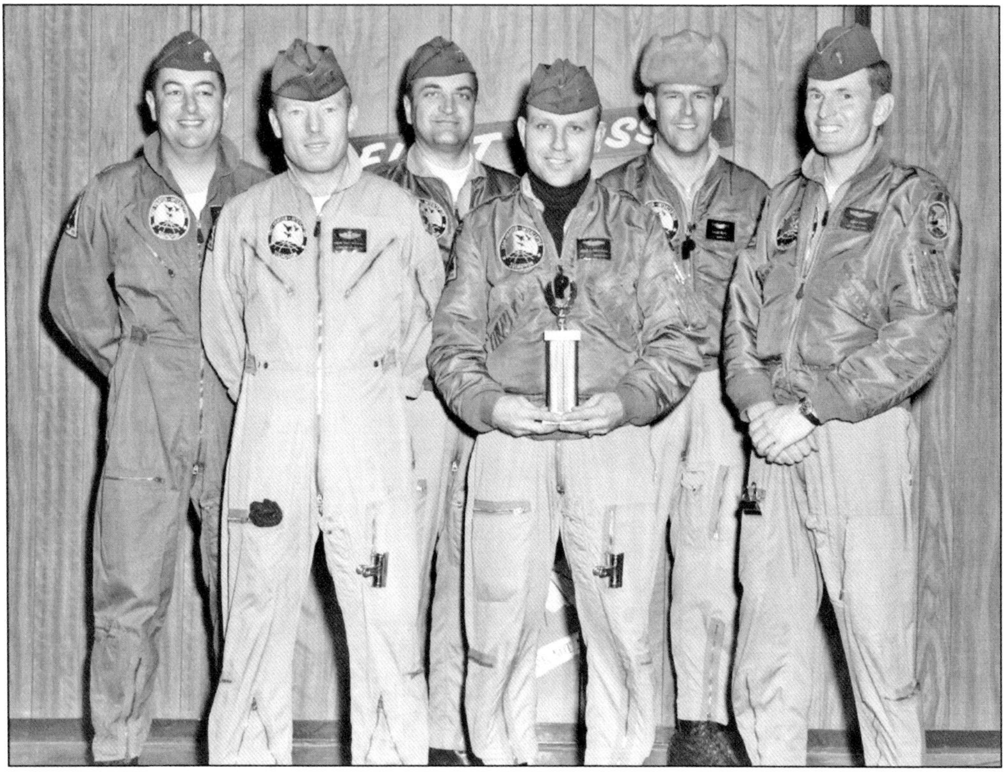

These F-102 pilots of the 190th received the Trail Award, created by Brigadier General Trail. It recognized an outstanding flight within the 190th Fighter Interceptor Squadron for having the best intercept success rate. Shown from left to right are flight commander Ed Parsons, Mac McCormick, Arnie Beaudreau, Jerre Kauffman, Wally Glass, and Ted Byrd.

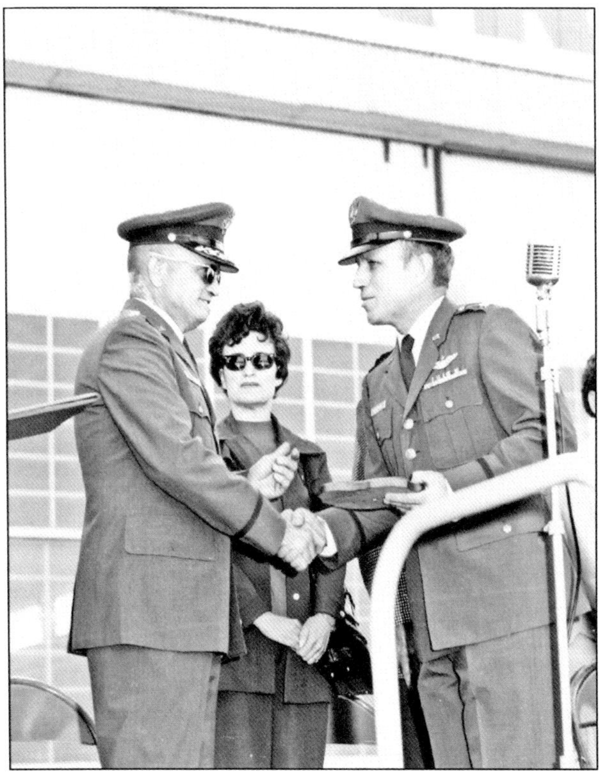

Capt. Jerre Kauffman served as the 124th Fighter Interceptor Group's safety officer in the late 1960s. Here he receives an award for safety excellence in both flying and ground aspects. In his role, Captain Kauffman was responsible for ensuring the airmen of the group followed safety practices and corrected deficiencies.

Bill Miller (right) discusses his recent flight with crew chief Glade Wakerlig (left). Miller served as a maintainer before being commissioned and earning his pilot's wings. He flew not only the F-102 but later the RF-4C Phantom and the C-26 administrative aircraft.

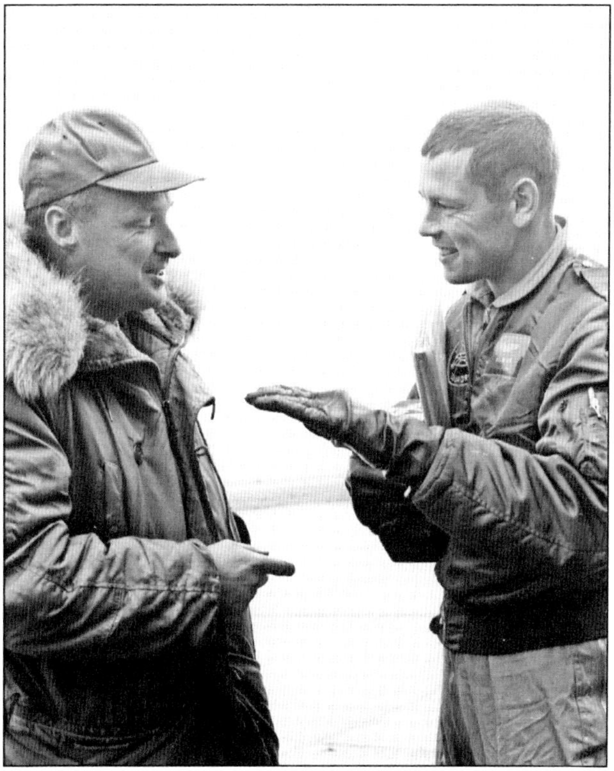

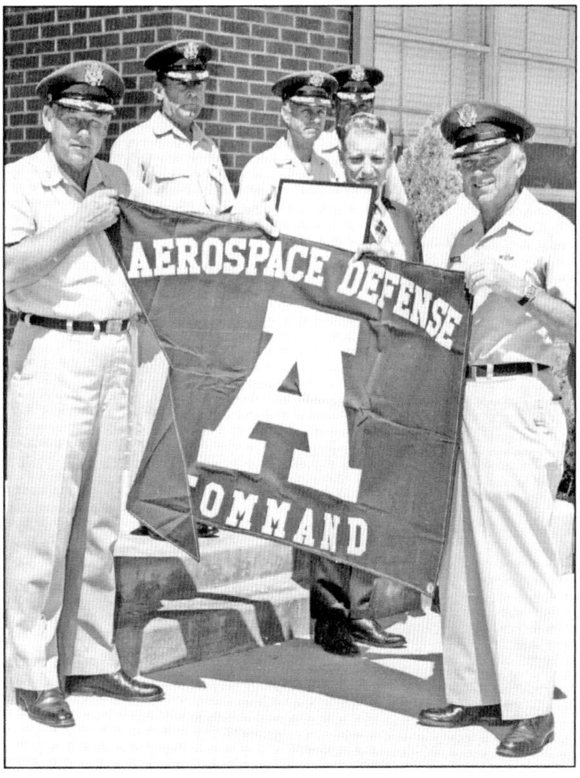

In 1969, the 124th won Air Defense Command's most prestigious honor: the A Award. Colonel Nordling is at right holding the flag. He felt that the awards the unit won were the result of the unit members' hard work.

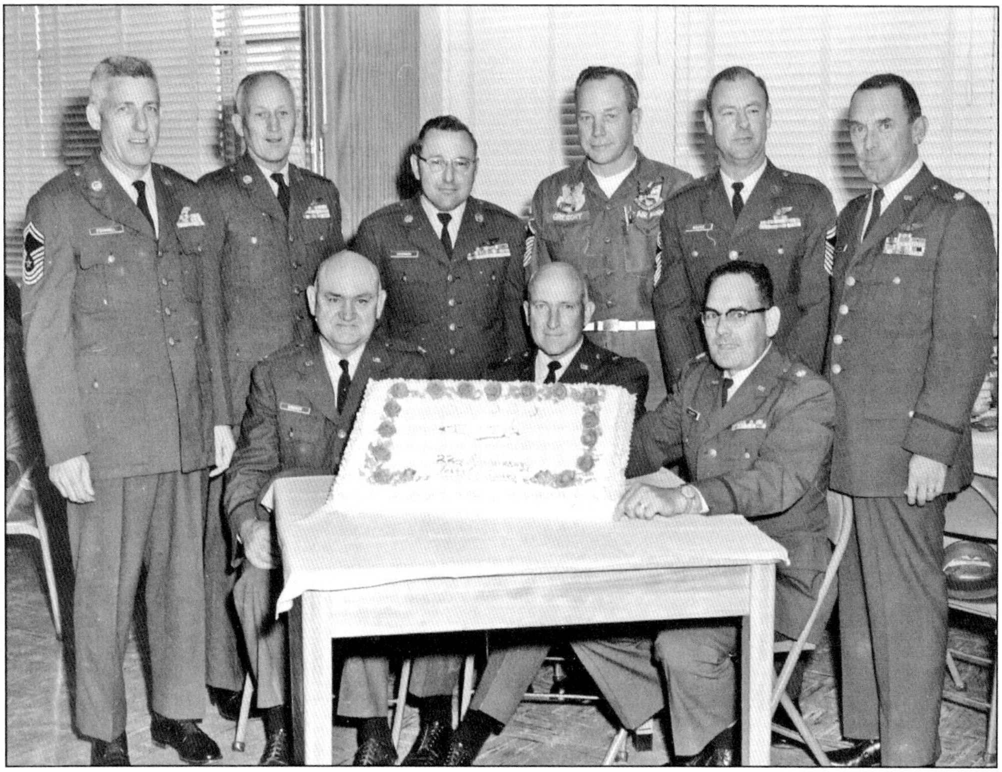

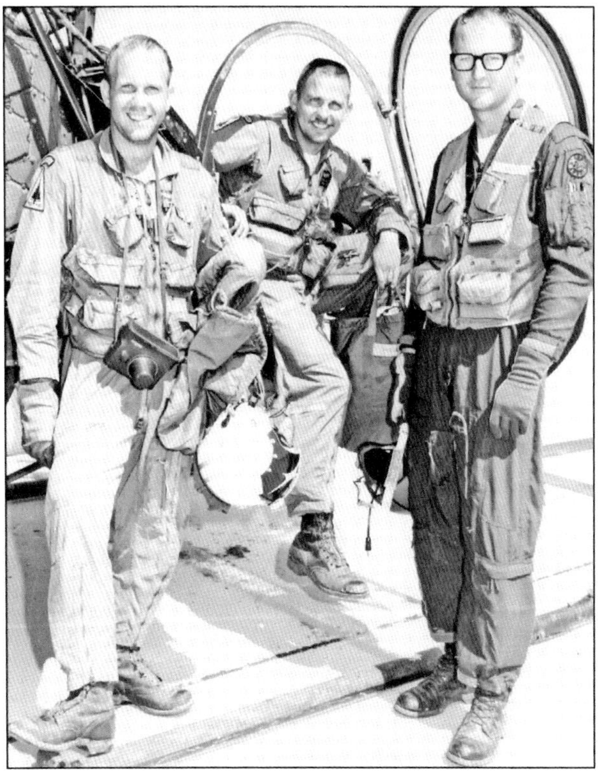

Nine original members of the Idaho Air National Guard pose for the unit's 22nd anniversary. Pictured here from left to right are the following: (first row) Lt. Col. Frank Bobbitt, Brigadier General Trail, and Lt. Col. Jack Flaherty; (second row) Chief Master Sergeant O'Donnell, CMSgt. Bill Fitzgerald, TSgt. Glenn Carringer, SMSgt. Clint Gregory, CMSgt. Holly Moore, and Lt. Col. W. D. Bozman.

Capt. Dean Jackson (left) and Capt. Dave Hudlet have been "rescued" by Lt. John Kane of the Idaho Army National Guard. To teach pilots survival skills, they were dropped off in the Idaho wilderness and left for 24 hours with only the contents of their survival vests. A Cessna, flown by an Air Guardsman with a private pilot's license, kept visual contact and dropped steaks to the poor "downed" fliers.

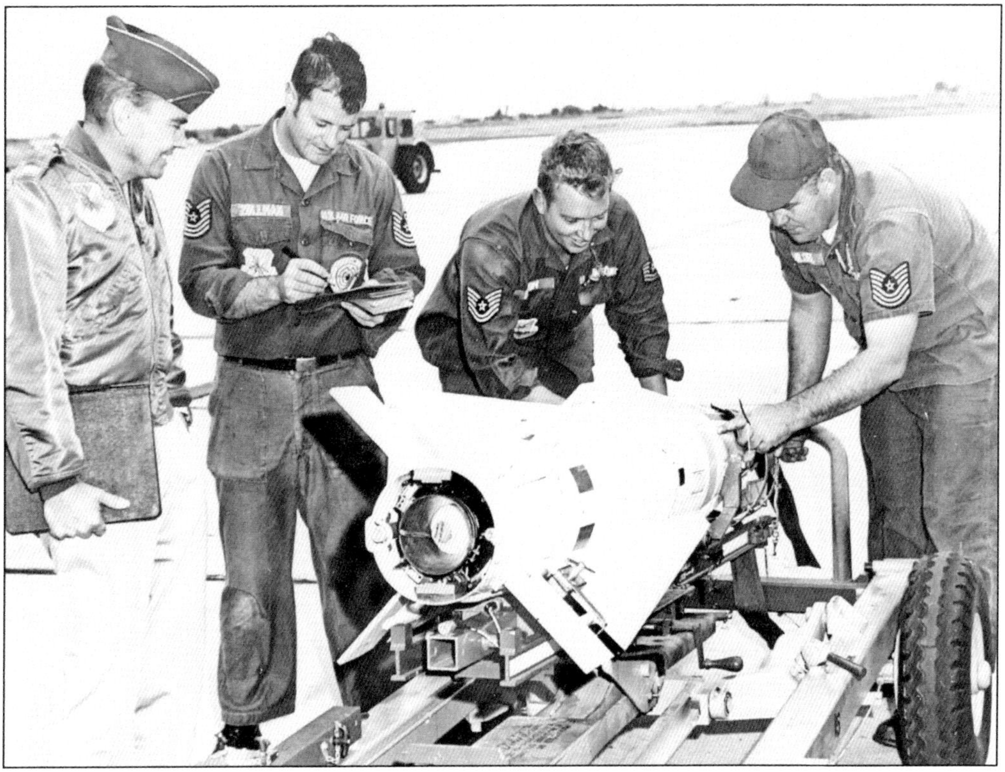

Some of the 124th's missile loaders inspect an AIM-4 Falcon at the William Tell Meet in 1970. The Idaho Air National Guard's missile-loading team won top honors at this meet. Some of the team members, pictured from left to right, were Capt. George Rich, MSgt. Dale Zollman, TSgt. Ron Bloom, and MSgt. Jack Wilder.

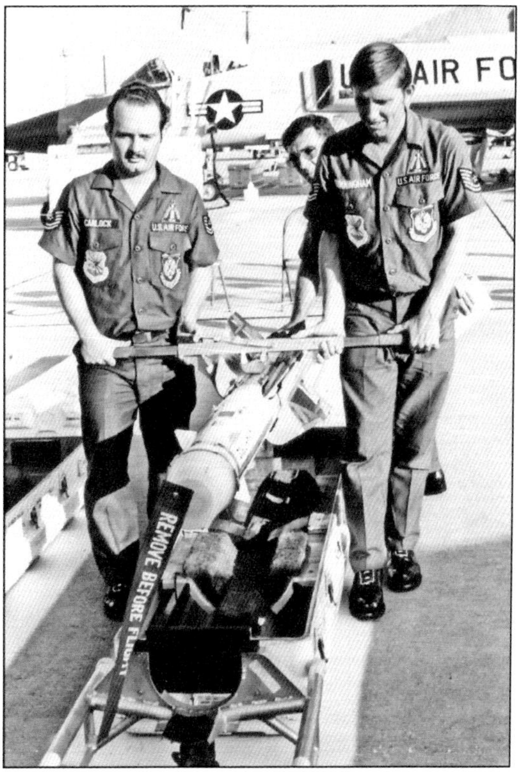

TSgt. Don Carlock (left) and TSgt. Dave Cunningham (right) were part of the 190th missile-loading team at the 1974 William Tell Meet. This Air National Guard team competed against 26 others to take third place overall in the missile-loading competition. In 1985, SMSgt. Don Carlock was named one of the "Twelve Outstanding Airmen in the USAF."

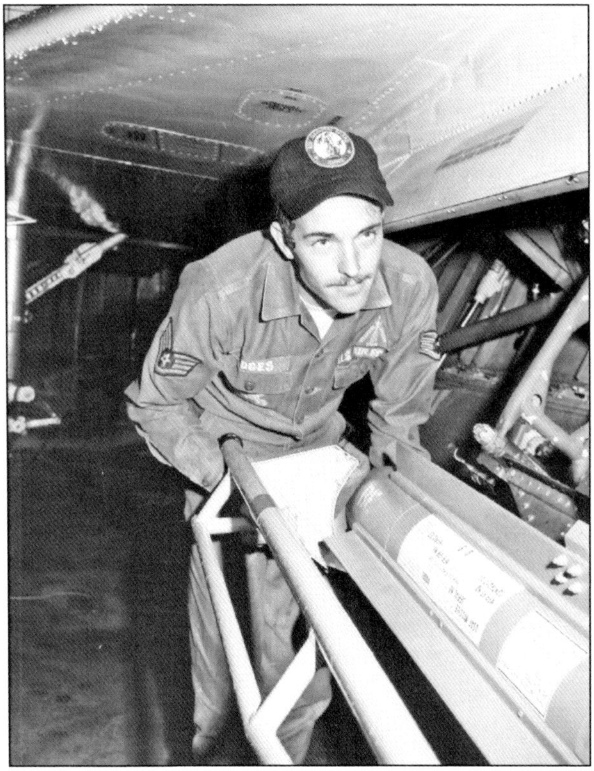

SSgt. John Hedges, a missile loader for the 190th, loads a Weapon System Evaluator Missile (WSEM). The WSEM was used to evaluate the performance of the F-102's fire-control system and ensure that the radar and aiming systems worked properly.

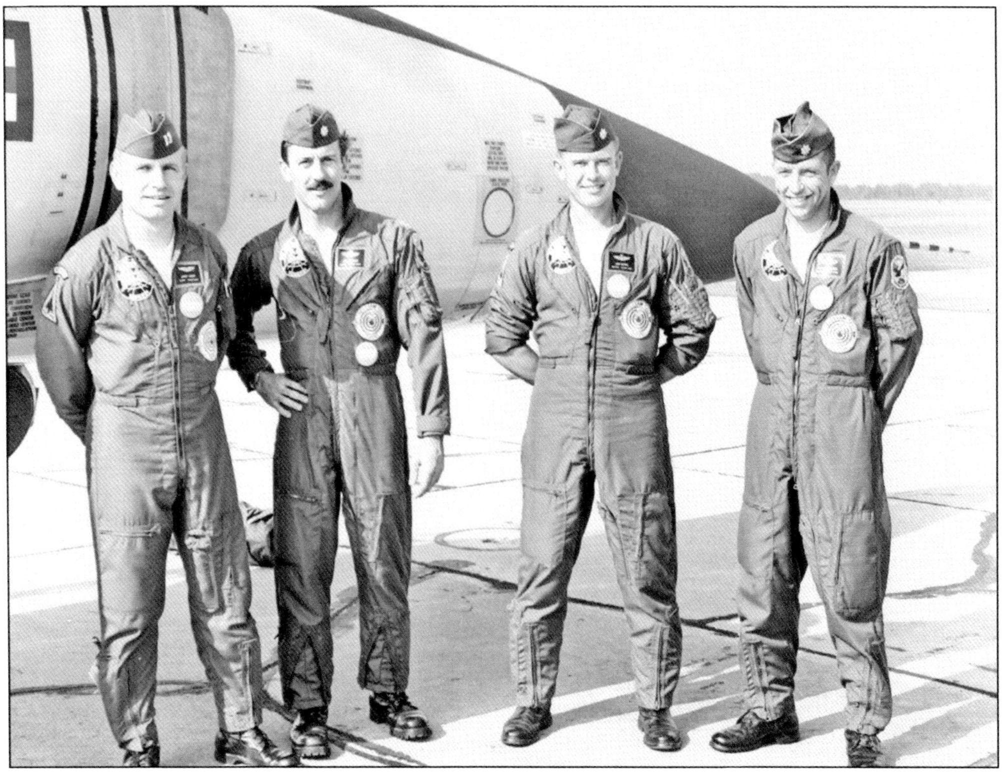

The 190th team that went to the 1970 William Tell Fighter Interceptor Weapons Meet included, from left to right, pilots Capt. Larry Leach, Lt. Col. Ron Weinert, Maj. Bob Bones, and Maj. Leland Bernasconi.

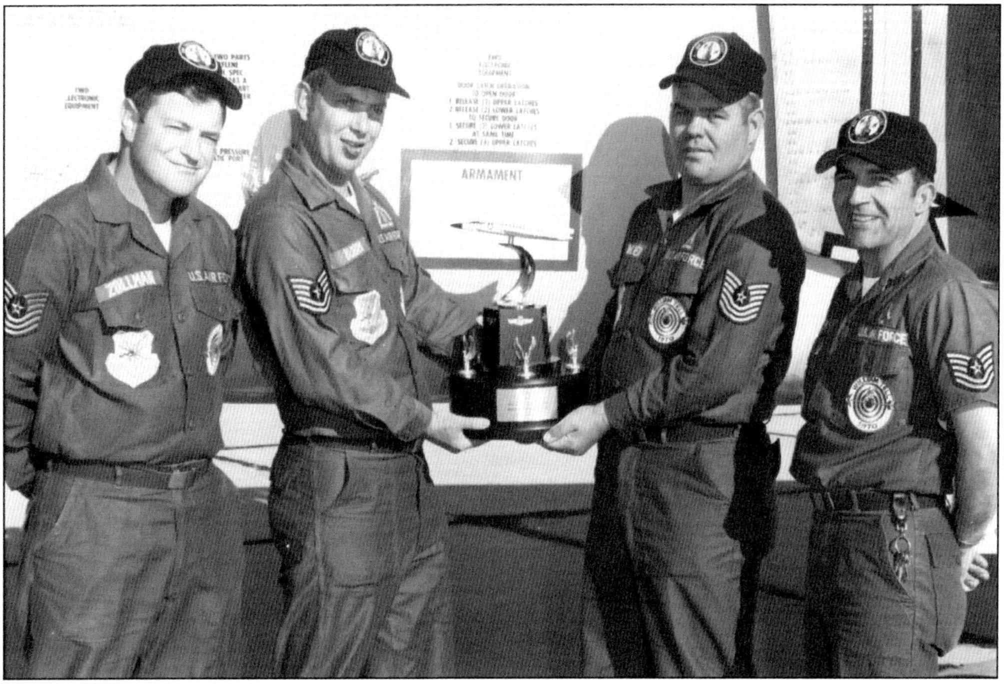

These four 190th airmen represented the team at the 1970 William Tell Meet that won the missile-loading competition over Air National Guard and active-duty U.S. Air Force units. Pictured from left to right, the team included Dale Zollman, Ron Bloom, Jack Wilder, and Curt Smith.

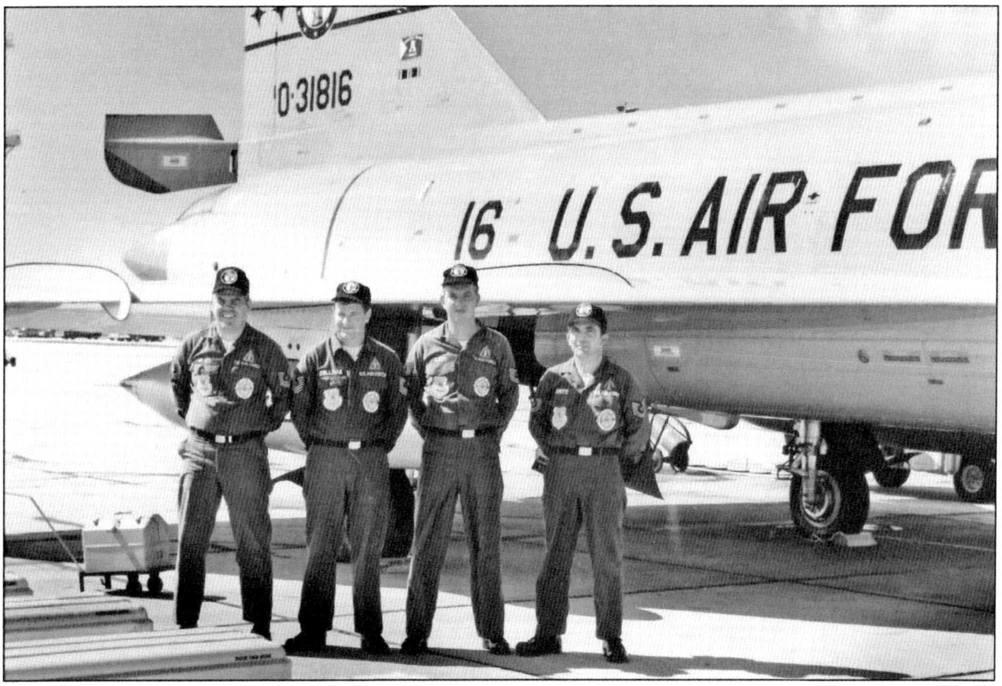

More of the 1970 William Tell missile-loading competition winners pose with one of their F-102s at Tyndall Air Force Base in Florida. Safety, maintenance, and speed were among the factors on which personnel were judged.

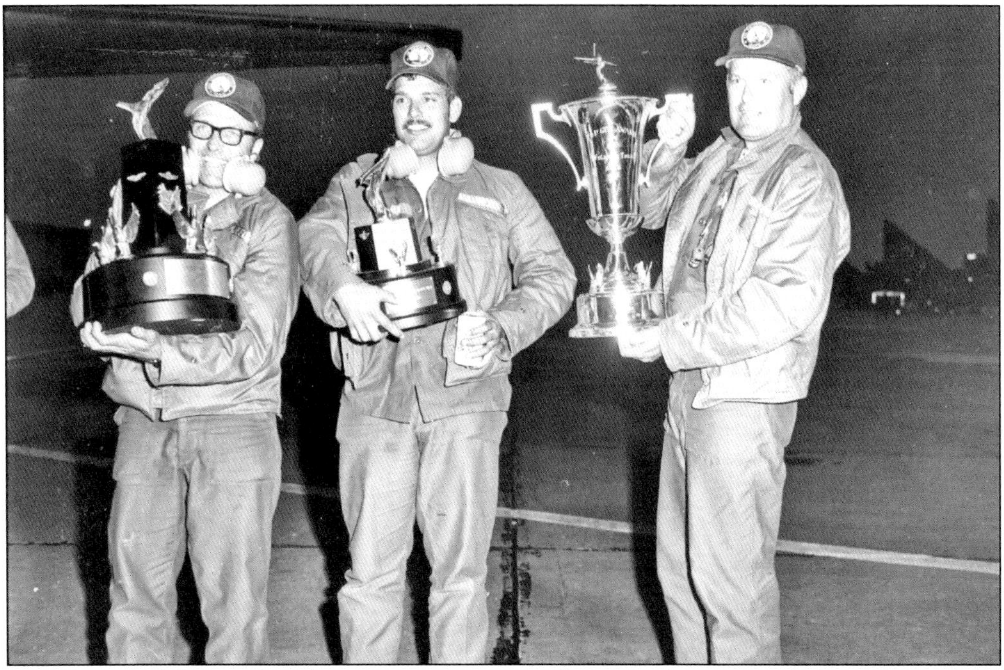

Maintainers of the 124th Fighter Interceptor Group have just been named the winners of the F-102 category as well as the overall winners of the 1974 William Tell Competition. The efforts of the maintainers, weapons loaders, and support personnel made the difference, along with the pilots who scored high in aerial gunnery. Seen here are Bob Busby (left), Steve Conklin (center), and Bill Parker.

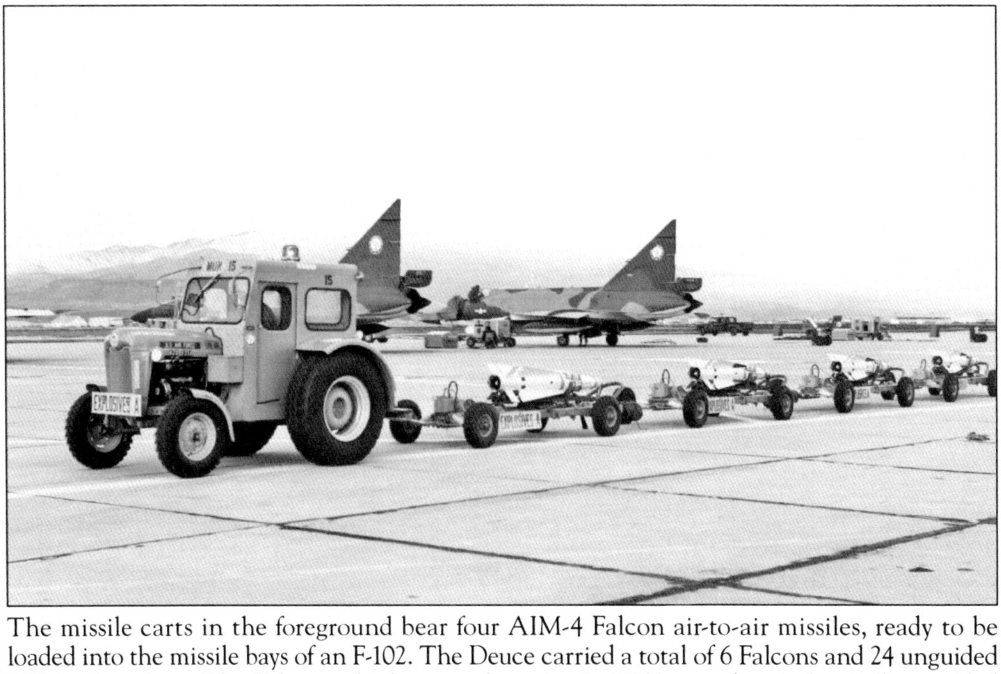

The missile carts in the foreground bear four AIM-4 Falcon air-to-air missiles, ready to be loaded into the missile bays of an F-102. The Deuce carried a total of 6 Falcons and 24 unguided 2.75-inch rockets. The Falcon, which entered service in 1955, was the air force's first guided air-to-air missile.

Mounted on the launch rails of the F-102 are a pair of AIM-26A Falcon missiles, the U.S. Air Force's only guided nuclear air-to-air missile. The AIM-26 was to be fired head-on at enemy bombers and was guided by the F-102's radar. Its nuclear warhead would be used to knock down large numbers of enemy bombers and missiles, much like a shotgun against birds.

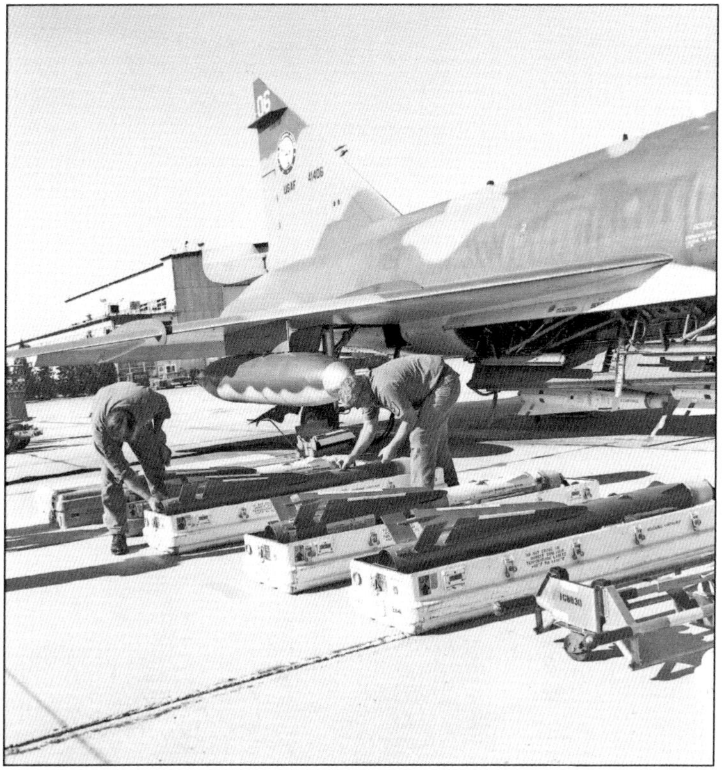

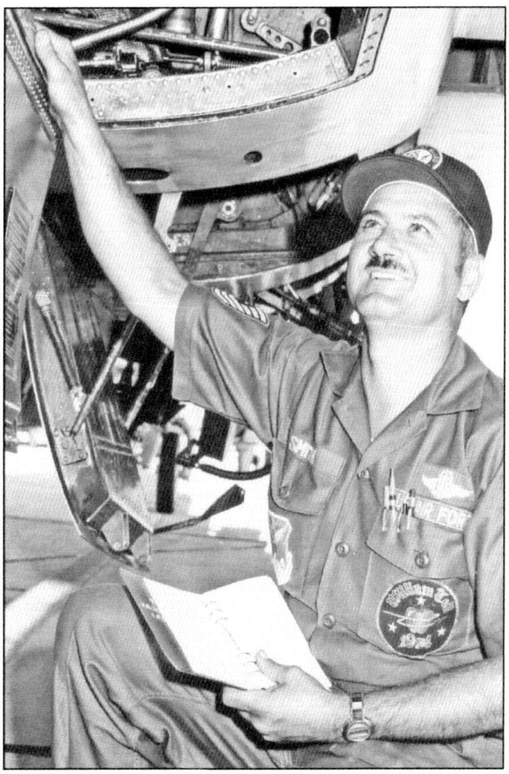

MSgt. Smitty Smith inspects an F-102's internal bays at the 1974 William Tell Meet. As crew chief, he was responsible for the overall maintenance of "his" F-102. He was part of the winning maintenance team at the meet. Normally, Smitty was crew chief on the 190th's support aircraft, the C-131, but he volunteered to serve as crew chief on the backup F-102 for the 1974 meet.

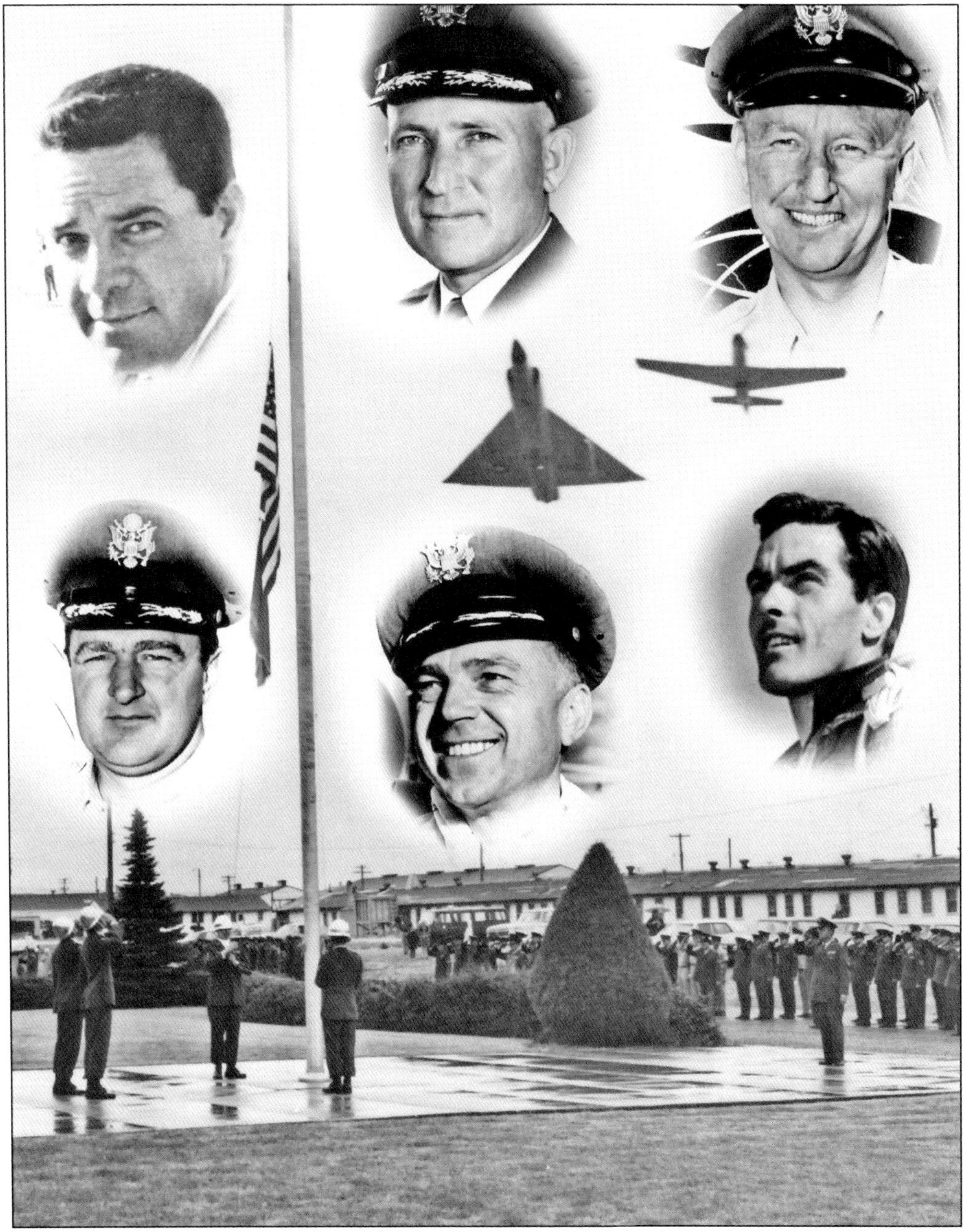

This special photograph was created for the Idaho Air National Guard's 25th anniversary. These officers were not only some of the first members of the Idaho Air Guard, but they also served as either squadron or group commanders at one time. From left to right are (top row) Col. Tom Lanphier, Brig. Gen. Jim Trail, Col. Dave Johnson; (bottom row) Col. Martin Johnson, Col. Ken Nordling, and Col. Bill Coburn.

Five

Phantoms Phorever

By the 1970s, the perceived threat of attack from Soviet long-range bombers had diminished. Many air defense units, including the Idaho Air National Guard's 190th Fighter Interceptor Squadron, changed missions. In 1975, the F-102s left Gowen Field and the camera-equipped RF-4C Phantoms arrived. This began the Idaho Air National Guard's 21-year involvement with the F-4 Phantom II.

The personnel of the 124th demonstrated a high degree of skill and proficiency in their new mission: tactical photoreconnaissance. The 190th's Tactical Reconnaissance Squadron RF-4Cs photographed the Teton Dam break in eastern Idaho in 1976 and monitored forest fires with infrared imaging. Additionally, Idaho Air Guard RF-4C aircrews, maintainers, and support personnel made deployments to Canada and Norway to maintain readiness.

Photoreconnaissance competitions helped Idaho Air Guardsmen hone their skills. Idaho Air National Guard fliers and maintainers won competitions at the air force's Photo Finish and the U.S. Navy's Photo Derby several times with team awards and maintenance awards. During the 1980s, the 189th Tactical Reconnaissance Training Flight was activated to train all Air National Guard crews in the RF-4C Phantom. The 124th retired its last RF-4C Phantoms in 1993.

In 1991, the Idaho Air National Guard assigned F-4G Phantoms to the 190th with a mission of suppression of enemy air defenses (SEAD), nicknamed "Wild Weasel." Idaho was the second of only two Air National Guard units to fly this dangerous and difficult mission—to locate and attack highly defended enemy radar and missile sites. The F-4G Phantom used special electronics and high-speed anti-radiation missiles (HARMs). The 189th trained active-duty and Air Guard crews in the Wild Weasel mission while the 190th remained an operational squadron.

The 190th Fighter Squadron's F-4Gs and personnel served multiple deployments between 1993 and 1996 for Operations Southern Watch and Provide Comfort to protect Allied aircraft in Iraq no-fly zones. Due to budget cuts, the F-4G Wild Weasel program was retired, and on April 20, 1996, the last F-4Gs in service left Gowen Field. The 124th Fighter Group was the final unit to fly the Wild Weasel mission.

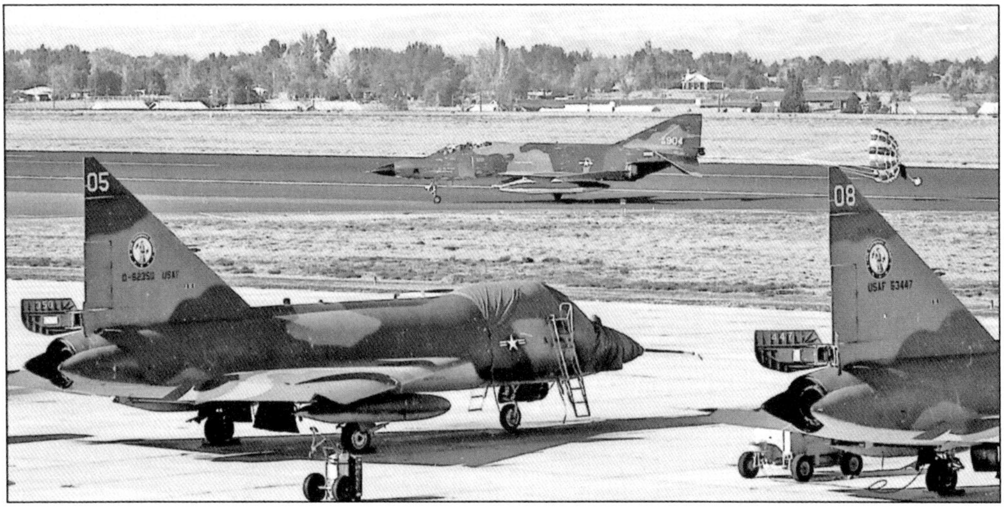

In October 1975, the Idaho Air Guard's first RF-4C, No. 65-904, landed in Idaho with Capt. Jim Davies and Capt. Gary Crowder at the controls. Though the F-102s in the foreground were retired, they remained an important part of Idaho Air National Guard history. The 124th had proved it was a professional Air National Guard unit that could maintain and fly advanced supersonic fighters as well as the active-duty air force.

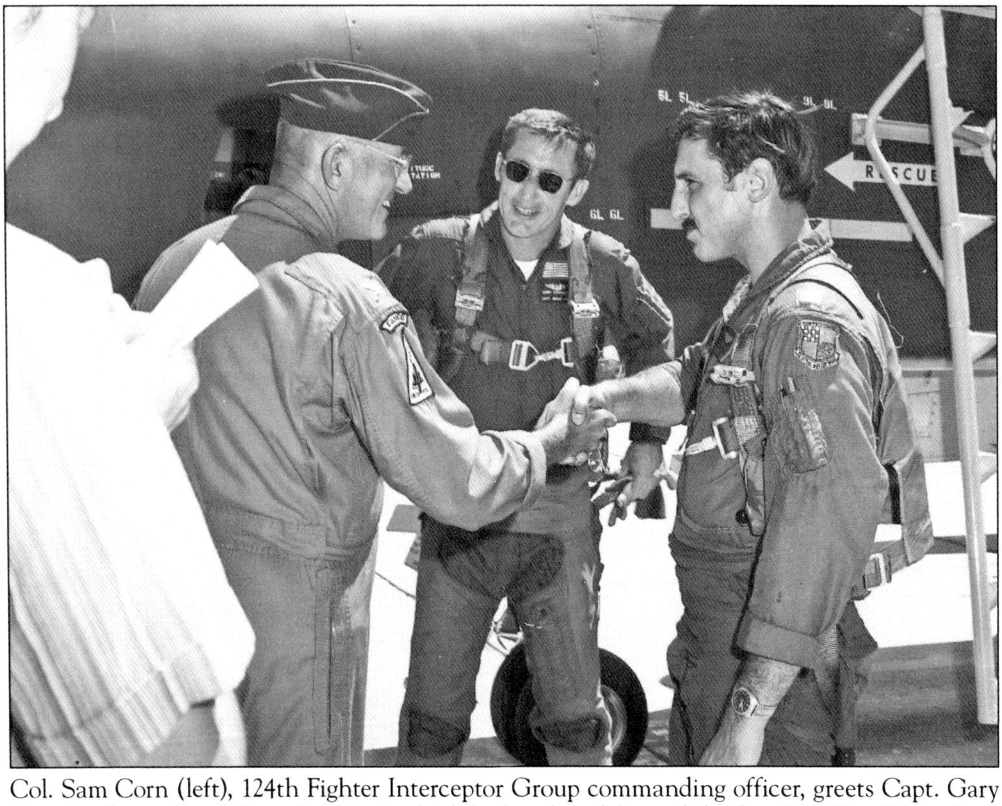
Col. Sam Corn (left), 124th Fighter Interceptor Group commanding officer, greets Capt. Gary Crowder (center) and Capt. Jim Davies (right) after they delivered the first RF-4C to Idaho from Shaw Air Force Base in South Carolina. By 1991, Jim Davies had been promoted to lieutenant colonel and had the honor of delivering the first F-4G to Idaho.

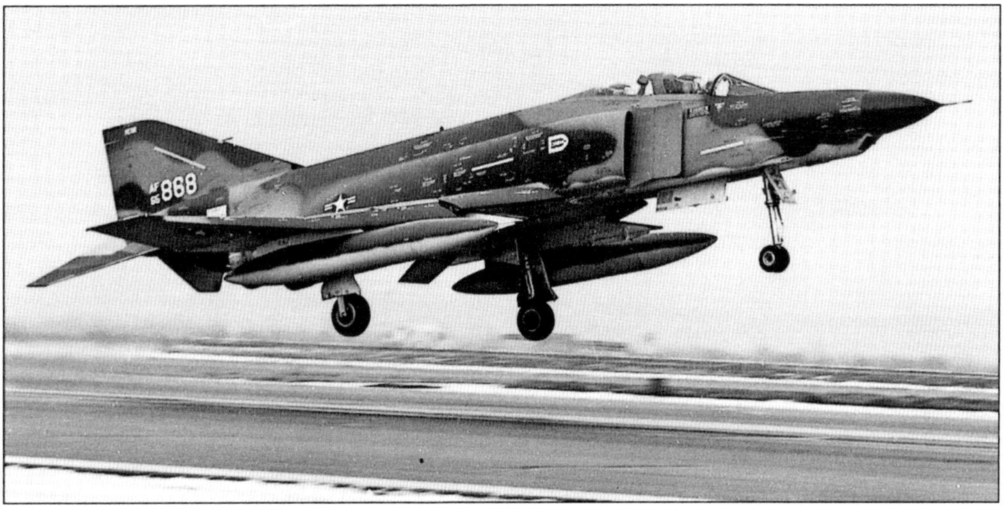

This aircraft was one of the first RF-4C Phantoms to arrive in Idaho and one of the last to leave. It was retired and transferred to the boneyard on March 31, 1992, just one year before the final Idaho RF-4Cs retired. A pair of J79 engines powered the Phantoms, as opposed to the single-engine F-102s. On low-altitude reconnaissance missions, the RF-4C relied on speed as defense.

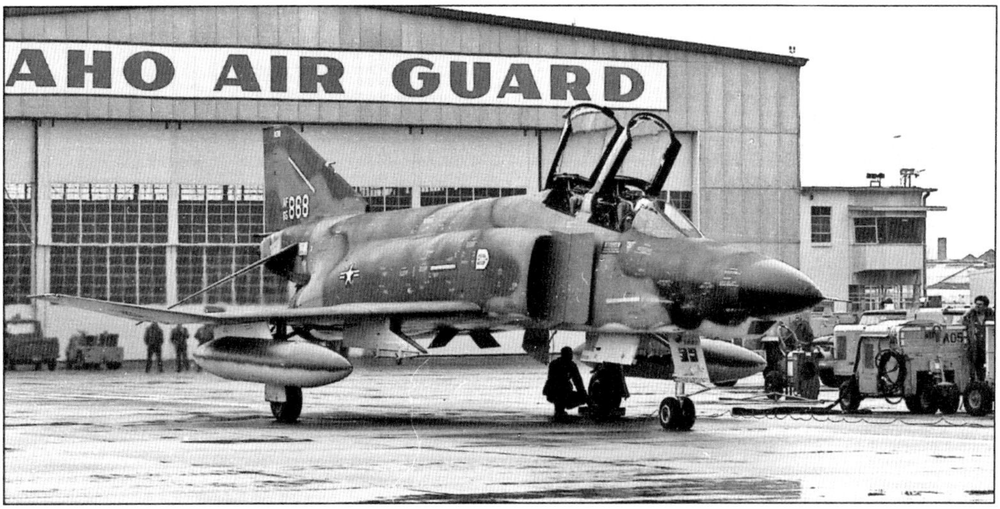

On a wet Idaho day, maintainers of the 190th Tactical Reconnaissance Squadron stand by as an RF-4C prepares to taxi. Within months of the transition to the photoreconnaissance Phantom, Idaho crews took photographs of the damage from the Teton Dam break in eastern Idaho during 1976. These images were important to relief and reconstruction efforts. The rainy weather may indicate this was taken at the time of the flooding.

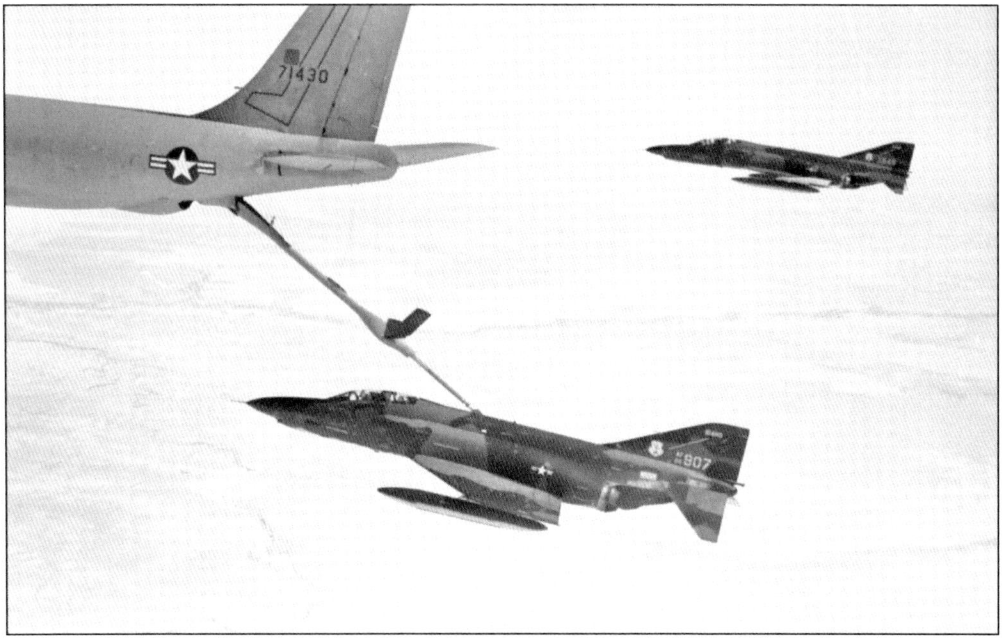

The first Idaho Air National Guard aerial refueling took place on March 5, 1976, with a four-ship flight of RF-4C Phantoms. Refueling is a difficult but critical skill, and the Idaho crews quickly learned how to accomplish the task. They would later use the skill during deployments to Norway and Alaska with the RF-4C.

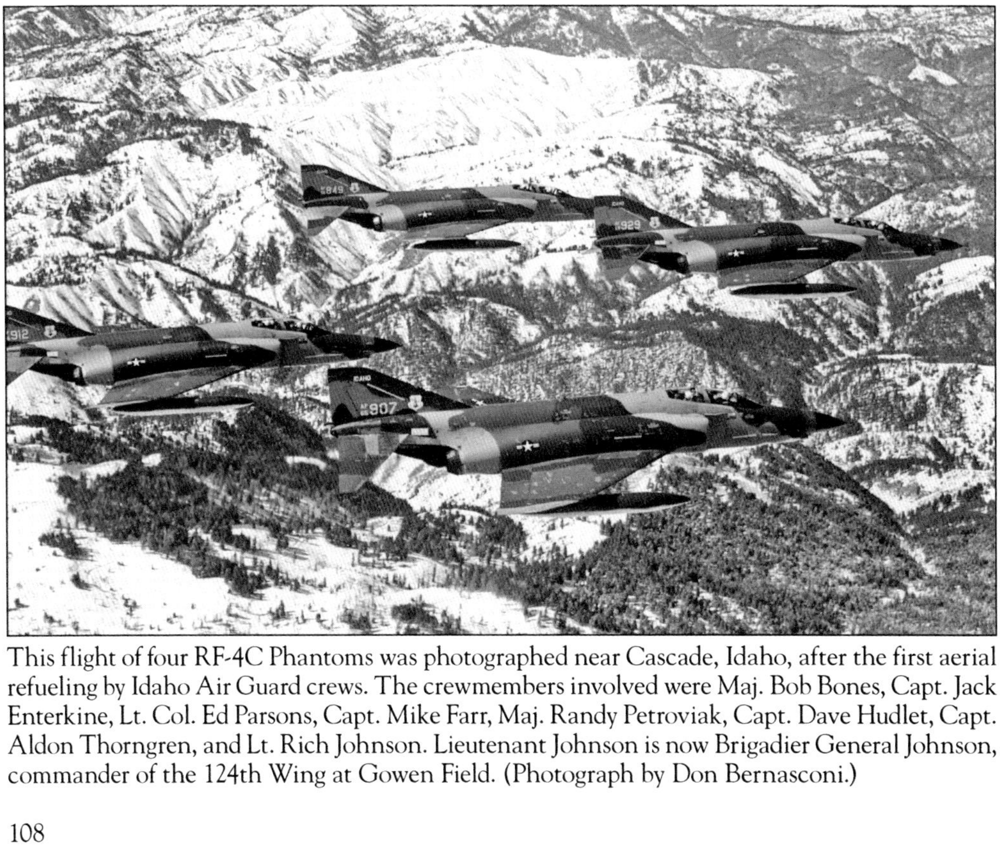

This flight of four RF-4C Phantoms was photographed near Cascade, Idaho, after the first aerial refueling by Idaho Air Guard crews. The crewmembers involved were Maj. Bob Bones, Capt. Jack Enterkine, Lt. Col. Ed Parsons, Capt. Mike Farr, Maj. Randy Petroviak, Capt. Dave Hudlet, Capt. Aldon Thorngren, and Lt. Rich Johnson. Lieutenant Johnson is now Brigadier General Johnson, commander of the 124th Wing at Gowen Field. (Photograph by Don Bernasconi.)

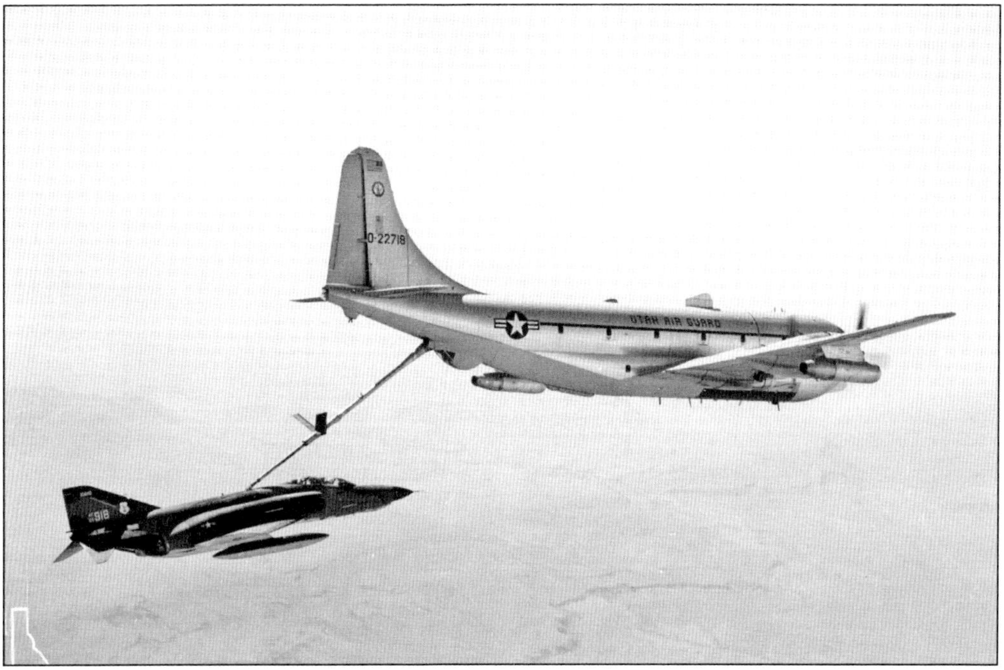

This Idaho Air National Guard RF-4C is seen with flaps down and throttle back for aerial refueling by a Utah Air National Guard turboprop KC-97. The faster RF-4C normally refueled with the KC-135 Stratotanker. Due to the Utah Guard's proximity and need to maintain proficiency in aerial refueling, this unlikely pair of jet and prop aircraft took place.

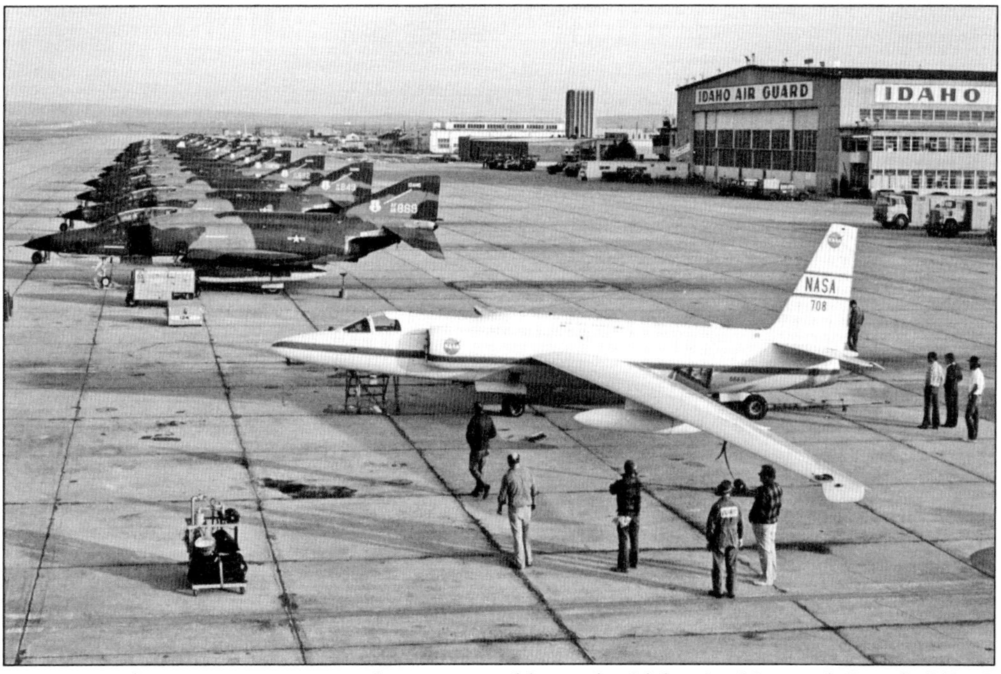

Two types of reconnaissance aircraft are pictured here: the Idaho Air National Guard's RF-4C Phantom and a NASA high-altitude U-2 that landed at Gowen Field in 1977. NASA U-2s were used to carry experiments into the atmosphere and engage in photographic missions over Earth.

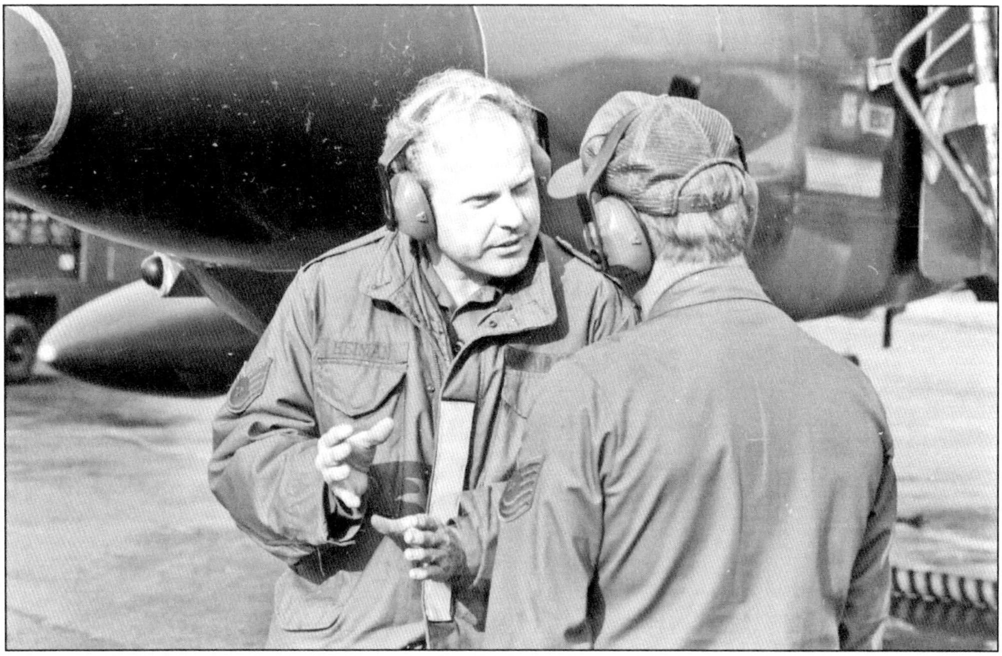

Crewmembers discuss maintenance issues by an RF-4C. SSgt. James Heiman (left) has opted not to wear a hat to minimize the danger of foreign object debris (FOD) being sucked into the air intakes of the Phantom. Hats are not normally worn on the flight line for this reason. Earmuffs hold down the unidentified technical sergeant's hat.

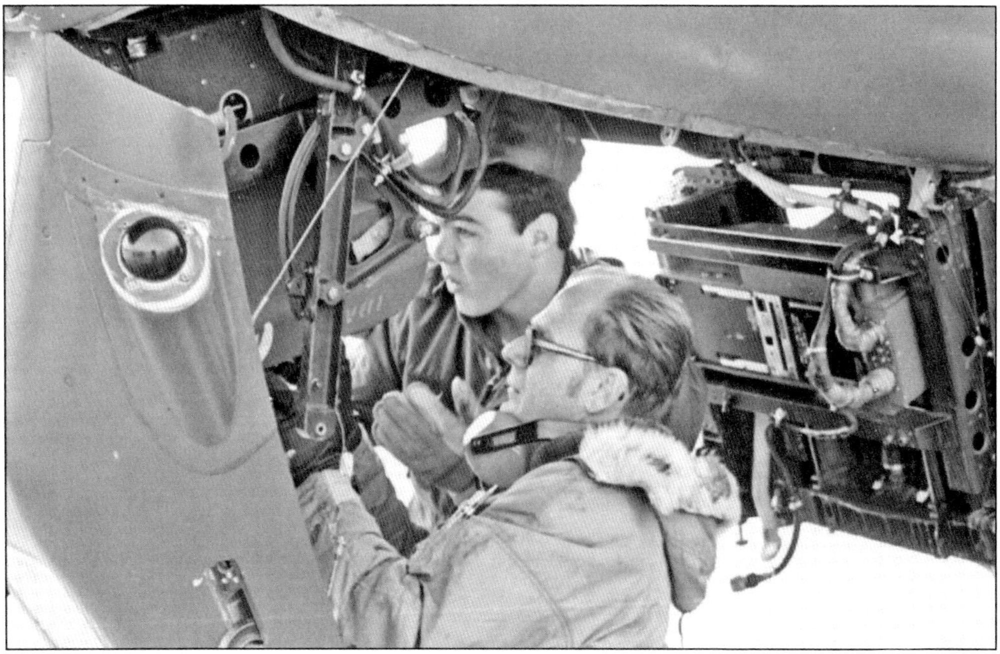

Idaho Air Guardsmen Lance Hock and Ray Greene service one of the cameras on an RF-4C Phantom II. This is camera station No. 1, a forward-looking station that housed a camera for either oblique or vertical daytime photography missions. The "Recce" (reconnaissance) version of the air force's Phantoms had three camera stations in the nose.

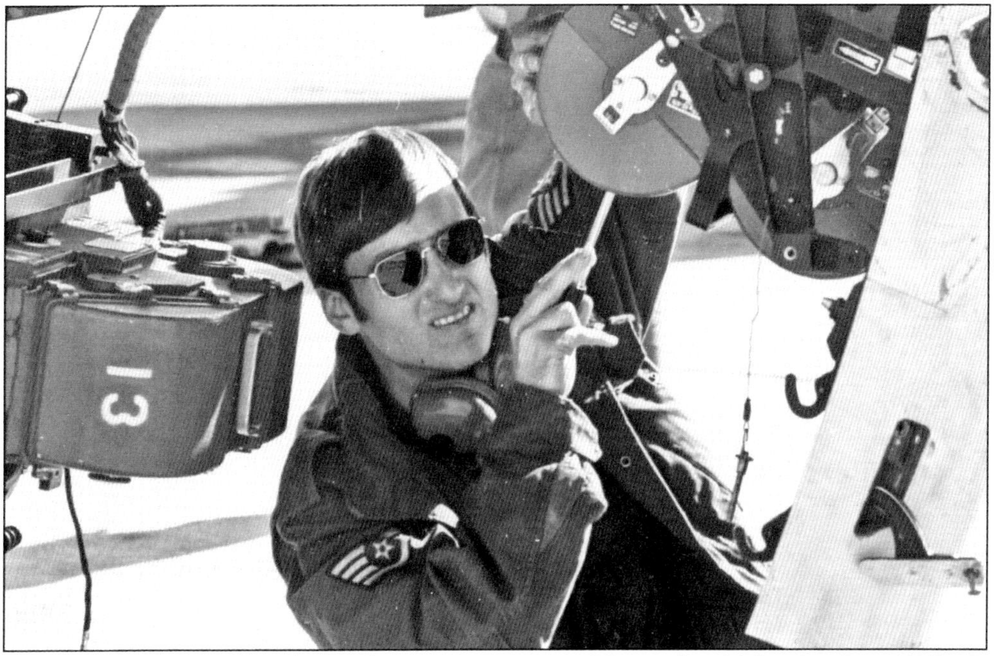

SSgt. Ronald Harwood works on the camera in station No. 1 of an Idaho Air Guard RF-4C. All camera stations were accessible through hinged doors that allowed for maintenance and the changing of cameras based on mission requirements. In addition to the daylight cameras, the RF-4C carried radar, infrared, and laser imaging systems, which allowed for nighttime reconnaissance capability.

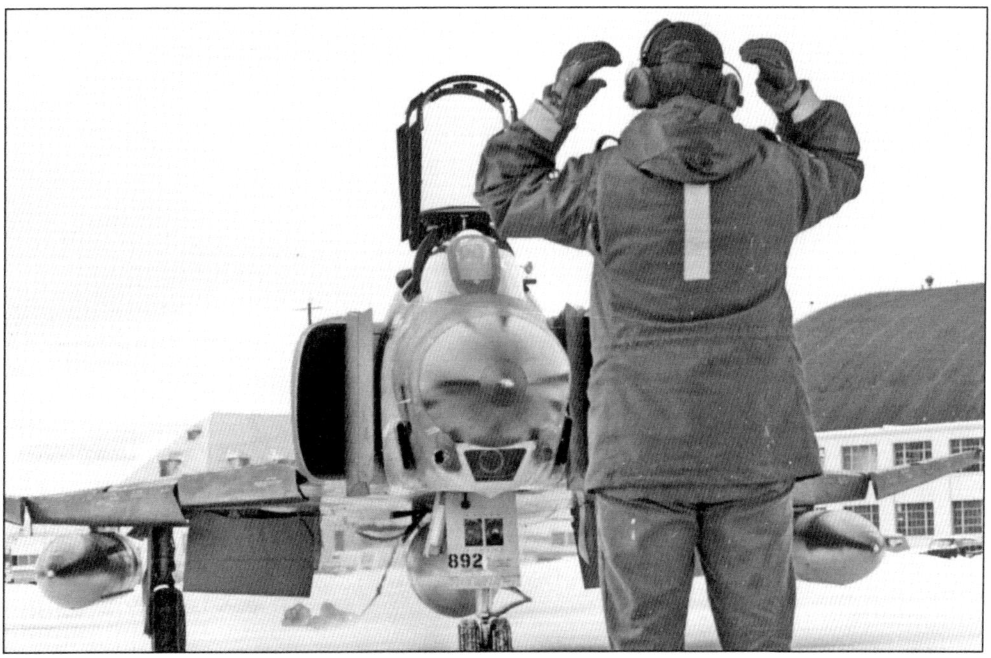

A crew chief directs his RF-4C to its parking spot after landing. The 190th Tactical Reconnaissance Squadron made regular deployments to Norway, Alaska, and Canada to conduct operations in cold-weather conditions, harsher than Idaho could provide for realistic training.

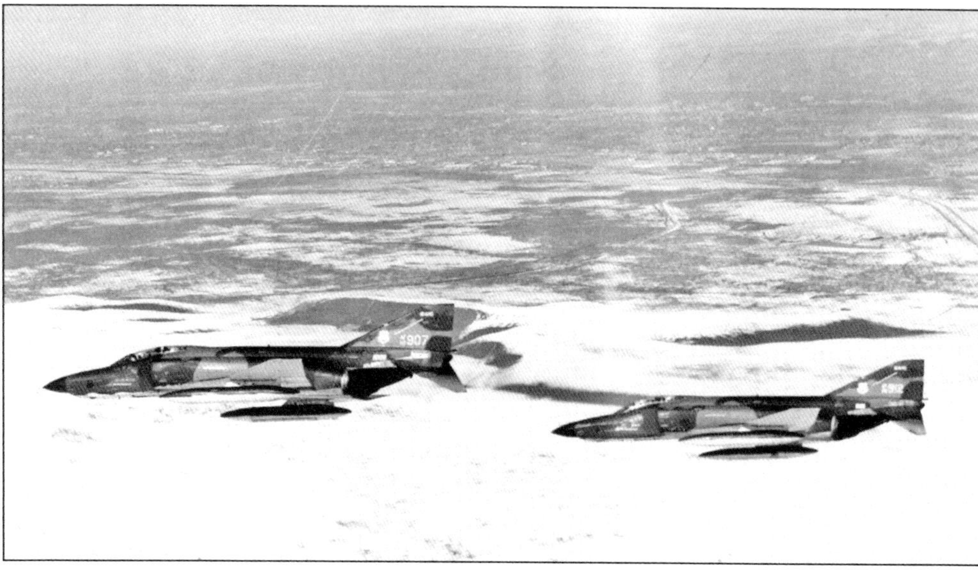

With Gowen Field visible in the upper left, two RF-4Cs are about to enter the pattern for their final approach. Although RF-4C photoreconnaissance missions were normally flown by single aircraft, formation takeoffs and landings were practiced as a means of recovering aircraft more quickly. This would have been essential should the 190th Tactical Reconnaissance Squadron ever have deployed in combat.

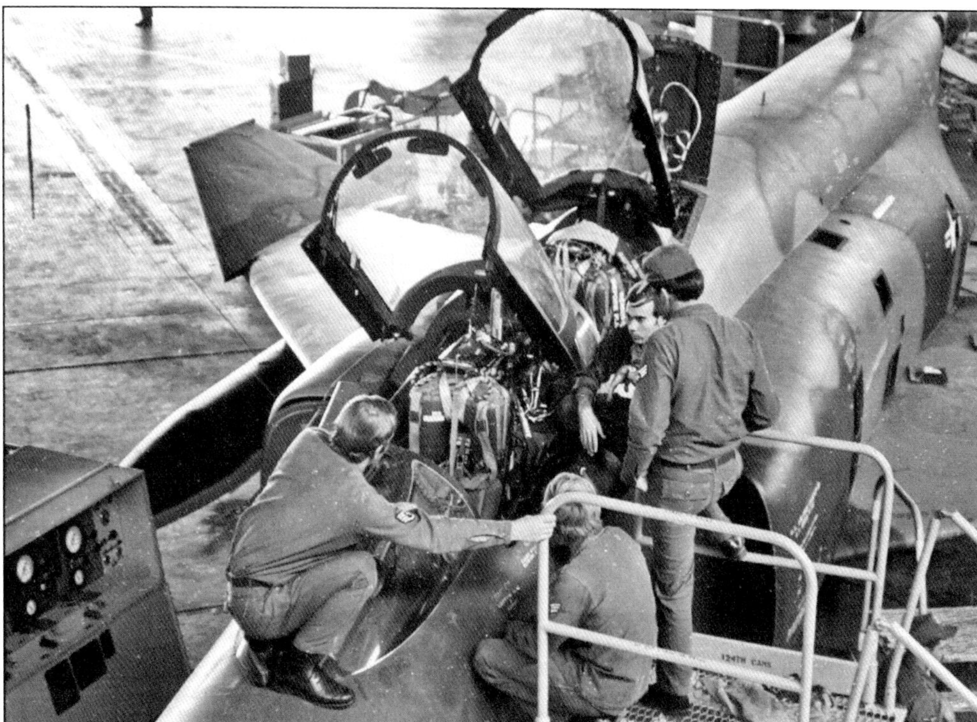

Maintainers inspect an RF-4C cockpit inside one of the Air Guard's hangars. The Martin Baker MK7 ejection seat where the crew is working is the type that saved two Idaho Air Guard crews who were forced to eject from their RF-4C Phantoms.

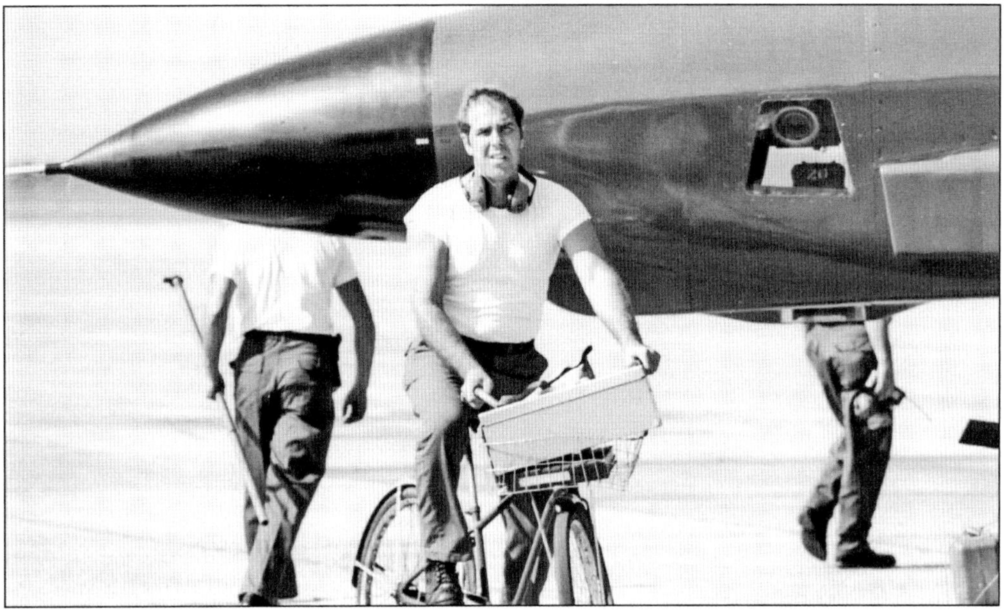

Low-tech solutions in a high-tech environment, bicycles have long been a mode of transportation around aircraft flight lines. Maintainer Mike Ciancia grabbed his tool kit and notebook and rode around the 190th flight line. From World War II through the 1970s, maintainers at Gowen Field used bikes to get around.

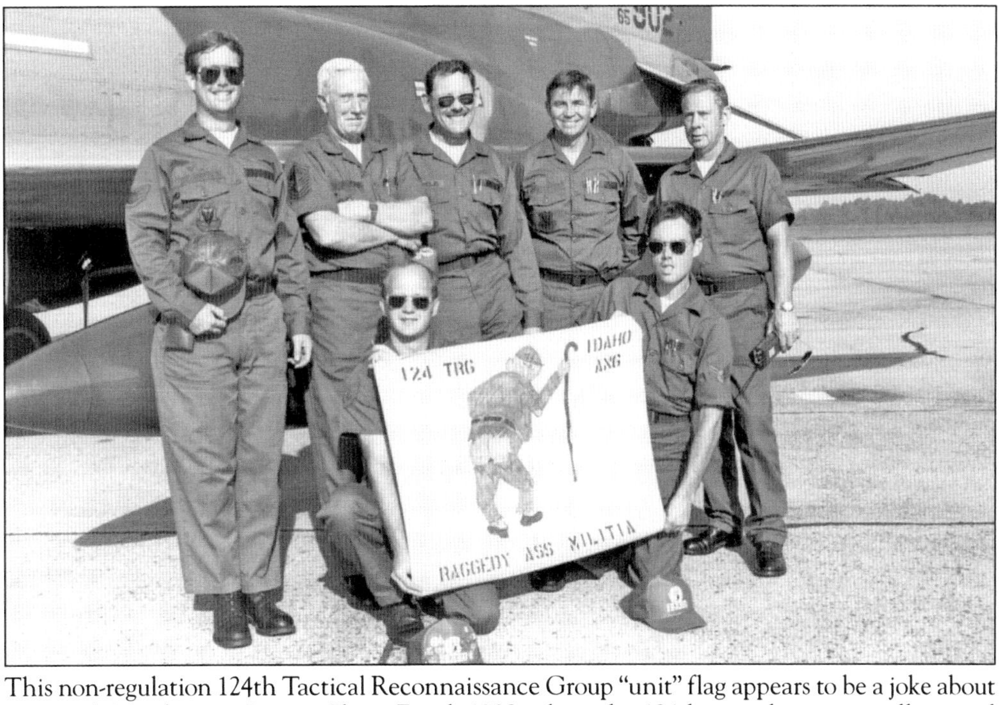

This non-regulation 124th Tactical Reconnaissance Group "unit" flag appears to be a joke about National Guard units. Seen at Photo Finish 1983, where the 124th won the top overall tactical reconnaissance unit, are the following, from left to right: (first row) TSgt. Harvey Dixon and senior airman Randy Tabbutt; (second row) Staff Sergeant Hunington, CMSgt. Don Noteboom, Dave Nicholas, TSgt. Don Votroubek, and CMSgt. Bob Demeyer.

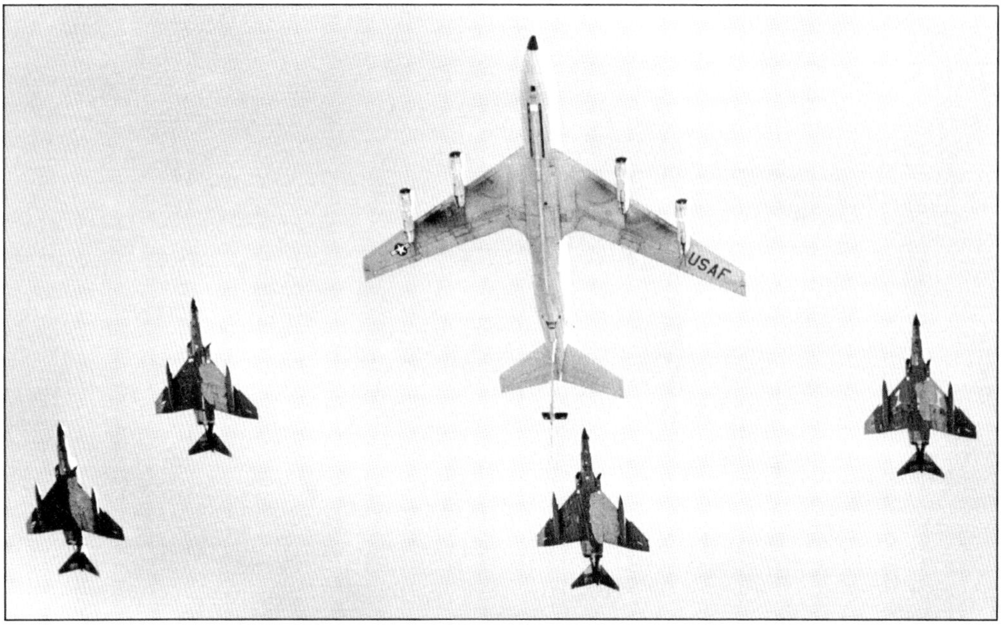

At the many air shows the Idaho Air Guard hosted over the years, spectators could always count on the 124th crews to perform a flyby with a KC-135 Stratotanker to demonstrate aerial refueling. This vividly illustrated for the crowds how close the tanker and recipient aircraft came in order to accomplish the task.

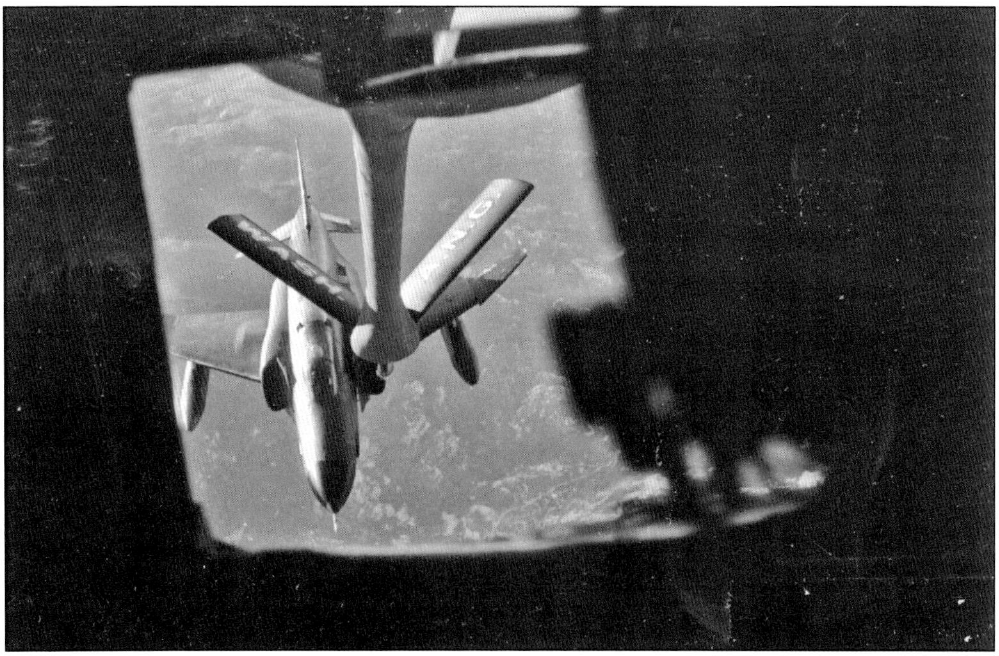

An Idaho Air National Guard RF-4C comes up to a Washington Air National Guard KC-135 Stratotanker to plug into the refueling boom. This photograph, taken through the boom operator's window, provides a good idea of how close the two aircraft must get to refuel. The boom operator controls the boom during this process and steers it to the refueling port on the receiving aircraft.

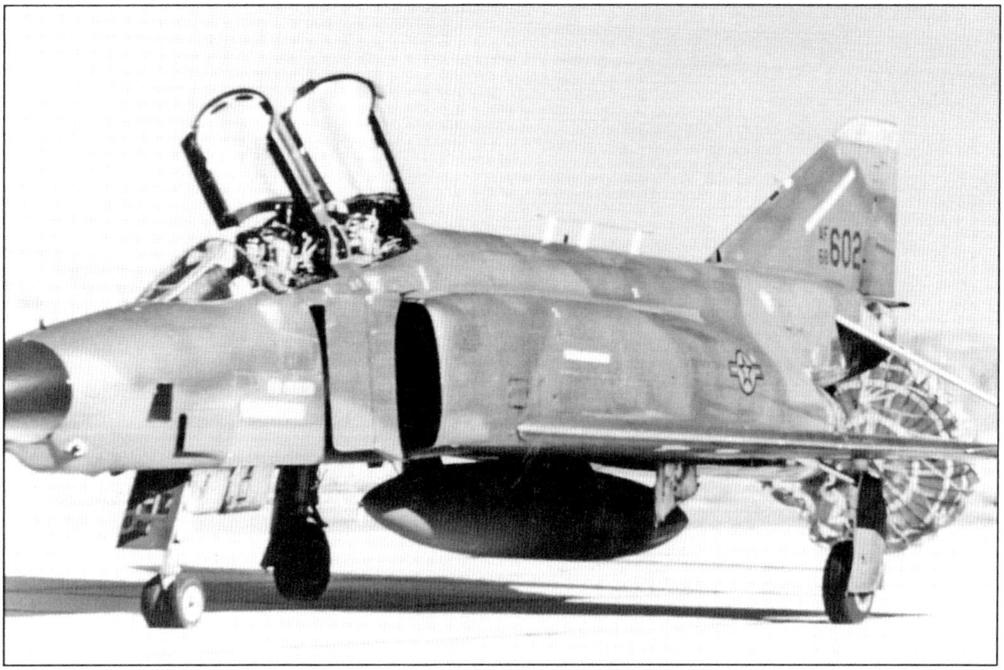

The RF-4Cs with towel-rack antennas on their spines, just forward of the tail, were equipped with long-range navigation (LORAN). LORAN was intended to increase the all-weather and night capabilities by measuring radio signals between fixed points to determine the aircraft's location. Unfortunately, the system did not always work, leading to navigational errors.

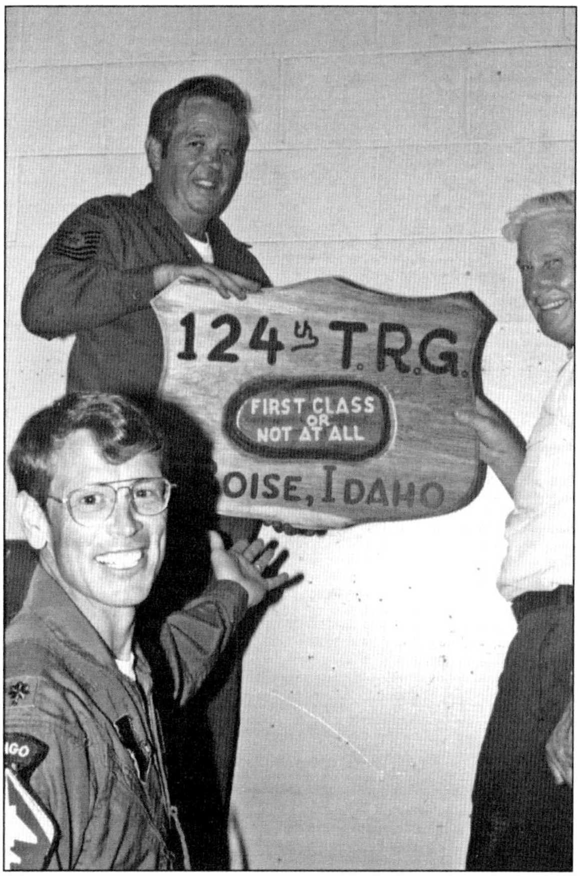

From left to right, Lt. Col. Bill Miller, MSgt. Jim Wenzell, and CMSgt. Don Noteboom pose with a plaque sometime between 1981 and 1983. In 1982, a whistling swan hit a 190th RF-4C in the cockpit during mission, disabling the pilot. Lieutenant Colonel Miller, in another RF-4C, responded to the distress call and joined up with the damaged aircraft. His calm leadership helped guide the back-seater of the damaged plane to land safely.

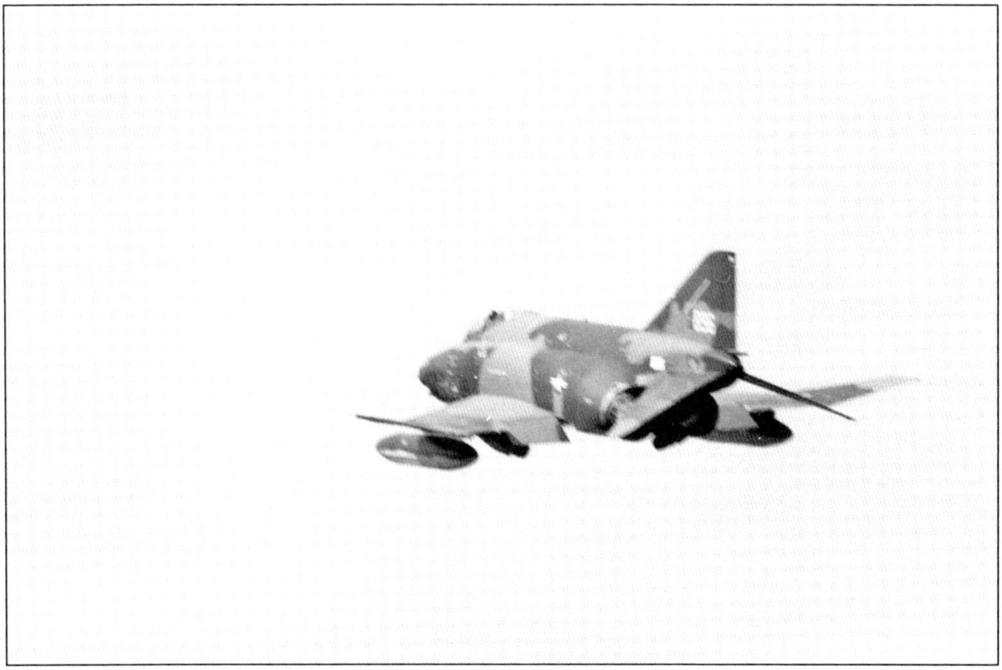

RF-4C missions were usually flown as single-ship flights in true reconnaissance form—alone, unarmed, and unafraid. The 124th crews practiced their skill day and night, not only to obtain good imagery but also to practice how to stay alive getting into and out of the target area.

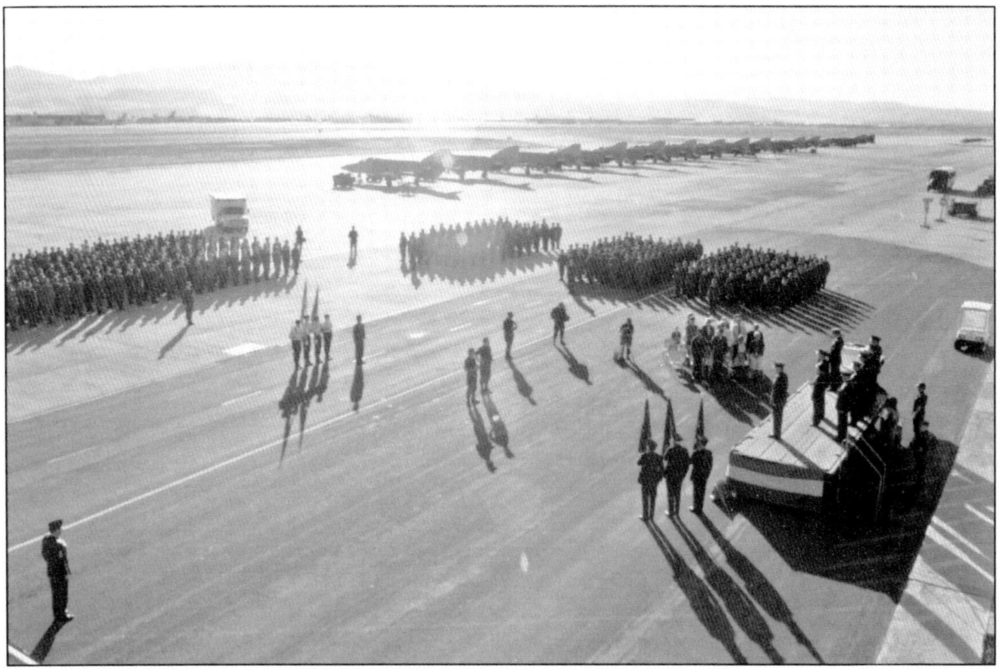

The 124th Tactical Reconnaissance Group is seen at a morning formation on the ramp at Gowen Field for an awards ceremony. In the background is a sight that has long been gone from Gowen Field: a flight line full of Phantoms. This photograph was taken before the 1991 arrival of the F-4Gs, as all of the aircraft are the Recce version.

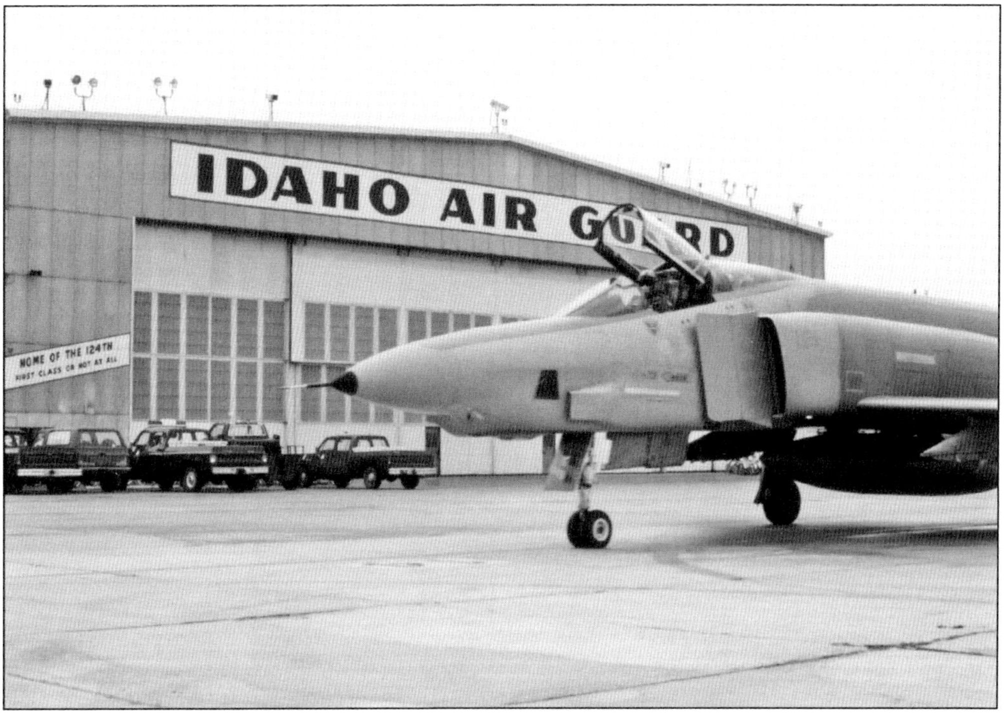

Taxiing past the maintenance hangar, this RF-4C reveals details such as the window for side-looking cameras as well as the yellow strip lights for night formation flying. In the late 1980s, the F-4 series of aircraft was painted in this two-tone gray camouflage scheme. Painted on the hangar at left is the motto of the 124th: "First class or not at all."

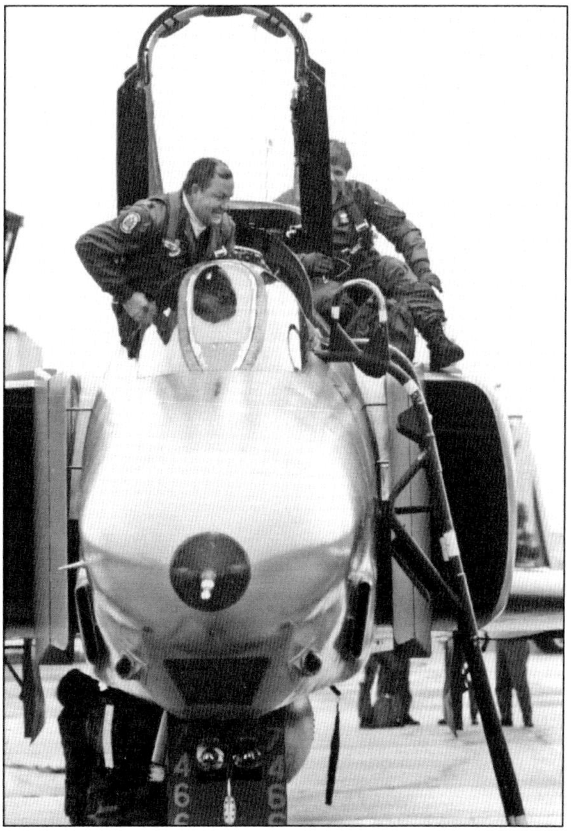

Lt. Col. Frank Fullmer climbs out of the cockpit of an RF-4C Phantom after his final flight with the 124th Tactical Reconnaissance Group. The tradition is to spray the crewmember with fire hoses and champagne immediately after he climbs down the ladder.

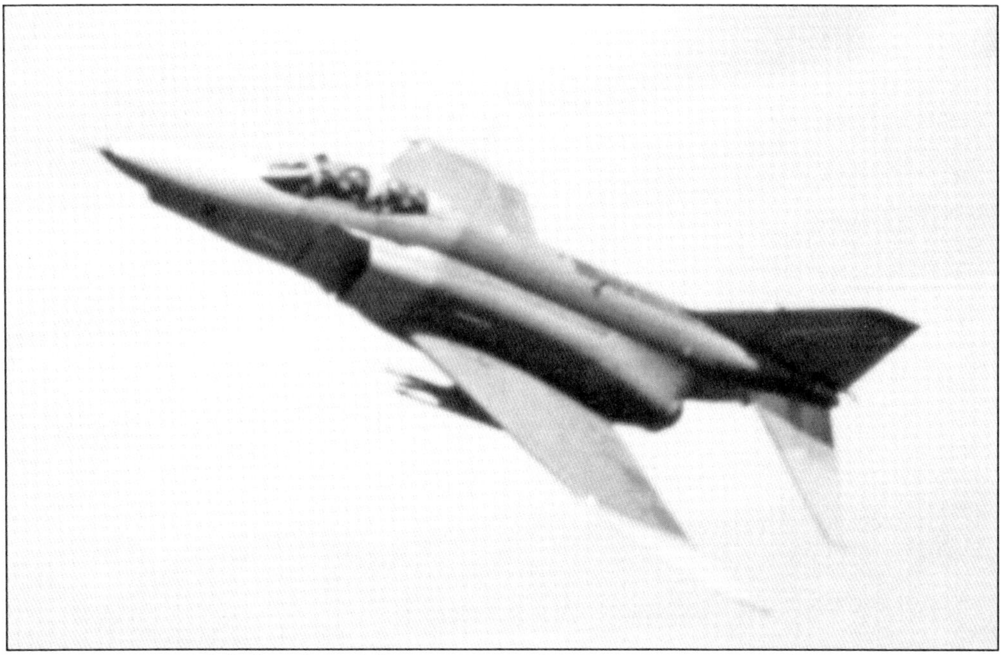

The last operational flight of an Idaho Air National Guard RF-4C occurred on March 31, 1993. Crews were already delivering Recce Phantoms to the bone yard at Davis Monthan Air Force Base as the group transitioned to the F-4G. This RF-4C, one of the last to remain in Idaho, banks one final time over the flight line at Gowen Field.

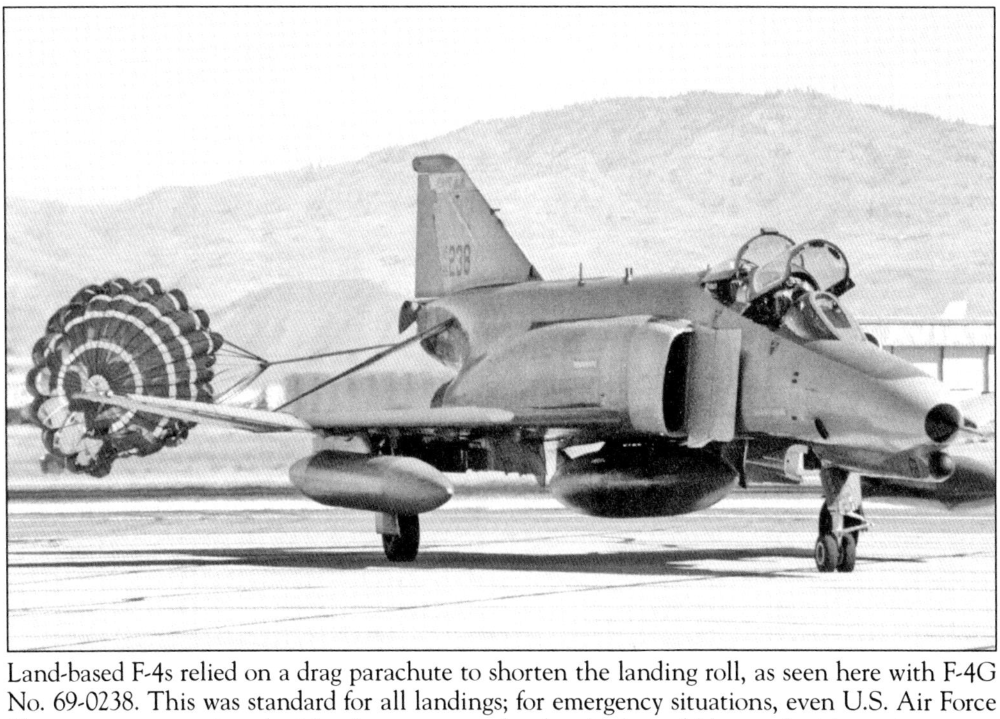

Land-based F-4s relied on a drag parachute to shorten the landing roll, as seen here with F-4G No. 69-0238. This was standard for all landings; for emergency situations, even U.S. Air Force Phantoms were equipped with a large arrestor hook, which could be used with a wire system on runways.

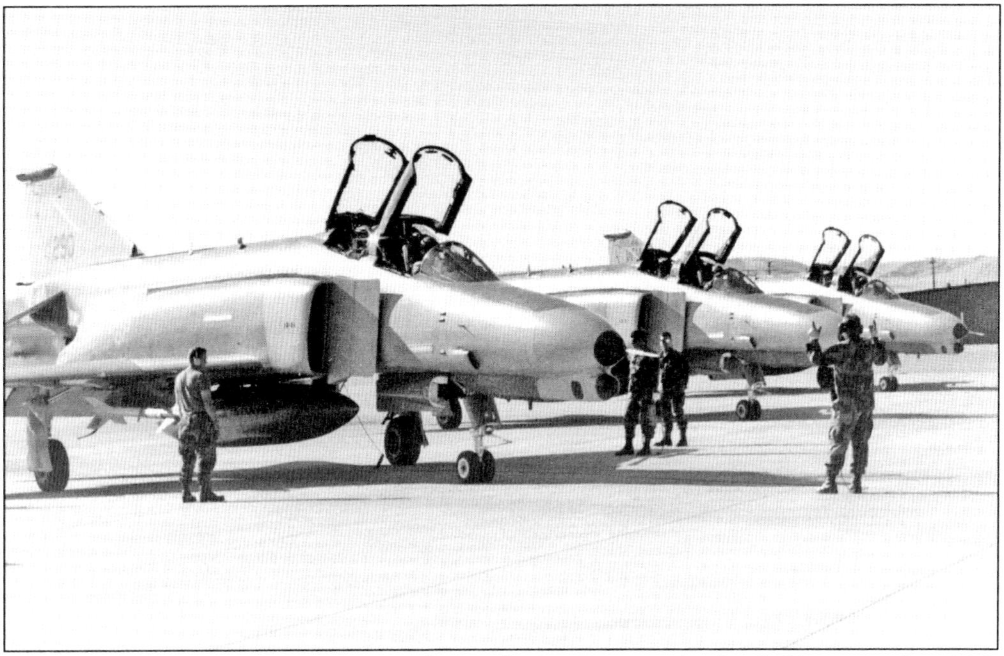

The Idaho Air National Guard received a total of 37 F-4Gs to be divided between the 190th Fighter Squadron and the 189th Fighter Training Unit. The 189th became the Wild Weasel School for all of the U.S. Air Force and Idaho Guard. A total of 125 students graduated from the school in four years. With the high demand for training students, the Idaho Air Guard's F-4Gs were flown daily.

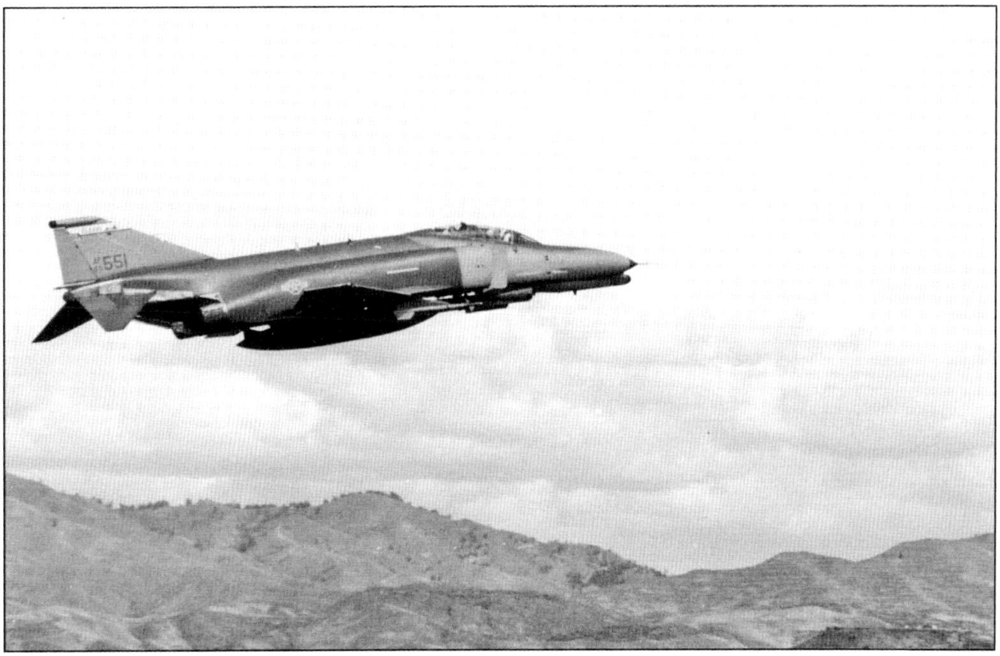

F-4G No. 69-7551, the first Wild Weasel Phantom delivered to the 124th Fighter Group, takes off for a training flight. In the summer of 1993, the Idaho Air Guard's 190th Fighter Squadron deployed to Saudi Arabia to enforce the Iraqi no-fly zone.

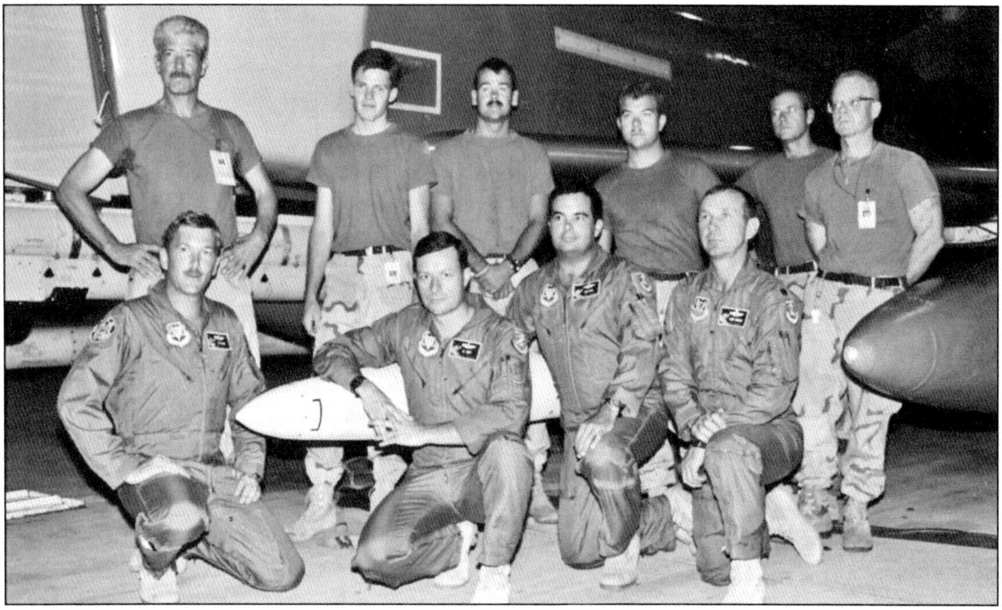

On a June 29, 1993, mission, two 190th F-4Gs were tracked by Iraqi early-warning radar, which indicated hostile intent. One of the F-4Gs fired a HARM and destroyed the radar. Personnel involved in the mission were, kneeling from left to right in the first row, Eddie Payne, Larry Kauffman, Mike "Taco" Bell, and Gary Sayler. The maintainers, standing from left to right, were MSgt. Bob Clinton, SrA. Kevin Forrey, SSgt. Craig Wood, SrA. Andy Reed, TSgt. Dean Sigman, and TSgt. Chris Adams. (Courtesy Brig. Gen. Gary Sayler.)

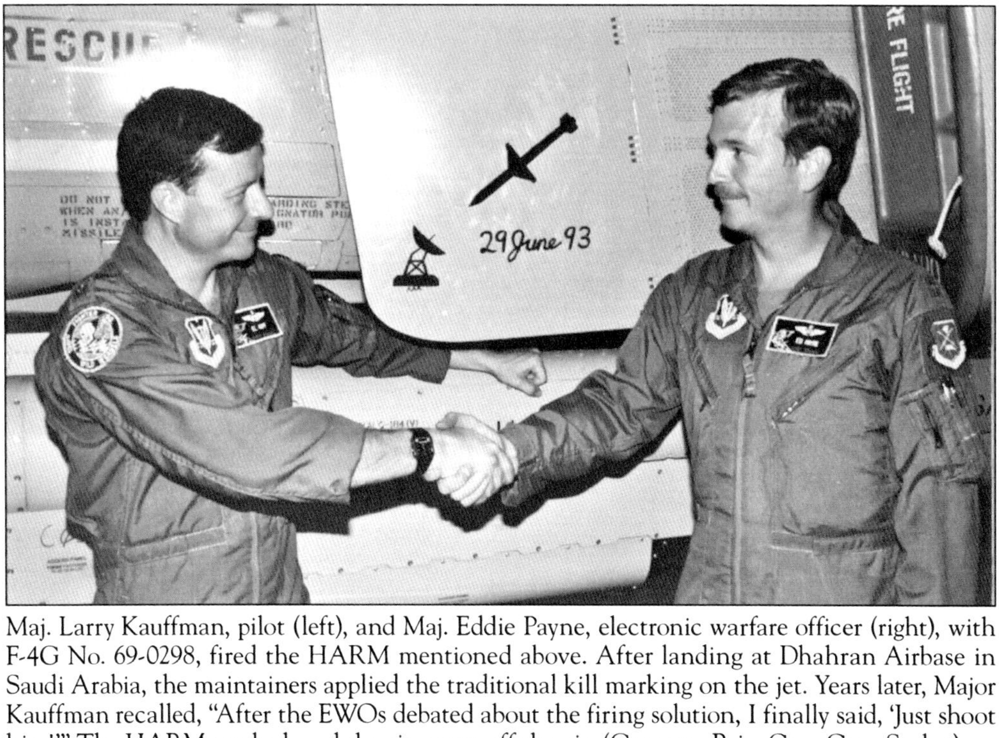

Maj. Larry Kauffman, pilot (left), and Maj. Eddie Payne, electronic warfare officer (right), with F-4G No. 69-0298, fired the HARM mentioned above. After landing at Dhahran Airbase in Saudi Arabia, the maintainers applied the traditional kill marking on the jet. Years later, Major Kauffman recalled, "After the EWOs debated about the firing solution, I finally said, 'Just shoot him!'" The HARM tracked, and the site went off the air. (Courtesy Brig. Gen. Gary Sayler.)

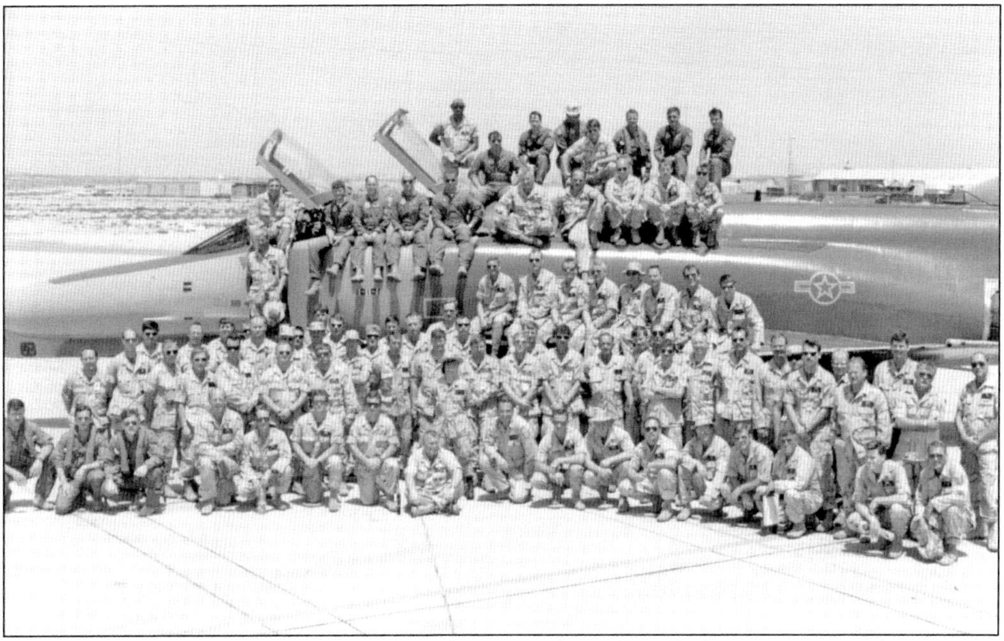

Pictured at the end of one of the 190th Fighter Squadron's first deployments to Southwest Asia, these happy Idaho Air Guardsmen and women are ready to leave the desert. No Allied aircraft were lost due to hostile ground fire while the Idaho Air National Guard crews were flying the Wild Weasel mission.

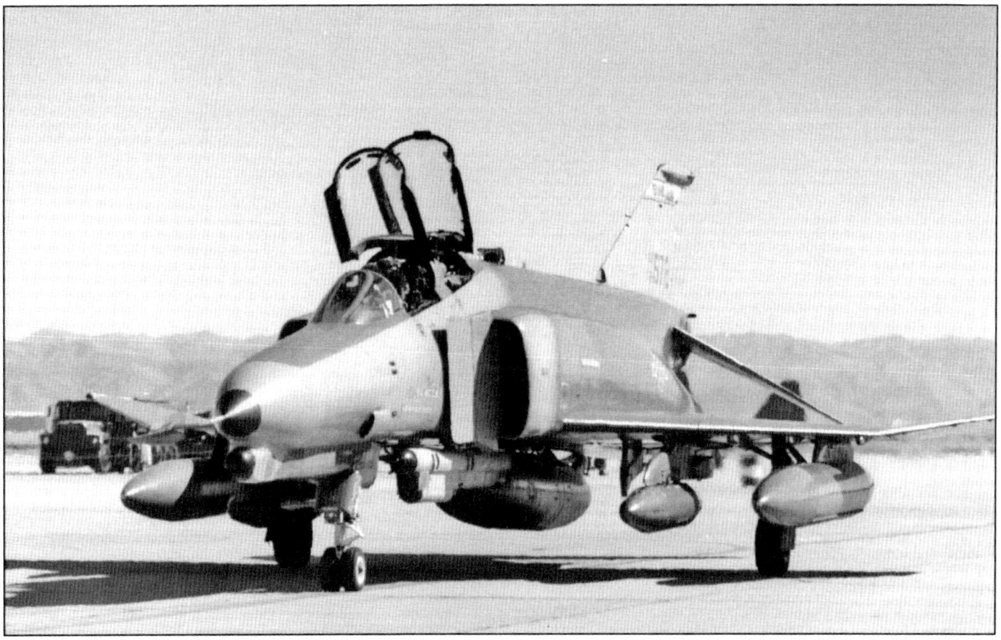

With the 190th Fighter Squadron's responsibility for the SEAD mission in the Middle East, its personnel and aircraft deployed frequently. This F-4G, No. 69-7572, appears ready to take off for a deployment. The aircraft has three fuel tanks plus travel pods under the wings for crews' luggage. The electronic countermeasures pod, hung in the forward missile well, is not usually seen on training flights.

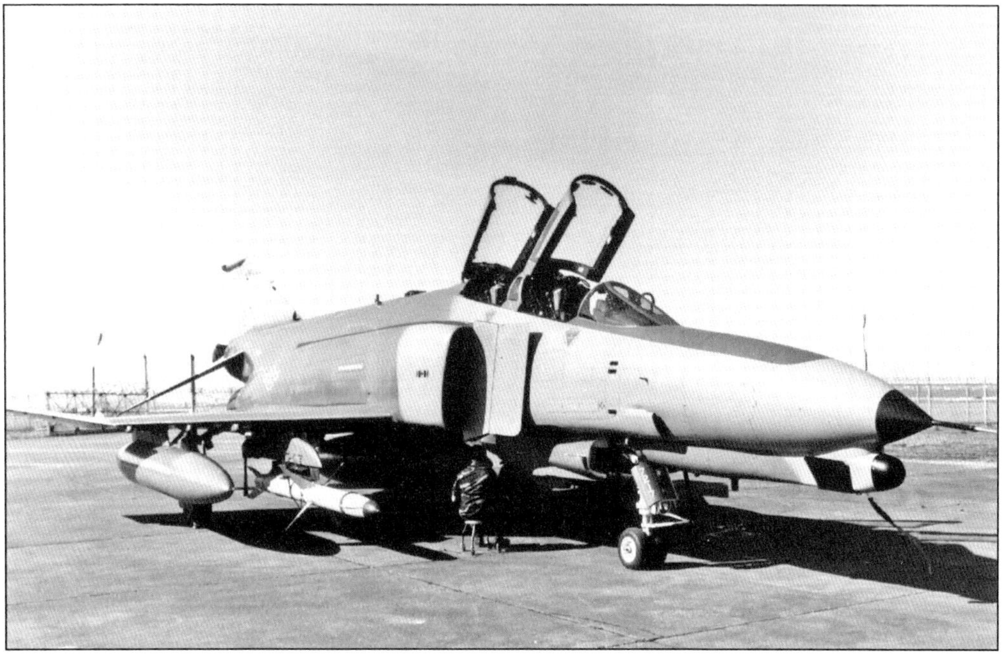

F-4G No. 69-7217, at Incirlik Airbase in Turkey, prepares for its next patrol over the Iraqi no-fly zone. Missions flown out of Turkey were in support of Operation Provide Comfort, the protection of Iraq's Kurdish population, which Saddam Hussein sought to exterminate. U.S. military forces patrolled the established demilitarized zones in order to keep Iraqi military from attacking the Kurds.

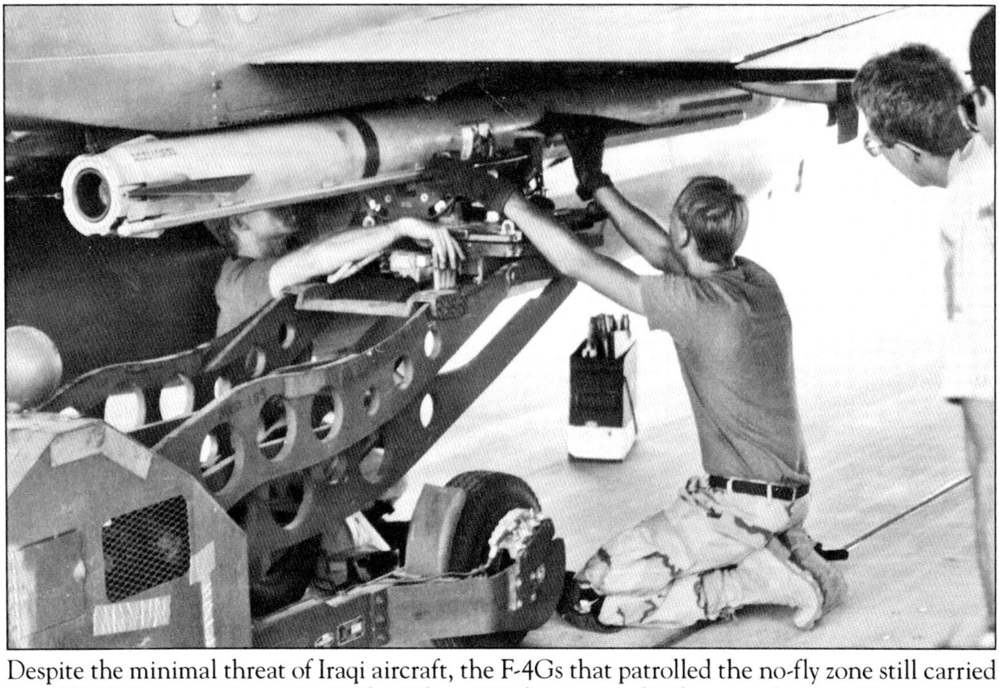

Despite the minimal threat of Iraqi aircraft, the F-4Gs that patrolled the no-fly zone still carried two AIM-7 Sparrow air-to-air missiles. These 190th weapons loaders are placing a Sparrow into the right rear missile well of an F-4G and will later add the fins.

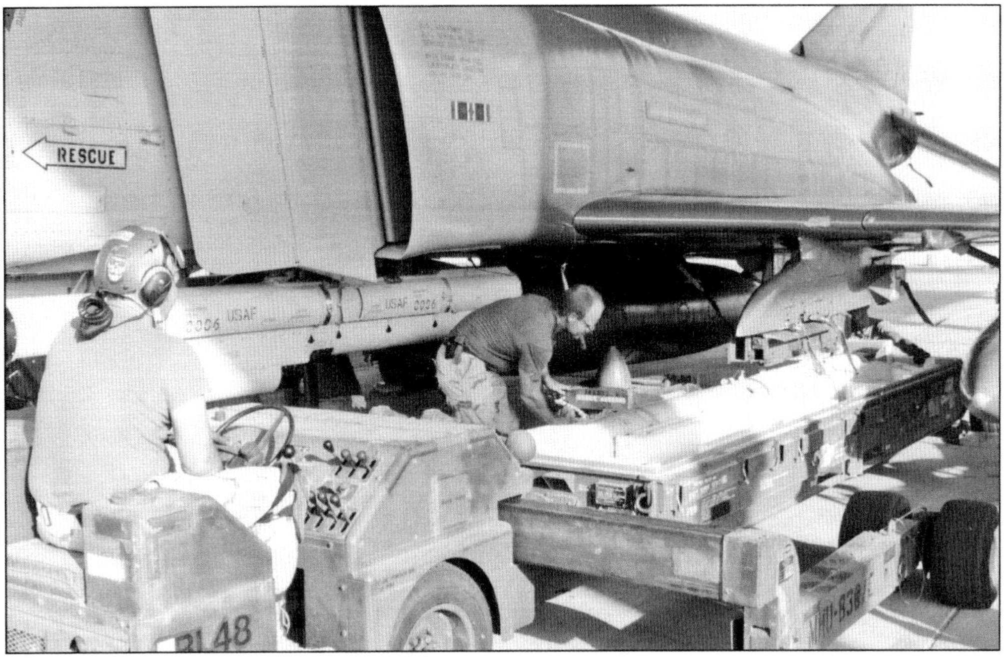

Using an MJ-1 jammer, weapons loaders of the 190th Fighter Squadron busily load an AGM-88 HARM missile onto F-4G No. 69-7207. The high-speed anti-radiation missile was the primary weapon of the F-4G Wild Weasel. It homed in on enemy radar transmissions and exploded over the transmitter into thousands of fragments. Hung below the F-4G's cockpit is an electronic countermeasures pod for jamming enemy radar.

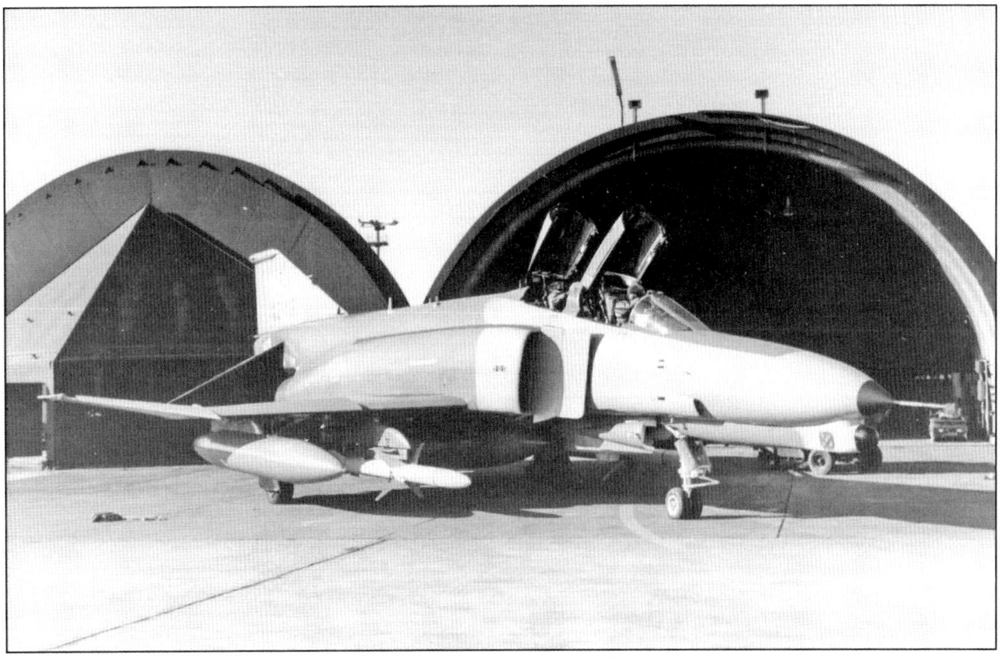

At Incirlik Airbase in Turkey, F-4G No. 69-0249 is readied for its next patrol with three bags of gas and two HARM missiles. Idaho Air Guard maintenance personnel consistently kept their Phantoms 100-percent mission capable and never missed a patrol along the no-fly zone.

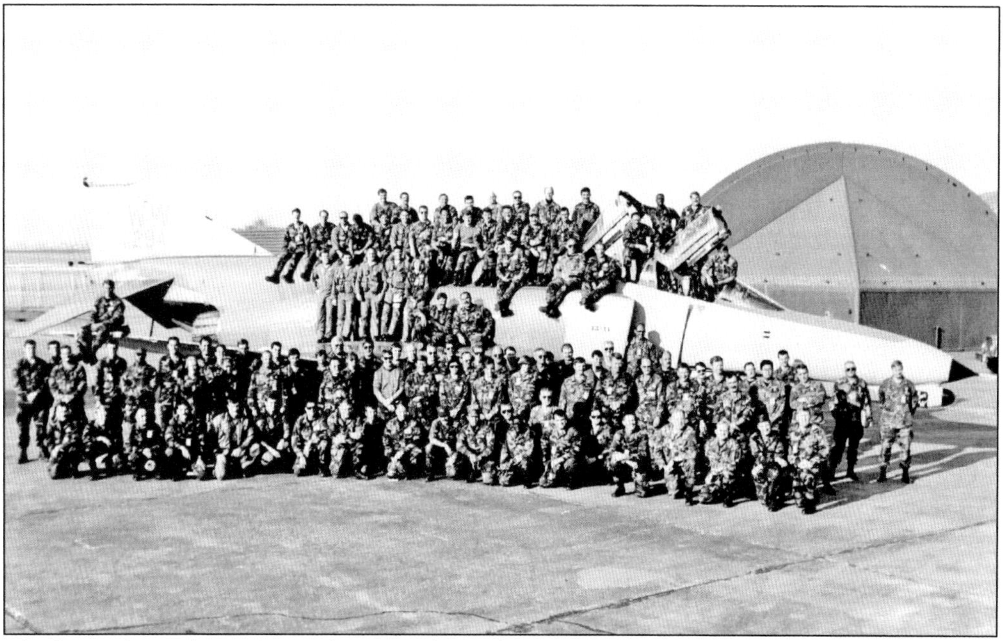

This hero's shot, taken in December 1995, shows the 190th Fighter Squadron detachment at Incirlik Airbase in Turkey during the last deployment of the U.S. Air Force's F-4s. F-4G No. 69-7294 was the 4,000th F-4 built. This final deployment marked the end of the Idaho Air Guard's ongoing rotations to the Middle East to provide Wild Weasel protection of Allied aircraft in Operations Provide Comfort, Southern, and Northern Watch.

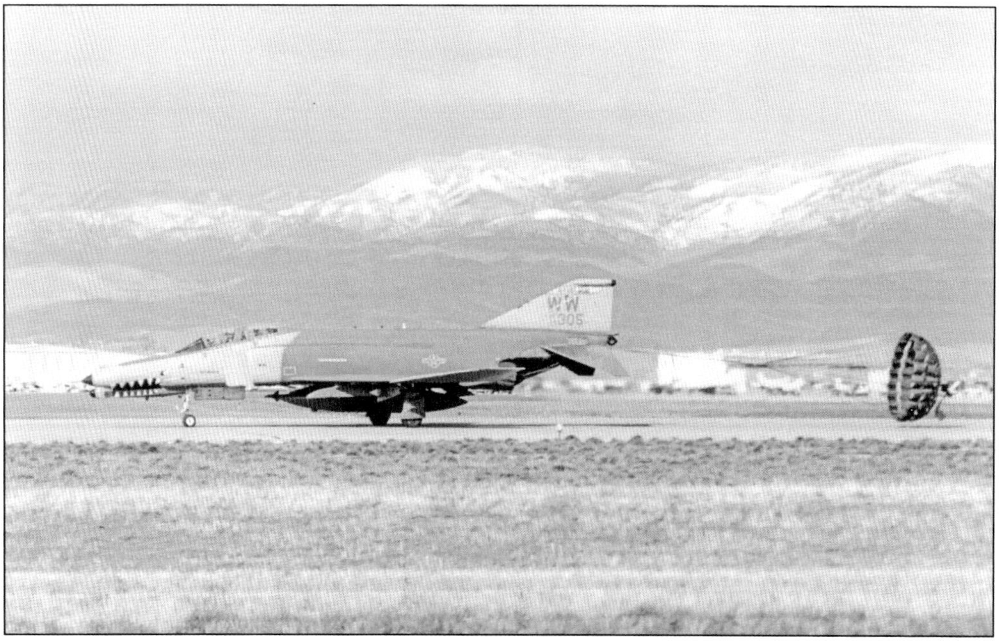

F-4G No. 69-305, just landed at Gowen Field, bears the distinct, Idaho-style shark mouth, which was adopted at the end of the 1995 Incirlik, Turkey, deployment. The tail code, "WW" for Wild Weasel, was also adopted by the 124th late in the F-4G's career. This aircraft flew the last U.S. Air Force Phantom operational combat mission.

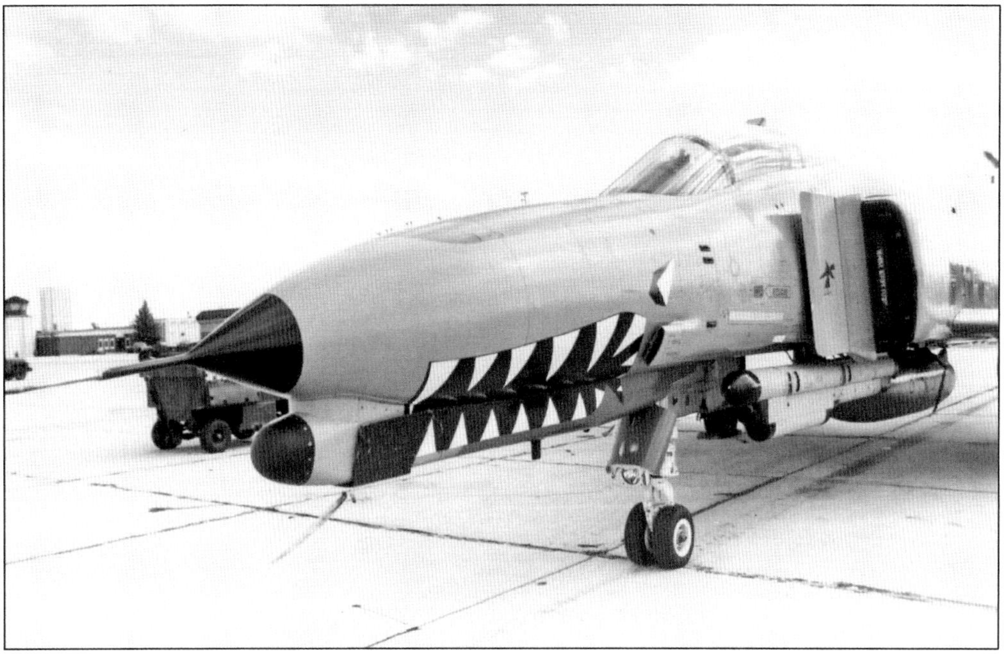

F-4G No. 69-0298, seen here, was credited with a radar site kill on June 29, 1993, during one of the 190th Fighter Squadron's first Operation Southern Watch deployments. It was crewed by Maj. Larry Kauffman and Maj. Ed Payne. The aircraft carries a kill marking, a black radar "dish" with HARM missile.

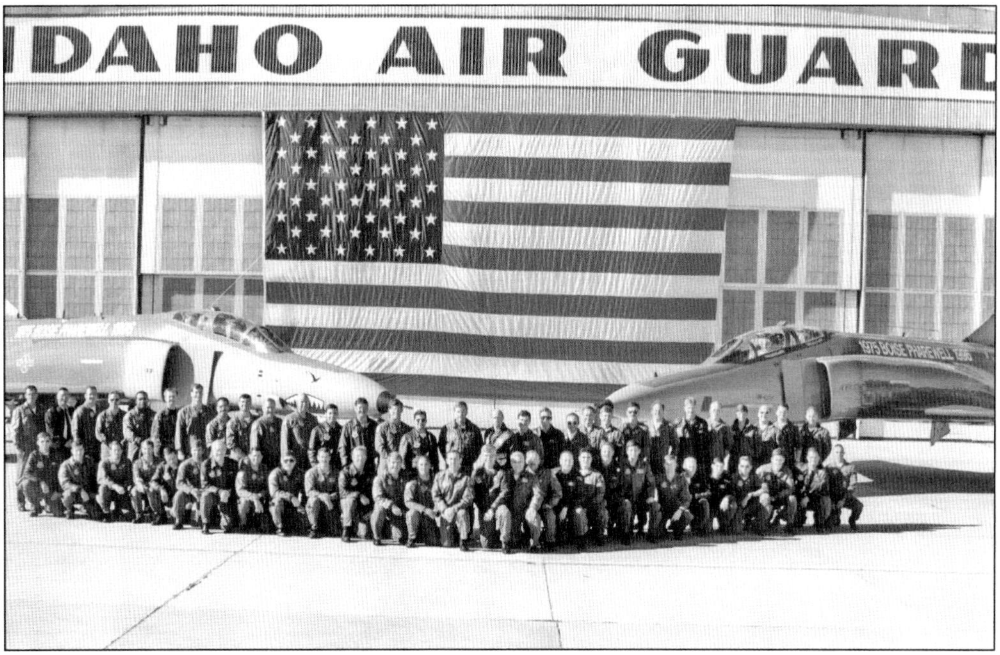

The last of the 124th Fighter Group's pilots and electronic warfare officers gather for a final photograph. Many of these fliers had been with the Idaho Air National Guard for the entire time the F-4s were in Idaho, some even before. The two pictured Phantoms were preserved for display aircraft and are now part of the airpark at Gowen Field.

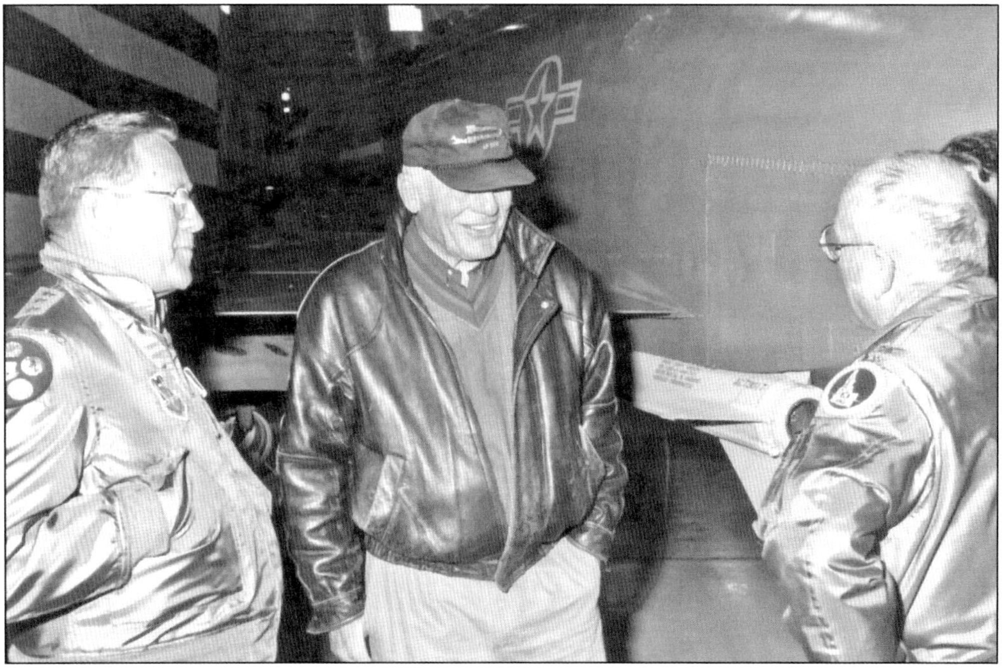

Some of the dignitaries who attended the Phantom Pharewell included Lt. Gen. James F. Record (left), commander of 12th Air Force, and Brig. Gen. Robin Olds (center), retired officer of the U.S. Air Force. Col. Jerre Kauffman (right) was a former 124th Fighter Group commander and longtime Idaho Air Guard pilot.

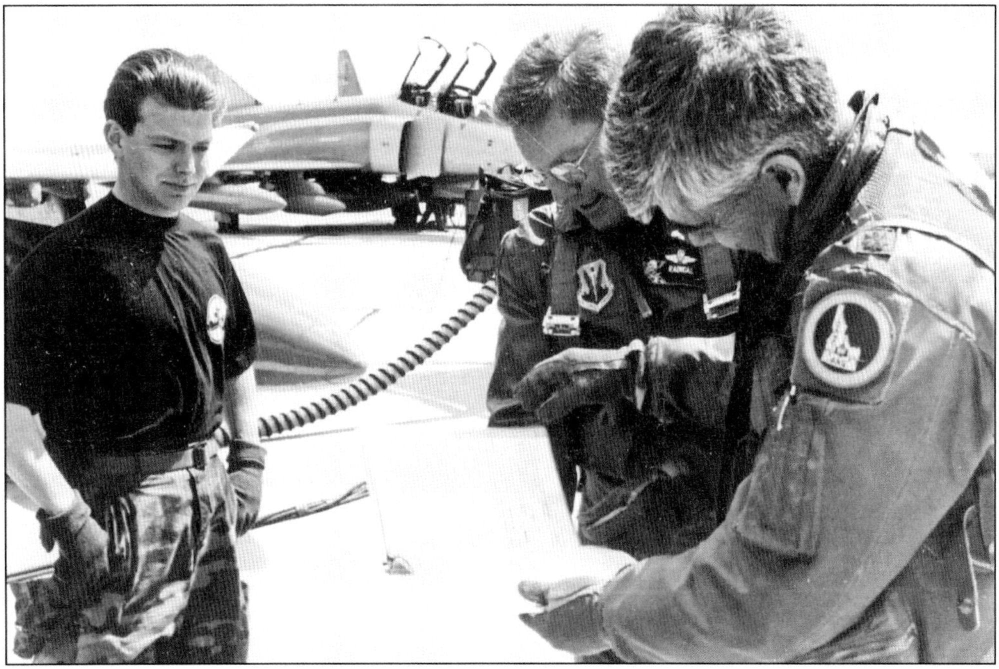

Maintainer Mark Klaudt (left) watches as Lt. Col. Tom Radeke, electronic warfare officer (center), and Lt. Col. Mike Palmer, pilot (right), check over maintenance forms prior to boarding F-4G No. 69-7557 for the Phantom Pharewell.

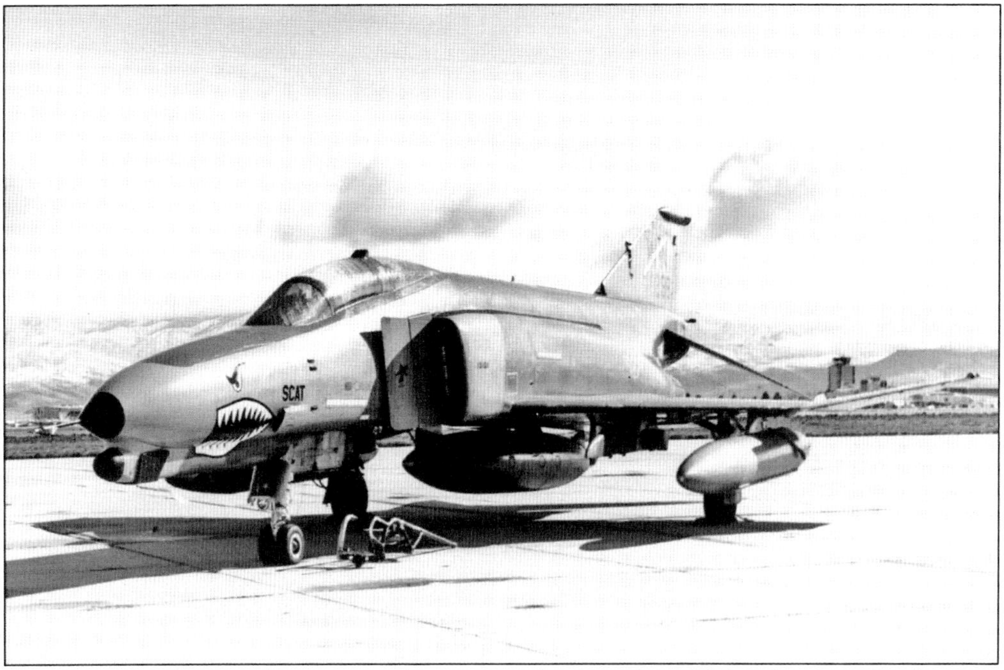

This photograph was taken on April 20, 1996, the day of the Idaho Air Guard's Phantom Pharewell. F-4G No. 69-0298 carries its radar-site kill marking. For the farewell, No. 298 also carried the nickname "SCAT" after the famous Vietnam War Phantom pilot Brig. Gen. Robin Olds, who had nicknamed his aircraft in that way. Maj. Larry Kauffman and Maj. Eddie Payne then flew No. 298 to the boneyard.

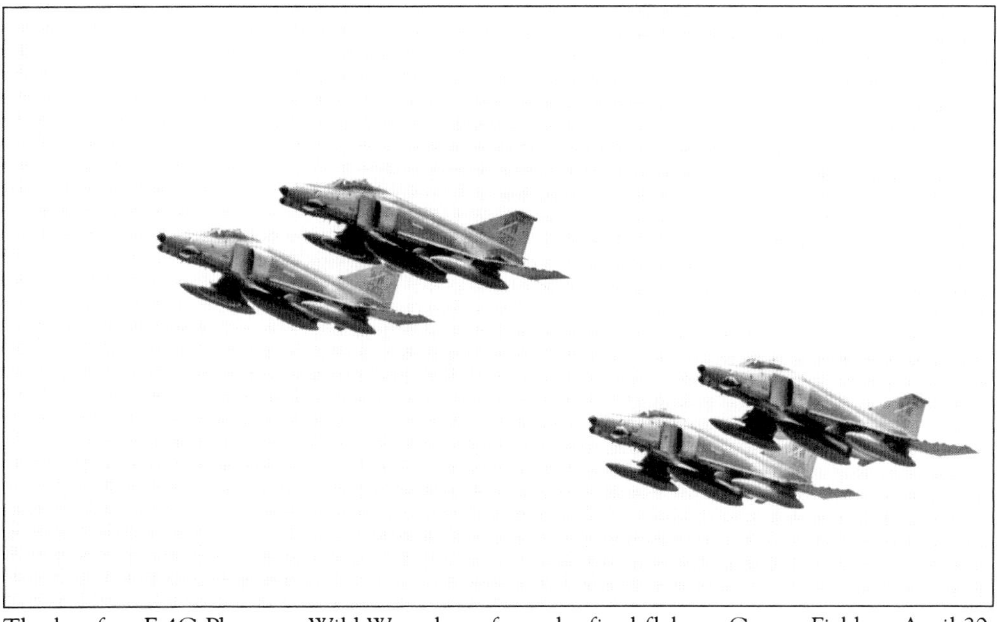

The last four F-4G Phantom Wild Weasels perform the final flyby at Gowen Field on April 20, 1996. The crews included Lt. Col. J. D. Merris, Lt. Col. Jay Stevenson, Lt. Col. Dave Gardner, Col. Gary Sayler, Maj. Eddy Payne, Maj. Larry Kauffman, Lt. Col. Tom Radeke, and Lt. Col. Mike Palmer.